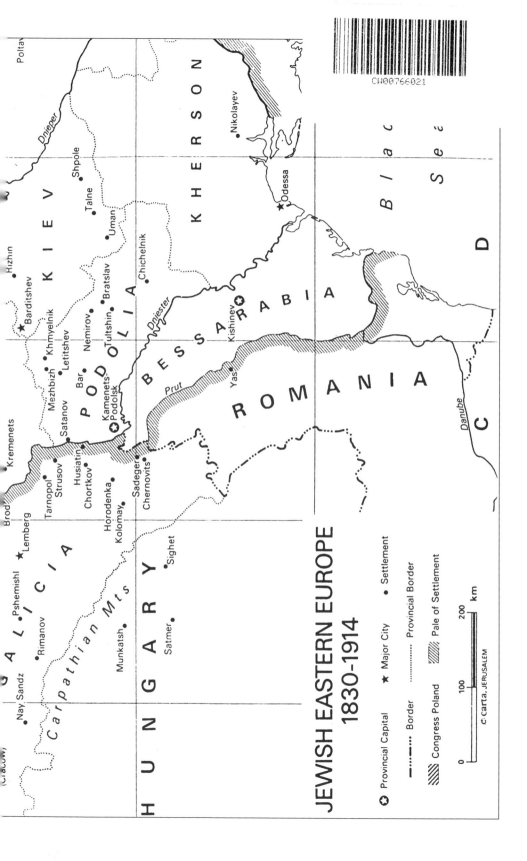

JEWISH EASTERN EUROPE
1830-1914

⊙ Provincial Capital   ★ Major City   • Settlement

‒‒‒‒ Border   ·········· Provincial Border

▨ Congress Poland   ▨ Pale of Settlement

0   100   200 km

© carta, JERUSALEM

Polta

Dnieper

Shpole

Talne

Uman

Hizhin

Barditshev

KIEV

Letitshev

Khmyelnik

Mezhbizh

Nemirov

Bratslav

Tultshin

Bar

POD OLIA

Satanov

Kamenets-
Podolsk

Dniester

Chichelnik

BESSA RABIA

Kishinev ⊙

Prut

Yas

KHERSON

Nikolayev

Odessa ★

Bl a c   S e a

ROMANIA

D

Danube

C

Kremenets

Brod

Strusov

Tarnopol

Husiatin

Chortkov

Horodenka

Kolomay

Sadeger

Chernovits

Lemberg ★

Pshemishl

GAL ICIA

Rimanov

Nav Sandz

(Cracow)

Carpathian Mts

Munkatsh

Satmer

Sighet

HUNGARY

Dearest David שיח',

As you attain this personal milestone perhaps
some wise words from one "Modest Genius" to
another may inspire you. As our Holy Rabbi's
have taught "Words that come from the heart
penetrate the heart".

Mazel Tov

Shlomo, Sharon,
Zach, Aharon & Sara-Leah

The Modest Genius

REB AISEL HARIF

Esther Rafaeli

PUBLISHING
JERUSALEM ◆ NEW YORK

THE MODEST GENIUS
Reb Aisel Harif

Published by DEVORA PUBLISHING COMPANY
Revised and Updated Edition

Text Copyright © 2004 by Esther Rafaeli
Cover Design: Ilana Dickman
Book Layout and Design: David Yaphe
Editor: Toby Weissman
Proofreader: Keren Diamond

Library of Congress Control Number: 2004112408

ISBN: 1-932687-04-1

Email: publisher@devorapublishing.com
Web Site: www.devorapublishing.com

Printed in Israel

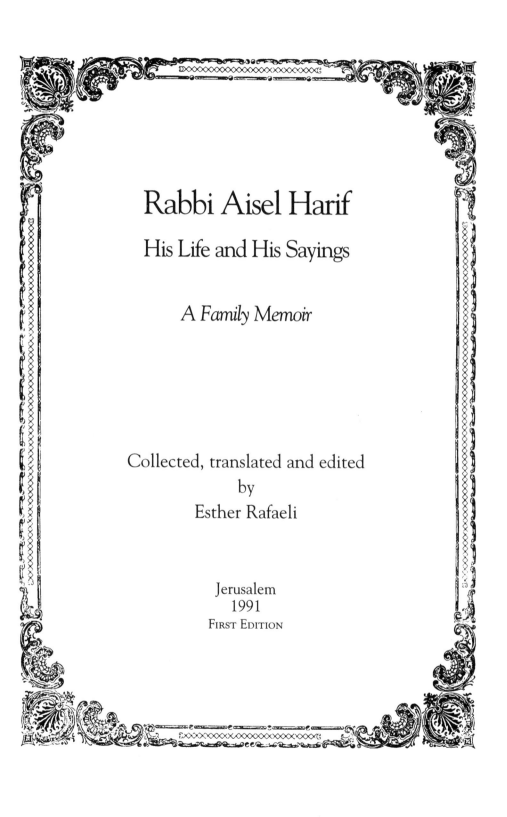

Rabbi Aisel Harif

His Life and His Sayings

A Family Memoir

Collected, translated and edited
by
Esther Rafaeli

Jerusalem
1991
FIRST EDITION

Ze'ev (Velvel) Shapiro (right, 1921) and son Alec Shapiro (1985) at Herzl's tomb, Vienna.

In memory of my father
Ze'ev (Velvel) Shapiro ז״ל
who kept the family lore alive for us

and

In memory of those members of the family
young and old
who perished in the Holocaust

CONTENTS

"Warm thyself
          by the fire of the wise."

(PIRKEI AVOT 2:15)

FOREWORD

I undertook the compilation and translation of this work in order to bring back to life the image of an illustrious ancestor, Rabbi Yehoshua Aisek ben Yehiel Shapira, or as he was more affectionately known, Reb Aisel Harif. Famous in his day as a giant in the world of Torah study as well as for the sharpness of his mind and his tongue, R. Aisel's witticisms and secular sayings still appear from time to time in rabbinic literature, Torah columns and anthologies of Jewish humor.

Although I had known of R. Aisel since I was a child, my interest in him was kindled in the 1970s, when my late father decided to collect and re-issue his works, since very few copies of the originals had remained after the Second World War. The fact that these limited editions were quickly snapped up was proof that Aisel Harif's reputation was still alive and well a century after his death.

As his descendants today live in Israel, England, Brazil and the United States, and since I do not know if there are any who can actually "learn" his works or appreciate the magnitude and quality of his scholarship, I thought it fitting to publish at least a short biography and a selection of his witty sayings and teachings, in English, so that they and his remarkable personality will be accessible to his descendants.

Although many writers have quoted the sayings of R. Aisel, I have relied mainly on four books: *Rabbi Aisel Harif* by Y.L. Levin, originally published in 1918, in Vilna, in Hebrew; *From the Mouth of R. Aisele,* by M. Reitzeson, published in Slonim in 1931, in Yiddish; *Der Yiddisher Oitzer* by A. Engelshar, reprinted in Bnei Brak in 1966, in Yiddish, from an edition originally published in Poland; and *Toldot HaYishuv HaYehudi b'Slonim,* by Kalman Lictenstein, published in Tel Aviv in 1960, in Hebrew.

Not all of R. Aisel's sayings lend themselves to translation, since many of them are based on allusions to the Talmud, or are puns on quotations from the sources; so I make no claim that this is a complete collection. It is, however, quite a comprehensive one, which I believe reflects R. Aisel's mentality and beliefs, and many of the stories are still appropriate and can be appreciated by us today. In addition, they are very useful in rounding out the portrait of R. Aisel, since there is little factual biographical data available. With regard to the dates of events mentioned, I have tried to be as exact as possible by comparing the various sources and assessing the information available.

One of the unexpected and surprising benefits of my research was the picture which gradually emerged of Jewish life in Poland and Lithuania in the middle of the nineteenth century, a picture that varies greatly from the idealised romantic perceptions which we tend to have of that period. I should like the reader to pay special attention to these elements, because they give the stories an added dimension of sociological history and tell us much about the lifestyle and customs of a great culture which flourished for centuries before it was destroyed in the Holocaust by Nazi Germany.

I would like to thank my brother Alec (Yehiel) Shapiro, for his encouragement and help on this project. As he worked concurrently on registering the family tree, we were able to contribute considerably to each other's work while enjoying the challenge of a family project.

I would also like to thank Rabbi Louis Jacobs of London and David Fisch of Jerusalem, for having read this manuscript and for their valuable suggestions. Also, Miriam Grossman and Sarah Lemann for their friendly typing services, and Norma Schneider for editing and giving the book its present form.

Finally I would like to thank my husband Alex for his patience in accepting R. Aisel into our daily life.

I hope those for whom I have written this book will enjoy reading it as much as I have enjoyed writing it, and, in the tradition of those I have written about, I give thanks that I have been able to record this chapter in the history of my family, in memory of those who have gone before, and those who were victims of the Holocaust.

Esther (Shapiro) Rafaeli

Jerusalem 1991

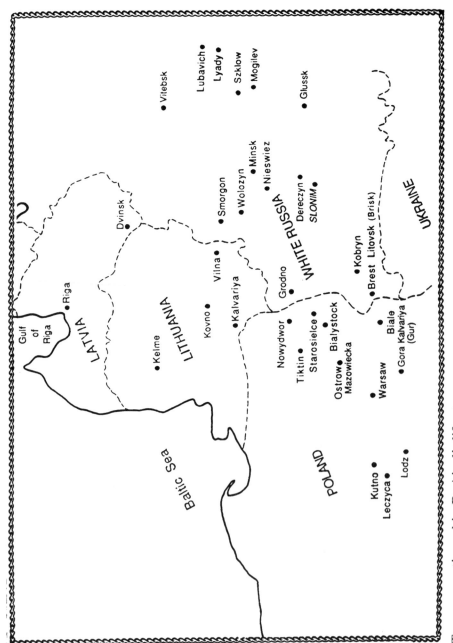

Towns mentioned in R. Aisel's life story

ANTECEDENTS

Yehoshua Aisek ben Yehiel Shapira, later to be known as Rabbi Aisel Harif, or Aisel the Sharp Intellect, was born in 1801 in Glovaki, a small village in the Vilna guberna. His father R. Yehiel ben Mordecai was the great-grandson of R. Yehiel ben Shlomo Heilprin of Minsk, who lived between 1660 and 1744. As both great-great-grandfather and great-great-grandson achieved lasting renown in their time, it is interesting to begin this memoir with a glance at the biography of the former.

R. Yehiel ben Shlomo was a Lithuanian Talmudic scholar and historian, the son of Shlomo Heilprin, the rabbi of Szklow in the province of Mogilev. According to his introduction to *Seder HaDorot,* Yehiel claimed descent through his maternal grandfather, from R. Shlomo ben Yehiel Luria, the renowned *posek* and Talmudist, who lived in the sixteenth century, and was known as the Maharshal. There is a strong tradition that the family is descended from Rashi through the female line. R. Yehiel studied the *Kabbalah* and is said to have performed miracles. He served as rabbi in Glussk, in the Bobruisk area, where his compilation of rules for the *Hevra Kadisha* was preserved in the original manuscript for many generations. In 1711 he became head of the leading yeshiva in Minsk, and also chief rabbi of the town. He taught according to his own method, which was based on logic and clarity of thought, contrary to the pilpulistic method, which was often devious and hairsplitting. The pilpulistic method was propounded by R. Arye Leib ben

Asher, author of *Sha'agat Aryeh* (The Lion's Roar), when he came as a young man to Minsk in order to found a new yeshiva. He challenged R. Yehiel's authority, but R. Yehiel won his argument and earned the support and admiration of his students. For some reason arising out of this conflict, R. Aryeh was eventually forced to leave the town.

R. Yehiel became famous for his historical chronology, *Seder HaDorot* (The Order of the Generations), which was first published in 1769 in Karlsruhe. It was re-issued in Lemberg in 1858, in Warsaw in 1878, and more recently in New York City. *Seder Hadorot* consists of three parts: (1) A chronology of events and personages from Creation to 1696, based on earlier chronologies and reference books. (2) Biographies and chronologies of the *tannaim* and *amoraim* (teachers of the Oral Law in the Talmudic and post-Talmudic periods), in alphabetical order. This section of the book, based on original research of the talmudic sources, and one of the first works written as modern biography, discusses the importance of the history of the *tannaim* to halakhic decisions. It is the most important part of the book. (3) Names of Hebrew authors and their books up to his own period, in alphabetical order, also taken from existing sources.

R. Yehiel also published annotations to the Babylonian Talmud, and a concordance called *Erkei Kinnuyim*, which lists names and verbs in the Bible and Talmud. While leafing through the Memorial Book on Minsk, published in 1985 by ex-citizens of that town, I found many references to R. Yehiel, who was also called "the Pride of Minsk" as well as "the Seder HaDorot," which shows that he had a very sound niche in the folklore of the town. In his entry,

Haim Levshai writes that R. Yehiel's grave still stands intact, although much of the old cemetery has been destroyed. The following story, from the Memorial Book, illustrates the kind of legend which grew up around R. Yehiel. It is taken from the records of the Minsk *Hevra Kadisha*:

"A short time after R. Yehiel ben Shlomo Heilprin (author of the *Seder HaDorot*) passed away in 1746, a certain peddler was making his way home to Minsk from his rounds. It was an icy winter's night, and deep snow covered the ground. Dozing from time to time as his horse plodded along, the peddler suddenly realized that the horse had stopped. Even though the peddler took the whip to him, the horse refused to move. Looking around to determine the cause of the horse's behavior, the peddler fainted upon seeing R. Yehiel standing nearby, wrapped in his shroud.

"When he came to, he heard the *Seder HaDorot* saying to him, 'Don't be afraid. If you look across the way, you will see a little house, with a candle burning in the window. Go there, and inside you will see a young maiden sitting alone, deep in thought. Knock on the windowpane, and when the maiden sees you, say loudly three times, "Your grandfather sent me to tell you not to change your religion." Then return here.'

"The peddler was afraid to move. 'Who will look after my horse and sleigh?' he asked the *Seder HaDorot*. 'I will guard them,' replied R. Yehiel, 'but you must do this for me as I am not permitted to go over there.'

"Doing as he was asked, the peddler heard a great cry from the young woman after he had spoken the words. He ran back as fast as he could, and found R. Yehiel still holding the horse's reins. 'You have done me a great kindness,' said R. Yehiel. 'How can I repay you?' 'When my time comes,' replied the peddler, 'I wish to be buried near you.' 'Oh, that is a very difficult request, but I shall try to fulfill it,' said R. Yehiel before he vanished.

"Many years later, the peddler passed away on a wintry night. As was customary, the *Hevra Kadisha* buried him as quickly as possible, even though this meant that the cortege had to set out in the midst of a snowstorm. When they finally reached the cemetery, they searched in vain for some landmark, until they suddenly saw a small plot right in front of them, clear of snow as if prepared for them. As quickly as possible they dug a grave and laid the peddler to rest. Although they registered the burial in their records, they noted that, because of the storm, they could not tell exactly where the grave was situated.

"Several years passed and an outstanding scholar died in Minsk. The community decided to honor him by burying him near the grave of the *Seder HaDorot*. But when the *Hevra Kadisa* came to prepare the grave, they found that someone had already been buried there. Hastening to the rabbi for advice, they checked the records of the *Hevra Kadisha* and concluded that the grave must be that of the peddler who had been buried years before on that stormy winter's night.

"Although the *Hevra Kadisha* was ready to move the peddler to another grave, the rabbi refused, saying that he must first talk to the peddler's widow, who was still alive. When the widow was brought before him, the rabbi asked her if she knew of any great *mitzvah* which her husband had performed. 'He was a very simple man,' she replied. 'He prayed and kept Shabbat. He ate only kosher food, and occasionally drank too much.'

"The rabbi kept pressing her to recall any unusual incidents in her husband's life. Finally she remembered that one winter's night he had come home so greatly agitated, that he was unable to talk. But eventually, after calming down, he had told her of his meeting with the *Seder HaDorot*. 'I didn't believe the story then,' she said, 'and even today I am still sure that he had simply had too much to drink.'

"After hearing the widow's story, the rabbi ruled that the peddler should not be moved from his resting-place."

R. Yehiel's descendent married R. Mordecai Shapira, a pious pillar of the community and serious scholar with close ties to rabbinic circles in Vilna and Wolozyn. Some sources say that R. Mordecai did not serve as a rabbi but studied for the love of study. However, in the preface to his book, *Birkat Moshe* (The Blessing of Moshe), R. Moshe Shapira, Aisel's second son, writes that Mordecai was rabbi and *Av Beit Din* (head of the rabbinical court) in Glussk and in Glovaki. This genealogy is included in the first edition of R. Aisel Harif's *Emek Yehoshua*, published in Warsaw in 1842, and is repeated and enlarged in later works of his son R. Moshe.

Mordecai's son, R. Yehiel Shapira, obviously named after his illustrious ancestor, followed in his father's path. God-fearing and scholarly, he is believed to have been a watchmaker by trade, but after spending some time with the renowned R. Shneor Zalman of Lyady, he became a *hassid*. Since there were no other *hassidim* or hassidic synagogues in Glovaki, Reb Yehiel spent much time away

17

from his family at the court of Shneor Zalman, neglecting his family and their financial situation.

When Shneor Zalman passed away in 1813, Yehiel followed his disciple, Aharon HaLevi Hurwitz of Starosielce, otherwise known as the Starsheler Rebbe, who led a variant group within the Habad movement. In contrast to the intellectual approach within Habad, R. Aharon HaLevi preferred exaltation in meditation and emotion in prayer, which he considered more conducive to love and reverence of God. Some of the most beautiful Habad melodies are attributed to R. Aharon. However, though he wrote many works expounding his theories, most of his disciples left him for the mainstream of the Habad movement and, with his death in 1828, his ideology died with him. It says something of Yehiel Shapira's ideas and personality that he was attracted to this group rather than to the mainstream led by R. Dov Ber and Menachem Mendel Schneerson of Lubavich (the forerunner of the Lubavicher *hassidim* of today). The latter lived until 1866, while Yehiel passed away in 1847.

From Childhood in Glovaki to Minsk

Yehiel's only child, Yehoshua Aisek, was born many years after his marriage. Although the poverty which beset the family didn't bother him, Yehiel made all efforts to give his son a proper Torah education. Like other villages in the area, Glovaki then consisted of a few hundred run-down wooden houses. The synagogue and *Beit Midrash* seemed to droop with the weariness of poverty, yet within its walls was a vibrant world of scholars and scholarship and a variety of ideas and methods of study. The scholars studied at night by candlelight as well as by day, and their learning was as rich as their income was poor.

As was customary at that time, Reb Yehiel put Aisele, as he was affectionately known, into *heder* at the age of three, and the boy soon showed signs of the precocity, inquiring mind and enjoyment of learning that would characterize him throughout his life. No one dreamt then that Aisele would eventually become the most famous rabbi of the old and historic town, Slonim. Aisele studied in the *heder* until the age of six, when it became obvious that he had outgrown its possibilities. His father then took on a special *melamed* for him. In later years R. Aisel told his son Berish, "Although my father took a special *melamed* for me — I don't know where the money came from — the fact is that I studied by myself."

When he began studying *Humash* Aisele immediately showered his teacher with questions. Thus it is reported that when studying the first portion of Genesis, he immediately asked how the sky was supported and why the portion starts with the second letter of the Hebrew alphabet, *"beit"* as in *"Bereshit"* and not with the first, *"aleph."* And why is the *"beit" of the word "Bereshit"* larger than all the other letters? And so on.

When Aisele began studying *Gemara,* he was in seveth heaven, taking it as a proof that he was now a "big" boy. A slight, frail child, "all eyes and soul," he never played with children. He studied incessantly, swaying to and fro over the large heavy volumes. His love of learning and of the Torah obliterated from his thoughts the poverty and hunger which nagged constantly at the family.

Even when he grew older Aisele remained a solitary person, and the few attempts which he or others made towards establishing closer relationships were not always successful. After he began to study in Minsk, two of the yeshiva boys invited him to study with them, but after the first meeting Aisele realized he had nothing to learn from them, and told them that he would not continue to meet with them since he had another partner who really knew how to study. A few days later, when the boys found him sitting alone with his books, they asked where his wonderful partner was. "Here, sitting right before you," he smiled in reply.

"Do you want to swallow up the whole Torah?" he was once asked. "The Torah was quicker and swallowed me up," he replied.

It is reported that once Aisele was walking with his father when the local rabbi happened to pass by. "Aisele," said his father, "if you keep on studying diligently you will soon overtake the rabbi." The child immediately ran after the rabbi until he not only caught up with him, but overtook him as well. Returning to his father, he said, "See papa, I have already overtaken him."

About this time Aisele was studying with R. Wolff, the *melamed* from Birz, who was well-known as a *talmid hakham*. But for some reason Aisele did not take to this *melamed* from Birz, and many years later he is recorded as having said to Y.L. Levin (the Hebrew poet known by his Hebrew acronym as Yehalel), when his father brought him to Aisel to be tested: "Your father did well in sending you to the *melamed* of Birz. I also learned with him. But always keep in mind that whoever did not learn with the *melamed* from Birz does not know how to learn. And the proof of this is in the fact that the *melamed* from Birz did not start with the *melamed* from Birz and therefore does not know how to learn."

This incident was also quoted by Yehalel in his autobiography, *Zichronot v' Hegionot*, which, by the way, gives us a vivid description of his trials and tribulations as a young *hassid* whose ambition was to write poetry. He eventually became a leading *maskil* and Hebrew poet, in spite of the opposition of his family and friends. Yehalel also mentions R. Aisel as being renowned for his stinging wit and "bitter sarcasm," a remark which suggests that R. Aisel's life was not a bed of roses.

One source says that the rivalry between Aisel and R. Wolff arose when Aisele began to teach some children in the villages surrounding Glovaki, in an attempt to alleviate the financial hardship of his family and stop his mother's tears. It seems that the *melamed* was incensed that a boy not even near *Bar Mitzvah* age should presume to compete with him.

Although small and not robust, Aisele was not afraid of anyone or anything. He loved challenge and overcame all obstacles with his strong will and determination, even the attempts of his mother and grandfather to indulge and coddle him. When he spent nights alone in the cold *Beit Midrash*, his mother was anxious and worried. "It is said that ghosts and spirits come to the *Beit Midrash* when there is no one there," she would plead with the boy. And he replied, "It says in the *Mishnah* that whoever sits and studies the Torah, The Holy One, Blessed Be He, sits and studies with him. So if He is there by me, why should I be afraid? If the ghosts come, the Holy One, Blessed Be He, will chase them away to the ends of the earth."

But the piercing cold of the winters did penetrate, not only into the study house, but into Aisele's bones as well. Once his family found him in the *Beit Midrash* with his hands and feet almost frozen, and had to work hard to warm them up. "You must have been studying cold Torah, that your hands and feet became frozen," they joked afterwards. "I don't study with my hands and feet but with my head, and that didn't freeze!" was Aisele's retort.

Sometimes Aisele was the only child among the adults learning in the *Beit Midrash* during the day, and the older men would ask him to run errands for them. At first he was very angry because the errands took him away from his learning, but on second thought he reasoned that he was studying to fulfil the Torah. "As I am not yet *Bar Mitzvah*, I have no obligations except that of charity, so I should be happy that the older men give me the opportunity to do good deeds and thus fulfil the precepts of the Torah." And then, he later recalled, he was able to go about his tasks happily.

Though he had an inquiring mind and a prodigious memory, it was only the Torah which interested him. Once he told his son Berish: "As a child I knew that I knew nothing, and that knowledge bothered me. I didn't want to look beyond the books. Sometimes I didn't want to see or talk to anyone. I was overcome with the thought that the Torah was so vast, and that I was so small and weak, and hadn't even begun the taste of it."

On another occasion, he related: "Everything was open for me in Glovaki: my bones to the cold, my body to hunger and my head to Torah. The cold affected my breathing and probably gave me my asthma, the hunger left no traces, and my head stayed open to the Torah. Through my studies I learned to pray. I was a small boy and sometimes I didn't completely understand a סוגיה or question, or would get involved in an interpretation and, being alone in the *Beit Midrash*, I would begin to cry and pray to The Holy One, Blessed Be He, to enlighten me. And then suddenly, the right answer would come to me. It seemed as if the very Heavens were learning with me."

Aisele's negative attitude to rabbis became apparent at an early age, when most children have not yet had occasion to form any opinions at all. When combined with his wit, which was also unusually precocious, many a rabbi was stung by his barbs. Once the rabbi of Glovaki came to the *Beit Midrash* and found Aisele studying. Picking up the *Gemara* which was on the table and opening it, the rabbi found that the first page had been torn. He scolded Aisele for being careless, and then, while leafing through the pages, tore a page himself. Laughingly, he said to Aisele, "I am being punished because I suspected you wrongly!" "Oh no," returned Aisele, "It is the *Gemara* which is punished. Your punishment is yet to come."

Later, while at the Minsk yeshiva, Aisele voiced criticism of the rabbis and was warned that he shouldn't make light of them because he himself was destined to be a rabbi. He retorted: "so I am making fun on account of the future!"

Once one of the elders teased Aisele, "You think you are a genius! At your age Rabbi Heschel was already studying in the big yeshiva with the advanced students!" "And at your age," quipped the young Aisel, "Rabbi Heschel was already studying in the yeshiva on high!"

Sometimes the elders scolded Aisele for his sarcastic tongue, asking him, "If you can't mind your tongue now as a child, what will happen when you grow up?" "I'll preach to the children," replied Aisele without a moment's hesitation.

By the time he was eight years old, Aisele was well-versed in many tractates of the *Mishnah*, and as there was no suitable teacher for him in his village, his father refrained from his customary visits to his rebbe and began teaching and studying with Aisel. This was no easy task, as the child continually pestered his father with his questions. But the time that Aisele spent studying with his father was to prove extremely important in that it provided the boy with a role model, for the boy absorbed much in manner, style and devotion to the *mitzvoth* from R. Yehiel. In later years, he always paid tribute to his father: "My father was a man of truth, a true *hassid* and a true scholar." Yet he did not choose to follow his father when Yehiel resumed his lengthy visits to Rabbi Shneor Zalman in Lyady, as soon as he thought that Aisele was capable of continuing his studies on his own. This Aisele did with great persistence and dedication, developing his own method of studying and searching out his own path in the Torah. At this point he already knew the Babylonian Talmud by heart and kept special hours for continuing study of the *Mishnah*.

The people of Glovaki, proud of their young genius, spread his name as a devoted scholar and sharp-tongued wit far and wide. Often they would tease him in order to provoke a sharp retort. At that time the leader of the Glovaki community was an aggressive, unlearned man, who was proud of his title "Head of the Community," but was called by the villagers "Foolish Head." Once he told Aisele: "Thanks to Glovaki you are a genius. In this little village you have no competitors. But if you lived in a city like Vilna you wouldn't have the same title!" "What an argument," replied Aisele. "In Vilna I would perhaps be a genius, or perhaps a child; but in Vilna you would still be a fool!"

Eventually Yehiel saw that the situation could not continue and that Aisele was in need of better supervision and guidance. Oddly enough he decided to apprentice Aisele to a tradesman. Thus, at the age of only ten or eleven, Aisele was sent to Minsk, where he was put in the care of a family friend, Reb Yitzhak Smorgoner, who was to teach him watchmaking. Left alone in the strange household, Aisele could not stop weeping over the loss of his beloved *seforim* (books). The good-hearted Smorgoner, unable to bear the unhappiness of the child, decided to take him to the Minsk

Yeshiva to have him tested. Much to Smorgoner's surprise, the *melamed* who undertook this task told him that the child had a brilliant mind "יניק וחכם הוא" (He is young and clever, a child prodigy) and was already well-versed in the *Shas* (*Talmud*) and the *Mefarshim* (commentators). The *melamed* felt that he himself was not qualified to continue Aisele's learning, and that the right place for the boy was no longer in the boys' yeshiva, but in the *Beit Midrash* with the advanced scholars.

From that day on Aisele was treated with great respect; all his needs were seen to and he ate at Reb Yitzhak's table. It was customary at that time for the wealthier people to invite the yeshiva scholars for meals on set days, the custom called *"essen teg"* or *"eating days."* Thus the boys were fed, and the patrons basked in the reflected glory of the guest's scholarship and in the doing of a *mitzvah*.

Smorgoner enrolled Aisele at Blumkas' *Beit Midrash*, the best yeshiva in Minsk, which was famous for the outstanding scholars who studied there independently, and there Aisele participated in the *shiurim* of the renowned Rabbi Avraham Dvoretzer. Aisele flourished from day to day in the special atmosphere of Blumkas'. His reputation spread rapidly in Minsk, where he became known as "the *gaon* (or genius) of Glovaki." Once an itinerant *maggid* gave a sermon at Blumkas', and when he finished, Aisele gave him a coin and said that it was a pity he had finished. "Why are you sorry?" asked the *maggid*. "You weren't even listening to what I said!" To which Aisele replied: "It is simply that while you were talking I had to concentrate harder in order that you shouldn't disturb me, and I enjoyed that deep concentration. Now that you have finished speaking I don't have to make that effort, and I'm sorry."

Aisele's reputation soon brought him to the attention of Rivka Blumkas, one of the wealthy ladies of Minsk and a member of the family which had established the *Beit Midrash*. Rivka took a special interest in Aisele, secretly hoping that she would eventually be able to betroth one of her daughters to him. It was then, as now, a great honor to have a תלמיד חכם (brilliant scholar) in one's family, and there was no longer any doubt that Aisele was destined to become famous in the Jewish world and would bring much honor to any family into which he married. In the course of time Rivka wrote to Reb Yehiel, inviting him to visit her in Minsk. Although she intended to propose the *shidduch* and write the *tnoyim* (terms of engagement) during Yehiel's visit, she gave no hint of this in her letter.

But this particular match was not meant to be. For, upon arriving in Minsk, Yehiel betook himself to Yitzhak Fine's house, his customary lodging-place, to refresh himself. Yitzhak Fine also had his eyes on Aisele as a son-in-law, and indeed, he did not let Yehiel leave till they had shaken hands on an agreement (*tekiat kaf*) that Aisele would marry Fine's only daughter and would be completely supported by Fine for the rest of his life. Such an arrangement was called "living on *kest*." Thus, when Yehiel came to Rivka Blumkas, and she made a more generous proposal, her overtures were too late. Yehiel declared he could not and would not go back on his word or break the agreement of the *tekiat kaf*. Aisele must marry the daught of Yitzhak Fine.

When Yehiel brought Aisele to meet Fine for the first time, they found a number of men in the room. "Aisele, do you know which one is to be your father-in-law?" asked Yehiel. Aisele pointed straight at Fine and said, "איך האב אם שוין פיינט" (I already dislike him), a Yiddish phrase that entered the vocabulary of our family and was used jokingly on appropriate occasions.

A short time later Aisele was married to Haya Fine at a wedding attended by all the scholars and notables of Minsk. Rivka Blumkas overcame her disappointment and attended, giving the young couple a handsome set of *Shas*, and a volume of *Poskim* (codifiers) as a wedding gift. Aisele was sixteen years old.

At the wedding, Aisele refused to give a *drasha*, or discourse, claiming, "I was tested before I got engaged. Now it is my turn to test others." But, as I often heard from my father, the marriage was not a happy one, and in the sources I have read, Haya is never mentioned as an active factor in Aisele's life. However, this may not be unusual according to the custom of the time. On the other hand, her son, R. Moshe of Riga, always mentions her in the dedications of his books.

Some years after the wedding Reb Fine's economic situation began to deteriorate, and it became impossible for him to fulfill his promise of full support to his beloved and revered son-in-law. "The sharpest [*harif*] amongst the knowledgeable [*beke'im*] and the most knowledgeable amongst the sharp," Fine used to say of him. Having to find other means of support, Aisele began teaching in the yeshiva as an assistant to R. Dvoretzer. During the day he supervised the studies of the students, and at night he applied himself tenaciously to his own.

Within a few years Aisele had become assistant head of

a yeshiva and a *maggid* (preacher) for the Hevra Kadisha Synagogue. Besides being a great scholar, Aisele was also a gifted speaker who easily won the hearts of his audience with his pleasant personality and wit.

At some stage during this period Aisele's father sent him to the court of his rebbe, R. Aharon Starsheler, where he acted for some time as a חוזר *(hozer)*, that is, the person who repeats and explains the rabbi's teachings to the assembled scholars and disciples. But Aisele did not remain there very long and returned to Minsk.

On another occasion during the difficult period that Aisele was still living on *kest* in his father-in-law's house, he received a letter from his father inviting him to return to Glovaki to live and study there. Aisele answered, "It is good to pray in Glovaki, "ממעמקים קראתיך הי" [From the depths, or valleys, I called upon the Lord], but it is better to study in Minsk."

Later on he left his position of *maggid* and assistant *rosh yeshiva* at the Hevra Kadisha Synagogue and became a *melamed* in nearby villages. When someone asked him why he had done so, Aisele answered with a quotation from Tractate Ketubot: כל ישיבה שאין עמה עמידה טובה הימנה, עמידה טובה סמיכה (*Amida* — standing, or a position — is preferable to any yeshiva — sitting, or a place of learning — which has no [back] support).

Together with his efforts to earn money, Aisele spent as much time as he could on his studies. In a relatively short time he reviewed the Babylonian and the Jerusalem Talmud many times over. He had a quick grasp and learnt rapidly, never forgetting anything. Clearly he had what we today call a photographic memory, and to this was added the gift of instant recall, but these were not mere mechanical talents. As we can see from his works, he had a powerful, original intellect as well.

Heikel Lunsky of Vilna, the biographer and author of *Great Jews*, relates that once at a wedding, the still young Aisele was asked to recite the Jerusalem Talmud by heart, and he offered to do so beginning at any point which was selected. Upon which one of the wedding guests asked jokingly whether Aisele also knew the Babylonian Talmud by heart. To the astonishment of those assembled, Aisele proceeded to recite the *Bavli* along with Rashi's interpretation and the *Tosaphot*. This was a feat that Aisele was called upon to repeat on other occasions.

Lunsky writes that R. Aisel completed the *Mishnah* 360 times in his lifetime, each study cycle taking about a month, and that Aisel also knew all of Rashi by heart. In his old age, when he needed a reader due to failing eyesight, he could pick up at any point the reader mentioned and continue both the text and the commentary from memory. Lunsky also relates that, although R. Aisel was born to a *hassid*, he often told jokes at their expense, and that although he was always in cheerful mood and rarely seen to be depressed or heard to complain of personal troubles, he wept such bitter tears when he prayed that his prayer book was often wet through.

Nonetheless, after years of living with his father-in-law and witnessing the latter's deteriorating financial situation, he realized that he must undertake the entire support of his family and become independent of both his in-laws and the "patrons and advisors" of Minsk. He decided to become a rabbi, and after mastering the *Shulhan Arukh*, he went to Vilna (which generally scorned the prodigies of other towns) and received his *smicha* from Rabbi Abeli Fosboller, one of the leading rabbis of the time. R. Fosboller was so impressed with Aisel that he offered him the post of *dayyan* (judge in the rabbinic court) in Vilna, remarking that "This small one will be great one day." This pun on a phrase from the circumcision prayers was a reference to Aisel's slight build. Aisel refused the post of *dayyan*, but used his time in Vilna to study Hebrew grammar. Quickly mastering its intricacies, he then returned to Minsk where he apparently resumed his position with the Hevra Kadisha Synagogue. He must have been about thirty then. There is correspondence at this period (1833) between R. Zacharia Yaloush of Lemberg and Aisele, showing that the latter was already making his mark as a scholar of outstanding logic: חריף ושנון בפלפול וסברא הלא בשמו הקדוש יקרא מוהר"ר יהושע אייזיק מ"ם דח"ק בק"ק במינסק (Sharp and clear in pilpul and logical thought, he will surely be known by his holy name, our teacher, the rabbi R. Yehoshua Aisek, serving as *Maggid* of the *Hevra Kadisha* in the holy community of Minsk).

It is quite likely that R. Aisel's tendency as a *mitnaged* (one who opposed Hassidism) was reenforced in the special intellectual atmosphere of Minsk and in the circle of important scholars in which he moved upon his return from Vilna.

KALVARIYA

After he returned to Minsk with *smicha,* many communities invited Rabbi Aisel to become their rabbi, but he was reluctant to take up a position in a community which was not to his taste, and to be at the mercy of the *parnassim* (leaders of the community). Eventually, in about 1833 or 1834, he accepted the post of rabbi in Kalvariya, a village situated on the border between Poland and Lithuania, in the Suwalki district, eighty per cent of whose residents were Jewish. Although Aisel was now over thirty, he still looked very young. Thus, when the new rabbi arrived the people of Kalvariya thought there must have been a mistake; perhaps this was the rabbi's son? The elders refused to address him as Rabbi, but called him *Rabad,* head of the *Beit Din* or rabbinical court. Ignoring this attitude since he could not do much about his youthful appearance, Rabbi Aisel merely remarked: "One must compose a new prayer for Kalvariya — cast me not out in my youth, rather than cast me not out in old age." And when one of the elders told him that he "would not have dreamt of entering the rabbinate at your age," R. Aisel retorted, "That is obvious even in your old age."

There is a puzzling situation here which implies that the old incumbent rabbi, Leib Broida, did not want to leave, perhaps because no other provision could be made for him. Thus it was only after R. Broida passed away in 1839, that R. Aisel finally moved from being a *dayyan* to rabbi of Kalvariya, at which time the community had no option but to acknowledge him. At this stage R. Aisel still did not know the *Poskim*, but when he heard that the community was complaining about this, he learned the שו״ת or response literature by heart in less than a year.

But R. Aisel was not happy in his new position. The village and its inhabitants were not what he had expected, and though part of the community tried to encourage and support him, the cool and unresponsive attitude of the others made his life difficult. Economic factors also contributed to his dislike of Kalvariya, for his salary, which was not always paid on time, was meager and insufficient for the needs of his family. When the *shamash* would inquire from time to time about his situation, R. Aisel replied: "Do you think it is easier for a rabbi to starve than for a *shamash*? Both suffer!"

When the situation became really serious, the community leaders decided that the rabbi should take on the management of the ritual baths in addition to his other duties, and keep the income for himself. When R. Aisel's supporters protested that even this would not be sufficient to support the rabbi, it was decided that he should also receive the income from the sale of yeast in the village. What a commentary this is on the life and times of the Jews in Eastern Europe in the middle of the nineteenth century!

R. Aisel was understandably unhappy with this undignified arrangement, and commented: "Now I understand the verse, 'He has filled me with bitterness, he has sated me with wormwood' (Lam. 3:15). The first part is a reference to Pesach, when no bread is baked, and there is no income from yeast. And the second part is a reference to Tisha B'Av, when no one bathes, and again there is no income."

One *Erev Shabbat,* the rabbi was accosted in the street by one of the more vulgar inhabitants of the village, who complained that there had not been enough hot water at the baths that day. Aisel asked him: "Isn't it enough that you have made me keeper of the baths? Do you want to make me into the bath-*goy* [gentile who does the jobs prohibited to Jews on the Sabbath] as well?"

"I used to make fun of rabbis and of the rabbinate," R. Aisel once remarked, "and now I have been punished with the worst rabbinical position there is."

During this difficult period R. Aisel visited Vilna, where he went to see Rabbi Fosboller, who had given him *smicha.* "You must not confirm rabbis for Kalvariya," Aisel told Fosboller. When R. Fosboller asked why not, R. Aisel replied, "Kalvariya needs a professional bath attendant and your honor confirms rabbis, not bath attendants!" Continuing to expand on the same subject, R. Aisel also said: "We have learnt 'love the trade and hate the rabbinate.' What is the connection between them? It must be a reference to the rabbinate of Kalvariya, which includes in its sphere the job of bath attendant."

On still another occasion R. Aisel is reported to have said, "If the people of Kalvariya would take my advice, they would select a professional bath attendant as rabbi, and not the other way round. The person chosen would be happy because he would not have to share his income with the bath-*goy,* and the people of Kalvariya would be happy too, because such a bath-attendant-rabbi would be superior to them not only in the ways of Torah but also in the ways of the baths."

"Indeed," he added, "the rabbinate of Kalvariya is like

the bath house. People rinse in it who are not pure, and soil it with their own uncleanliness." These undignified jobs with which R. Aisel tried to supplement his salary were an additional burden on his work.

Once he remarked: "As rabbi of Kalvariya I must walk through fire and water. The *halakhah* is likened to fire, and whoever errs in it is burnt, while the *aggadah* is likened to water, and whoever is thirsty may drink from it. There are rabbis in Vilna who are strong in *halakhah* and others who are strong in *aggadah*, because there are many scholars in the town who are only interested in one or the other. But in Kalvariya I must be strong in both because there are few scholars. I must preach about *aggadah*, because there is no preacher in the town, and I must also give new interpretations of *halakhah*."

The *shamash* of the *Beit Din* in Kalvariya was unpleasant and mean in outlook. He was stingy with candles for lighting the study rooms and tardy about bringing R. Aisel's salary on time. Once, in sheer aggravation, Aisel said to him, "Listen, there are three kinds of shamash in the Jewish religion: the *shamash* of the *hanukiah*, the *shamash* of the fringes and the *shamash* of the Beit Din. The *shamash* of the *hanukiah* gets burnt up, the *shamash* of the fringes gets twisted round and round (in Yiddish, *fardreyt* also means crazy), but one can never get rid of the *shamash* of the *Beit Din*; he doesn't get burnt up and he doesn't go crazy!"

R. Aisel's personal problems never dulled his wit; they may even have sharpened it. Once two men came to him for a *Din Torah*. Both were called Leib (lion), and both argued their cases with great obstinacy. R. Aisel sighed, "Motti the wagon-driver has it easier than I. He has two horses which he claims are like lions, while I have two Lions who are like horses."

As head of the *Beit Din*, R. Aisel once commanded a leading member of the community to appear at a *Din Torah* over a complaint lodged against him by a widow. The man refused to come and threatened to have the rabbi expelled from the town if he continued to bother him. "I am not afraid that they will expel me from the town," said R. Aisel. "A rabbi who serves without salary will be welcome anywhere."

In the same vein, R. Aisel once declared: "I am much better off than Moshe Rabenu. When Korah and his followers rose up against Moses and wanted to take his place, 'Moses heard and fell on his face.' Why? Because it is no small matter to lose a position as leader of the Jews. But such an attack would not bother me too much, because it is not difficult for a rabbi to find a position without salary."

After the *baal-keriyah*, or Torah reader of Kalvariya, had held his position for forty years, the congregants came to R. Aisel to complain that his voice was weak and he could no longer be heard. R. Aisel advised them to take a young man with a strong voice. The friends of the old reader came to protest the dismissal, saying that he had been on the job for forty years, he had a claim on it. "In order to have a claim," said R. Aisel, "one must have a voice, for without a strong voice, one can not make a claim."

Another story is told about R. Aisel's situation in Kalvariya and the reason for it. The congregation was accustomed to visiting the rabbi on festival days, after prayers and before the festive meal, in order the hear his *Divrei Torah*. Once he said to them, "Come, I will explain this custom to you. A festival is half for the Almighty — the prayers — and half for you the meal which you enjoy. In order to make a separation between the two halves, it is usual to visit the rabbi. Here there is no "Almighty," and no "congregation", because if the rabbi is not concerned with Torah, but has to look for additional sources of income, he is not fulfilling the half which belongs to the Almighty. And if the congregation does not pay the rabbi's salary, it is not fulfilling the half "for you" (i.e., the rabbi hasn't enough for the festive meal).

In spite of his deep resentment and unhappiness over his situation, R. Aisel outwardly maintained his humor and wit. Since the good citizens did not trouble him very much, he was able to devote a great deal of time to his learning, plunging ever deeper into the sea of the Talmud which had drawn him since childhood. When he sometimes took time off from his studies to attend to matters of charity, the elders criticized him for "neglecting the Torah." To this Aisel replied, "Is there a greater neglect of Torah than to refuse to give or do *zedaka?"*

It was also during this period that R. Aisel began devoting time to the completion of his first book, *Emek Yehoshua*, which he had been working on for some years. Published in 1842, the book created a sensation in the scholarly world of Torah, and Aisel was hailed as a giant amongst the wise men of his time. In his introduction to this work, R. Aisel mentions that his father encouraged him to publish the book and thanks him for having accustomed him from boyhood to the demands of the Torah, and seeing the pleasantness of the Holy One: ("על אשר הרגילני מנעורי לעול התורה ולחזות בנועם ה'"). Aisel

Kalvariya

expresses himself with the modesty which was characteristic of him throughout his life, even inviting the reader
to inform him of any errors in his logic or interpretation:
"אודה ולא אבוש טעיתי"; I will thank him and not be ashamed
that I made a mistake). He also asks the reader to check
everything he has written or referred to, because according to the Talmud *Yerushalmi,* one should not rely on the
thoughts of a young man.

R. Aisel explains the title of the book, *The Valley
of Yehoshua,* by saying that he didn't want to take
an exalted position on the mountain but preferred to
be in the valley: ממעמקים קראתי לה' להושיעני בתורתו הקדושה
(From the depths, or valleys, I called on the Holy One
to save me with his holy Torah) He gives a reference
to the book of Joshua and the date of publication, in
gematria (1842 = (תר"ב = "ויושע של הלכה בעמק יהושע וילן").

Now R. Aisel's congregants basked in his reflected glory.
"R. Aisel has nothing to complain about in Kalvariya," said
one of them. "He came here a gifted young man and will
leave as a great leader in Torah."

With the passing of time and Aisel's increasing renown,
the members of the community came to appreciate more
and more his personality and witticisms, as well as his
stature as a scholar. Although they began to repeat his sayings to all, R. Aisel's attitude to Kalvariya did not change.
He had suffered too many indignities in the years he had
spent there.

It seems that all of R. Aisel's children were born in
Kalvariya, although the oldest, Issachar Ber, may have
been born in Minsk. The only birth date that is certain is
that of Moshe, who we know was born in 1835. All the

39

other evidence is circumstantial. It comes as a surprise to realize that Aisel's four children were born eighteen to twenty years after his marriage, when he and Haya were in their thirties. We don't know if there were any unsuccessful pregnancies or still-births, or whether it was their difficult economic situation or poor personal relations which influenced them to wait so long. This is one of the big questions to which I have no answer.

Interior of synagogue at Kalvariya, Lithuania. Photographed by Bruce Kahn, 1994. The stone synagogue was built in 1803 after a fire destroyed the wooden one. There was a beautiful elaborate Aron Kodesh and paintings of animals on the walls. There were two sections for women on either side of the building

Interior of synagogue at Kalvariya, Lithuania.
Photographed by Bruce Kahn, 1994.

The so-called Rabbi's house, photographed by Saul Isserof in 1994, may have been the home of the incumbent rabbi, or perhaps the Beit Midrash, which I have seen described as a separate building. There were also many small prayer-halls (klois) in Kalvariya, so there must have been a varied mix of residents.

KUTNO

After R. Aisel published *Emek Yehoshua*, he received many invitations to serve as rabbi in communities wealthier and more renowned than Kalvariya.

One such delegation, from the central Polish town of Kutno, offered him especially favorable conditions: a good salary, good housing, free time to devote to his studies and only two sermons to be given during the year, on *Shabbat Hagadol* and *Shabbat Shuva*. Impressed by these generous conditions and by the size of this well-established community, R. Aisel decided to accept the position in Kutno, despite the efforts that Kalvariya was now making to keep the rabbi who was bringing honor and fame to the community.

But, although the Jewish community of Kutno welcomed him with much enthusiasm, R. Aisel soon found that he had made a great mistake. He had neglected to investigate the nature and quality of the community, and was not aware of its strong hassidic character. True, Aisel's father had become a *hassid* and he himself had served as a *hozer* for a short period in his youth in the circle of the Starsheler Rebbe. But while his father became a disciple of R. Shneor Zalman, R. Aisel was never tempted to join any hassidic sect. He preferred instead to follow the path of his grandfather, Mordecai, who had enjoyed a close relationship with the Vilna Gaon and prayed in the same style. Thus, he became a *mitnaged*, a strong opponent of Hassidism. We can wonder today whether it was Yehiel's long absences from home at the court of his *rebbe*, and the ensuing poverty of the family, which provided the emotional basis for Aisel's antagonism to Hassidism, and which he later clothed with his preference for intellectual study as opposed to emotional inspiration.

Not only was Kutno a strong hassidic community, but there was no common language between Aisel and the Jews of the town. R. Aisel spoke with the Lithuanian lisp and was accustomed to the austere Lithuanian style and behavior. Thus the two could not understand each other, and the leaders of the community began to question his credentials and his scholarship. But Aisel refused to be examined by them. "If you have come to show your greatness in Torah," he told the examiners, "then your trouble is for nought. And if you have come to examine me, then let us see if you are worthy to be examiners."

Very soon there was open conflict between the rabbi and the elderly *dayyanim* who were loathe to accept the authority of a younger man. Once R. Aisel questioned the severity of one of the *halakhot* advanced by the older *dayyan*, and asked why the *dayyan* had not sought Aisel's opinion. "I pray to the Holy One to open my eyes to the *halakhah*," said the *dayyan*, "and then I decide. I don't go in search of conversation." "Instead of praying for your eyes to be opened," Aisel replied, "it would be better to pray for clear thinking, because a *dayyan* mustn't adapt the *halakhah* to his own fears, but rather his fears to the *halakhah*."

To another *dayyan* Aisel advised, "Instead of being too strict in *halakhah*, it is better to be strict in common sense and logic. If he (the *dayyan*) wishes to find the answer, he will refuse to make the decision alone."

The same subject would also arise many times in later years, when Aisel was serving as rabbi of Tiktin. To one of the senior *dayyanim* in that town who tended to hand down very severe decisions, R. Aisel once said: "You enjoy forbidden things." "What do you mean?" asked the *dayyan*, deeply offended. "Simply that you enjoy your own severity and forbidding matters to others."

On another occasion R. Aisel remarked to the *dayyan* of Tiktin, "There is not one *zaddik* (pious man) who has not himself sinned at some time. Therefore it is clear that both you and I will also go to *gehenom* (hell). I will not remain there, but you will, because when the Heavenly Court decides that we must go through *gehenom*, I will take a lenient stand. After a certain time I will say that I have done my duty and run from there. But you will be so concerned as to whether you have really served your time that you will stay on and on, and never leave."

On still another occasion, when R. Aisel could not prevail upon the *dayyan* of Tiktin to change his mind, the latter claiming that the *halakhah* clearly prevented him from accepting the rabbi's opinion, Aisel took a firm stand. "It is clear from the *halakhah* that I am the authority here, and therefore you must accept my opinion."

R. Aisel's problems in Kutno were not only with the *dayyan*. For example, he felt that the *hassidim* had too many feasts, wasting time that should have been spent learning Torah. They in turn vented their anger on him because their candidate for rabbi, R. Yitzhak Meyer, had been passed over when Aisel was appointed. It is even said that Aisel barely escaped injury one year, when stones were tossed into his *succah* by *hassidim.*

R. Aisel soon realized that it was not in his power to change the people of Kutno, and ceased making efforts to do so. And it was not long before he decided that he must take the first opportunity to escape from the town, and not allow himself to get adjusted to the lifestyle and mentality of its people. Nevertheless this decision did not prevent him from continuing to make remarks and criticisms about the *hassidim,* which certainly did not endear him to them. Of their communal feasts, he is reported to have said, "A beast stuffs his belly, and a man should fill his head, but the *hassidim* exchange the head for the belly."

Sometimes the *hassidim* tried to provoke him in turn, but R. Aisel was always ready with a sharp retort. Once one of them asked Aisel why he did not wear a silk *kapote* (coat) as other rabbis did. "There are rabbis who consider themselves perfect beings, without fault. If these men wish to say 'I am a worm and not a man,' they must wear silk from the silkworm; otherwise no one will believe them. But, as I am a simple man, with many faults, I can say 'I am a worm' without having to wear a coat produced from the silkworm."

Once the keeper of the bathhouse prepared a great feast and invited R. Aisel to participate and hear what his children had learned. When asked what he thought of the boys' knowledge, R. Aisel replied ambiguously, "I wish someone would say that about my children." When asked what he meant by this remark, R. Aisel answered, "Surely they can learn better than their father, and I mean that I wish the same could be said of my children."

R. Aisel was always amongst the first to finish the

Shmoneh Esrei, because he did not like to keep the congregation waiting. Once, when asked why he prayed so fast, he explained: "There are men whose hearts and minds are at peace with their Maker and with themselves. They are not troubled by strange thoughts and ideas during their prayers, and so they have plenty of time to pray. But I am not like them, so I must hurry and finish my prayers quickly." In another version of this story, R. Aisel explains, "Sometimes a *baal agalah* sees young rascals hanging onto the back or sides of his wagon. So he starts to drive faster in order that they will have to jump off. So it is with me. Sometimes when I pray strange thoughts and ideas come into my mind, and I must finish praying quickly so that I will get rid of them."

Another congregant asked R. Aisel, "Why does the rabbi hurry through the *Shmoneh Esrei?* We are used to rabbis who extend the prayers." "And I," retorted the rabbi, "am used to *baalei-batim* (landlords, bourgeoisie) who turn their eyes to heaven when they pray, and not to the feet of the rabbi!"

When one of the townspeople criticized the rabbi for hurrying through prayer when it was his responsibility to pray for the whole congregation, the rabbi replied laughingly: "If I pray for all of you, I shall never finish!"

On the other hand, when R. Aisel noticed a man praying so rapidly that he finished within a few moments, kissed his *siddur* and turned to go, he stopped the congregant and remarked: "In *Megillat Esther* we read that Ahashverosh reigned from India [הודו] to Cush [כוש]. Our sages asked whether this implies that these countries were close to each other or far apart. I have learnt from you that they are indeed close together, for you covered the distance from the prayer Hodu [as in India] to Cush [a kiss in Yiddish] as fast as an arrow."

On the subject of his attitude towards the length of the service, R. Aisel once said: "I don't like to draw out the prayers, but I support the right of other rabbis to do so, since it written 'המאריך בתפילה מאריכים לו ימיו ושנותיו.' (He who spends much time in prayer, his days and years are lengthened).

"And," he continued, "rabbis are in need of such consideration, since it is written in tractate *Pesachim*, 'Woe to the rabbinate which buries its incumbents.'"

When those in his company asked, "But, as your honor is also a rabbi, is he not in need of such special consideration?" R. Aisel replied with a smile: "אני מקדם רפואה למכה I bring the cure before the illness. Instead of the rabbinate burying me, I hasten to bury the rabbinate."

This characteristic of refraining from lengthening prayers unnecessarily seems to have become a Shapira trait. My father told me that his own father, Yehiel, had similar feelings. Though not a rabbi, Yehiel was a popular *baal tefillah* in the town of Lenczyza, and was always careful not to draw out prayers, especially at the close of Yom Kippur. (He and his wife, Esther Leah, died in a typhoid epidemic in 1916 within a few weeks of each other).

A well-known story which circulated in Kutno concerned R. Aisel's dismissal of the *shochet* (ritual slaughterer), who did some slaughtering while drunk. It relates that when the *shochet* came to the rabbi with some of his colleagues and asked on what basis he had been fired, R. Aisel replied: "On the basis of *Had Gadya*. For it is written, 'the Angel of Death came and slaughtered the slaughterer.'" But the aggrieved man would not give up so easily. "Why should the *shochet* pay with his life if the animal is to be slaughtered anyway?" he asked. "Because he slaughtered on the Eve of Passover, after four glasses of wine, and therefore he was drunk, and that was his guilt."

R. Aisel seems to have harbored a prejudice against ritual slaughterers in general. One *shochet* came to him for advice. "I am offered a bridegroom for my daughter. He is from a good family and makes a good impression, but he is very quiet and never talks. Should I agree to the *shidduch?*" The rabbi replied that "not everything the *shochet* slaughters is always kosher, just as not everything a wise man says is always clever. As long as the silent one keeps quiet, no fault can be found with him."

Later, when a *shochet* in Slonim transgressed the law, R. Aisel fined him by forbidding him to slaughter cattle (*behemah* in Hebrew) and limiting his work to the killing of chickens. The *shochet* asked R. Aisel the reason for such a sentence. "A man who sins is a *behameh* [fool, in Yiddish]. Therefore he may not kill a *behemah* [cattle]. Because it is written, 'לא תעמוד על דם רעך' ["Do not stand by when the blood of your friend is spilt," (*Kedoshim* 17)].

When asked why *hazanim* (cantors) sometimes also served as ritual slaughters, the rabbi replied: "In order to illustrate the verse 'רוממות ה' בגרונם, וחרב פיפיות בידיהם' [Praise of the Holy One in their throats, and a double-edged sword in their hands.]"

In a similar vein, a *hazan* once said to the rabbi, "People say that *hazanim* are fools, but I am witness that this is not so." "You can't be a witness," answered R. Aisel, "because one does not take evidence from fools."

Unlike the poor village of Kalvariya, Kutno was a large town with a wealthy population, in which R. Aisel had more scope for his many and varied charitable works on behalf of the poor and the sick. Even though he planned to leave, he did not neglect this aspect of his work. When the leaders of the community came to him once about the *eruv* (wire demarcating the boundaries within which one is allowed to carry things on the Sabbath), which was in frequent need of repair, he said, "First let us examine whether you are accustomed to giving something out of your possession on weekdays, for instance to charity. Then we will worry about the *eruv*. For, if you don't give anything away on weekdays, you will surely not be giving anything away on Sabbath." (For additional stories about R. Aisel's thoughts and deeds regarding charity, see the chapter "The Rabbi Against the Rich.")

Dissatisfied with his situation in Kutno, R. Aisel accepted with alacrity when he was invited to serve as rabbi in the city of Tiktin, even though it meant a cut in salary, for Tiktin was considered a town of scholars, one which honored the Torah. Although there were many *hassidim* there, they were men of learning, and the community had the Lithuanian flavor which was so close to R. Aisel's heart.

Aisel's stay in Kutno had been short, and his departure was brief. But, although they were happy to see him leave, no sooner was he gone than he was missed, for he had managed to leave his mark during his brief stay in the town, and the congregation now realized they had lost a scholar of great genius. They decided therefore to invite him back at a larger salary and with the promise that they would be more amenable in their behavior towards him. But Aisel refused. "In a year of hunger I gave a *heter* [permit] for *kitniot* [pulses forbidden on Passover, and a pun on Kutno], but it was only a temporary *heter*, not a permanent one." On the same subject, he added, "A rabbi is like a *talmid hakham*, and a *talmid hakham* like a *kohen* — he is forbidden to remarry his divorced wife." As to the raise in pay offered, R. Aisel commented, "If Kutno has the extra money, let them spend it on *tzedaka*, because the money belongs to the poor and not to the rabbi."

R. Aisel proceeded to Tiktin in 1849, when he was forty-eight years old.

View of Tiktin Synagogue and Beit HaMidrash, now a museum.
A. Shapiro 1988

51

TIKTIN

Tiktin (or Tykocin in Russian) is situated in northeast Poland, in the Bialystock province, near the border between Poland and Lithuania. It was mentioned already in the thirteenth century, and Jews had lived in the town since 1522, when ten Jewish families from Grodno were invited to settle there. Given sites where they could build their homes, they were later allowed to establish shops, a synagogue, a cemetery and their own autonomous community. A 1536 charter provided that the rabbi and the head of the town council should jointly judge cases between Jews and gentiles. The Jews engaged in the wholesale trading of salt, spice and cloth, and by 1576 there were fifty-four homes owned by Jews. Their rights were renewed by royal charter in 1576 and 1639. In 1642 a baroque synagogue was built which remained the finest building in the town till 1740. Although the Nazis ruined the interior and the women's section, the synagogue building still stands, preserved as a historical site, and the *Beit HaMidrash* has been made into a museum. I have included a photograph taken by my brother in 1988.

Tiktin produced many famous rabbis in its early years, including several important authorities on *halakhah*. Its importance in Jewish life was greatest in the seventeenth and eighteenth centuries and many of the rabbis who served there went on to outstanding careers in other well-known towns and centers of learning. In 1857, shortly after R. Aisel had moved from Tiktin to Slonim, the community

Door of Beit
HaMidrash, Tiktin,
now a museum and
cultural center

of 3,456 Jews constituted seventy percent of the population, but the figure gradually declined towards the end of the century.

The salary offered to R. Aisel in Tiktin was meager, but when he asked that it be increased, he was told that one didn't need much money in Tiktin because fish were plentiful and cheap. "If you are offering me קדחת [fever, suffering, or, in slang, something worthless] for salary, then you can't expect me to eat fish, for fish is bad for a fever."

Besides scholars and tradesmen, the Jewish community of Tiktin also comprised a large population of poor and indigent people who lived in pitiful conditions, and R. Aisel devoted much time and effort to trying to alleviate their suffering. To those who claimed they sympathized with the poor in their suffering but did little to help them, R. Aisel said, "I never saw a man sitting in a warm house and shivering because he felt sorry for the poor, who are sitting in their unheated huts, freezing with cold."

With further regard to the giving of charity, R. Aisel used to say, "Whoever doesn't find it in is heart to give *zedaka* doesn't have a Jewish heart. We have studied in the *Yerushalmi (Terumoth)* that all the body's organs are dependent upon the heart, and that the heart depends upon the pocket. Therefore, if there is no pocket, there is no heart, and if we say 'A Jew up to his pocket,' we mean 'a Jew up to his heart'."

While many of the wealthy of Tiktin gave generously to charity, there were others who were mean and unfeeling. One of the latter had been declared by the *gabbaim* (synagogue managers) as being impervious to any appeal. Although the *gabbaim* tried to convince R. Aisel that it was useless to approach this man for a donation, Aisel insisted on calling upon him. But when the man saw who was knocking at his door, he simply refrained from opening it, and when he came to the synagogue for evening prayers, he approached the rabbi and said in a bragging tone: "The rabbi is supposed to be so clever, but what foolishness was this to come to my door? Surely the rabbi was told that I do not give *zedaka* and knew that he was troubling himself for nought!" "Oh," replied R. Aisel, "I didn't come for a donation, I came to warn you. I heard that pork has become so expensive that gangs of thieves are going about at night stealing pigs and selling the meat to gentile butchers at high prices. So I was afraid that they might try to snatch you and sell your flesh too. I just wanted to do my duty and warn you."

In his sermons R. Aisel always tried to influence his congregation to do good deeds and give charity, praising the generous and criticizing the miserly. Once someone remarked, "The rabbi preaches only about charity and loving-kindness, but there are many other matters with which the rabbi should concern himself." To which Aisel replied, "I am not the rabbi of those who refuse to give to charity."

R. Aisel came to another wealthy but mean villager to ask for a large sum of money, but the man offered only one ruble, saying that while he never refused anyone, he also never gave more, because he thought that was a generous enough sum to ensure that he would get into paradise. R. Aisel countered with the following story: "Once there was a rich man who never refused to give *zedaka* but always gave only small sums. When he passed away and came to heaven for judgment, he proudly told the heavenly court of his deeds. Upon checking his claim and finding it to be true, the court accorded him "limited" paradise — a small windowless house which was hot during the day and cold at night. When the man returned to the court to protest his lot, he was told: 'You are a clever merchant, surely you know the value of money. Yet for your odd rubles, which would barely buy a hut, you expect to have a palace!' And you," concluded R. Aisel to the villager, "you will get to *Gan Eden* because you gave charity, but what kind of paradise do you expect it to be?!"

On another occasion a wealthy tax-collector gave R.

Aisel a large sum of money thinking that the rabbi would surely put some of it aside for his own old age. He was surprised when R. Aisel was back again within a short time to ask for more, saying that those who had received the money had already spent it and were in need of more. "But our sages of blessed memory said one must not give away more than a fifth of one's money, and the rabbi has given it all away. How is that possible?" Aisel replied: "In order not to go to *gehenom* it is enough to give one fifth, but in order to get into paradise one must give much more."

On another occasion, one of Tiktin's misers commented to R. Aisel, "We thought that the new rabbi, a genius and a sharp scholar, would capture us with new thoughts and new ideas. But he merely repeats the old cry that poor people need money and that a lot of poor people need a lot of money." "Well," replied Aisel, "you behave like a son of Noah before the giving of the Law, and you want to hear new thoughts which came after the giving of the Law." (In Hebrew, misers are called "sons of Noah" after the Talmudic phrase "הנהרג על פחות משוה פרוטה"; he could be killed for a matter worth less than one *prutah*.)

Similarly, when R. Aisel called upon one of Tiktin's wealthy tight-fisted men about a matter of public concern, the man told him, "It's a pity you troubled yourself, Rabbi. Don't you know that I am בן נוח (one who refuses to give charity)?" "But Noah had three sons, and I wonder why you chose to be a חם [Ham, in Yiddish, means an ignorant peasant]."

In accordance with his feelings about the importance of *zedaka*, R. Aisel treated the poor and sick with more respect and attention than he gave to the wealthy men of the town, and the poor came to look upon him as a true friend, often appearing at his home in search of help. Thus, it used to be said of him that his standards were the opposite of everyone else's; he was more impressed by rags and poverty than the trappings of success. "If you want to influence R. Aisel, or get some help and attention from him," people would say, "dress more simply and shabbily, for the more unfortunate you appear the more successful you'll be."

According to the conditions of his contract, R. Aisel did not have to deal with היתר ואיסור (the daily problems and questions about forbidden foods and related matters). He could leave this work to the *dayyanim* and supervise only the more difficult cases. He did, however, have to take part in the *Beit Din*, where he soon earned a reputation as a wise, learned and incorruptible judge, who loved truth and justice. So many people began to flock to the Tiktin *Beit Din* from far and wide that R. Aisel soon found his precious study time endangered.

Although he tried to limit the number of cases brought before him by insisting that he would only hear those brought by the residents of Tiktin, his sound judgments merely served to increase his popularity and bring more plaintiffs to the town. While the Jews of Tiktin basked in the fame of their rabbi, and the renewed reputation of the rabbinate of Tiktin, the rabbi himself wondered how he could free himself from this time-consuming work.

The *Beit Din* sat in a building with windows that had been fitted with iron bars by the community leaders some years previously. This had been done to prevent the flight of poor and orphaned children who had been forcibly rounded up for military service by agents of the czar. These children, who were known as *"cantonistim"* or "kidnapped," were sent away to other areas to live with non-Jewish farmers and peasants. Very often they were forced to convert to Christianity, a common phenomenon in the early part of the nineteenth century. When they were old enough for army service, they were forced to serve for a period of twenty years.

R. Aisel demanded that these iron bars be removed from the public rooms, as he could not bear to see them. When the community leaders refused to do this, Aisel suspended the *Beit Din* and heard no cases. The leaders eventually gave in, but most unwillingly and ungraciously. As a result, relations between R. Aisel and the community leaders worsened and he became increasingly outspoken against them. They responded by criticizing him for being too aggressive and nonconformist, complaining that he was shaming the rabbinate and estranging the rich by going from door to door asking for charity and spending too much time with the poor. When one of the *parnassim* asked R. Aisel whether it wasn't demeaning for him to be seen so often and so at ease in the company of tradesmen and simple people, R. Aisel asked in return: "And aren't you ashamed to demean yourself by your snobbishness and your bragging!"

On the other hand, the *parnassim* were afraid to anger the majority of the congregation, who admired and loved R. Aisel, with their critical and offensive behavior. In an attempt to placate everyone, they decided to increase the rabbi's salary by one ruble a week. But when he heard of this R. Aisel remarked, "I am afraid that even if they raise my salary by a ruble a week, they are cursing me ten rubles' worth."

Another wealthy man who refused to give *zedaka* once asked the rabbi whether he didn't think his associating with the poor was disrespectful of both the Torah and himself. "If I thought the respect of the rich was something important and worthwhile," R. Aisel replied, "your question would be valid, But, since respect of the rich is not 'respect,' so their disrespect is not disrespect." Furthermore, R. Aisel is supposed to have said: "I have known many rich men in my life, and they all wished to be respected for their wisdom rather than for their money. Is there any better testimony that their wealth is not worthy of respect? And as for their wisdom, that is something we will consider when they lose their wealth!"

R. Aisel did not always trust the community leaders. He knew it was very difficult to do public work honestly and in good faith. Thus, he said, the prayer "מי שברך" (May He who blessed our fathers), in which we ask that all the sins of those who work for the community be forgiven, was composed for those who did engage in this work. (This prayer is recited after the reading of the Torah.)

R. Aisel once allowed a seat at the eastern wall to be rented out to a wagon driver who had become rich and who gave a lot to charity. The wealthy congregants and other notables who had seats there were angry, and took it as a personal insult. When they complained to the rabbi, he replied: "There are so many *ferd* (horses or blockheads, in Yiddish) sitting at the eastern wall that we need a wagoner to look after them."

Once R. Aisel praised a community leader who had

worked for a charitable cause. "The rabbi praises the man, but the man denounces the rabbi!" remarked his companion. "Well, he made a mistake, and I too sometimes make mistakes," answered R. Aisel.

The *shamash* of the Tiktin synagogue became too old to fulfill his duties, and the *parnassim* dismissed him without providing him with any other source of income. The *shamash* called them to a *Din Torah* before R. Aisel, but the leaders refused to come, saying that since they would not accept the rabbi's ruling in the matter anyway, there was no point in troubling him. But R. Aisel did not accept their refusal to attend the *Din Torah*. "If you do not come, I will not allow you to continue living in Tiktin," he warned them. "For a community which does not respect a *Din Torah* is not a community, and therefore has no representatives."

Unperturbed by the attitude of the *parnassim*, R. Aisel continued to act in accordance with what he felt was just, ignoring those who disagreed with him. Thus, when the *shochet* of the town was caught in a misdemeanor, R. Aisel dismissed him, refusing to reinstate him even though the leaders begged him to do so, and the man was prepared to admit his guilt and repent. "A man does not sin unless some foolish spirit enters into him, and a fool is not permitted to be *shochet*," declared the rabbi.

Though his personal stature grew, and his popularity increased despite his difficulties with the leaders, R. Aisel became increasingly disillusioned with his position in Tiktin. It no longer gratified him. "A rabbi does not realize how weak he is, what little real strength he has, and the village policeman doesn't realize how strong he is. Who would dare to tell the policeman what to do? The

61

congregation of Israel survives by virtue of the innocence of rabbis who believe in their strength and the stupidity of policemen who are ignorant of their own power."

But, when the people of Radom, a developing town in central Poland, invited him to be their rabbi at a handsome salary, he refused, saying: "Radom is a town of *hassidim* in need of מופתים [wonders]. But my strength is only in אותיות [signs or letters]."

Another offer came from the town of Kalish, whose representatives came to interview the rabbi in his home to find out if he was really all that he was said to be. They were charmed by his personality, but on seeing his simple home and life-style, they politely remarked that it did not seem to be in keeping with his standing. "If you find fault with the quality of my home, I am not suitable to be the rabbi of your town."

R. Aisel's dissatisfaction began to be known to his congregants. In order to prevail upon him to stay in the town, they launched a plan to build a large yeshiva where the rabbi would serve as *rosh yeshiva* as well as rabbi of the town. But Aisel refused to accept this added responsibility, and continued his policy of encouraging young men to study in the big *yeshivot* of Lithuania. He believed that it was good for the young scholars to leave their homes and familiar surroundings, and to study hard and diligently in difficult and strange environments. Refuting the popular notion that babies learn Torah in the womb and therefore need not continue studying after coming into this world, R. Aisel pointed out that the angel who tapped babies on the upper lip so they would forget the Torah, and thereby shaped the depression in its center, did so in order to oblige Jews to study and master the Torah consciously. "What is learned easily is quickly forgotten," he said. "Only learning accomplished through real effort and diligence is retained."

During the tranquil early period in Tiktin, R. Aisel Harif wrote his second work, *Nahlat Yehoshua,* which was published in Warsaw in 1851 to great acclaim in scholarly circles. Two years later, in 1853, Aisel Harif was invited to Slonim, to take over the position of R. Berish Ashkenazi, who had become rabbi of Lublin. Aisel was happy at the opportunity to move on to such a prestigious town, and he remained in Slonim for the rest of his life, a period of about twenty years. The years in Slonim were to be the most fruitful and productive of all.

Alec Shapiro at restored synagogue of Tiktin. June 2004

SLONIM

The town of Slonim is in the Grodno district of Belarus. It was first heard of in the eleventh century, when it was a wooden fortress situated on the banks of the Szczara River, in the flat marshy territories between the Slavs and the Lithuanians. The area was contested between the two peoples until 1569, when it was unified with Poland, under whose rule it remained until 1795. Although the Polish parliament sat there at one period, the fortunes of the town fluctuated considerably during these years and until the end of the eighteenth century, when the area passed to the Russians, who held it for the next hundred and twenty years. Its situation gradually improved, and in the middle of the nineteenth century Slonim became an important provincial town with a growing population, increased industrial power and trade connections through Russia. At the end of the nineteenth century, Jews made up over seventy per cent of the population. But after 1915, when the Germans defeated the Russians, the occupation brought great suffering to Slonim, and it never regained the status it had held earlier.

The first privileges to Jewish inhabitants of Lithuania were granted in 1388, in an attempt to attract Jews from Poland to develop Lithuania's economic life, but Jews were probably living there before then. The main evidence of Jewish settlement in Slonim in this period are tombstones that date from the late thirteenth and mid-fourteenth centuries. Unfortunately, legal records and documents pre-

The Great Synagogue
in Slonim. Built in 1642

served in Slonim date only from the mid-sixteenth century, but there are indications that the town played an important part in the political life of Lithuania, even though it was only fourth or fifth in importance to other towns such as Brisk and Grodno.

In 1583 Slonim was mentioned as one of the communities declared exempt from a special tax, and Jewish merchants from the town traded with Lublin and Posen. According to the records of the Council of Lithuanian Jews, the town was listed as an independent community or *kahal* in 1563. Although a magnificent stone synagogue was built there in 1642, Slonim's Jews then suffered waves of persecution. In the seventeenth and eighteenth centuries there was trading in wheat and timber with Koenigsberg, and wealthy merchants went to fairs in Leipzig. Contracting for the army, the manufacture of alcoholic beverages and other crafts (prayer shawls, *tefillin* and ritual items) were part of the flourishing Jewish economy.

In 1847 there were 5,700 Jews, and in 1897 there were 11,435, which meant that the Jews comprised seventy-eight percent of the population. By the nineteenth century there was also wholesale trading in timber, furs and hides, transport contraction, iron foundries, agricultural machinery, brick kilns and steam mills. The first textile factory was opened by a Jew in 1826; it had thirty-five workers, twenty of whom were Jews.

In 1881 anti-Jewish hooligans destroyed some homes, but the Jewish population continued to grow, partly due to expulsions from nearby villages. By the end of the century labor unions and self-defense groups were established, and many Jews began to be active on the Jewish and

Polish political scene. Slonim of the twentieth century was a far cry from the Slonim of the nineteenth century. Apart from the economic upheavals and hardships of the First World War and the Polish occupation, the influence of the Enlightenment had led to modern education and secular culture, involvement in government on local and national levels, and a broad spectrum of Jewish political and religious activity. There was a Jewish vice-mayor, and Jewish representatives were elected to the *sjem* or parliament. All that was destroyed in the Second World War.

Due to internal problems, the community of Slonim had remained without a rabbi since 1844, when R. Berish Ashkenazi left the town. The *parnassim* had been seeking a strong personality who would lead the community justly and not allow divisive elements and interested factions to disrupt its life as had happened in the past. They felt that in R. Aisel Harif they had found the man they were looking for — a great scholar steeped in learning, as well as a wise judge who was recognized as one of the greatest of his generation throughout the countries of the diaspora.

The community heads got their first taste of R. Aisel's famous wit when they came to Tiktin to bring him his official letter of appointment. Upon telling him with pride that Slonim was a very old town, and that it was commonly believed that Rashi's great-grandchild was buried there, Aisel replied, "If the great-grandchild of Rashi really is buried in Slonim, that is not so bad. But you had better make certain that Rashi himself is not buried there, because if he is I will certainly not come to serve as your rabbi." The implication being of course, that if scholarship was dead in Slonim, Aisel was not interested in serving that town.

Before accepting the position in Slonim, R. Aisel put forth many demands to the congregation. First of all, he demanded a high salary so that he would not have to seek additional sources of income as he had been forced to do in the past. Any additional moneys that he received from selling *hametz*, etc., he wished to spend as he saw fit, mainly on charity. Moreover, he asked to be freed from the practical work of deciding questions of היתר ואיסור, requesting that this be left to the *dayyanim*. Finally, he told the community leaders, he wanted the right to absent himself from the town whenever he wished, and to be free from having to give sermons, although he was prepared to preach if and when he felt like it (which he usually did before Passover and on Yom Kippur).

Although the community leaders first tried to bargain with R. Aisel, they eventually agreed to all his conditions and agreed to pay him eighteen rubles a week, double the salary of the previous rabbi. And so during the autumn of 1853, R. Aisel and his family moved to Slonim, into the refurbished house of the rabbi that had been vacated by R. Berish Ashkenazi several years previously.

Many visitors came to greet and to inspect the new rabbi, perhaps even to bait him, in order to enjoy a witty response. One of the older residents approached him saying, "It is said in our town that it is a good sign for the rabbi and for the congregation if rain falls when a new rabbi comes. And here the new rabbi has come, but the sky is clear and the sun is shining. What kind of a sign is this? "Well," replied R. Aisel, "the rains are according to the rabbi. An indifferent rabbi brings just a slight shower; an average rabbi, an average rain; and a great rabbi brings

Tashlich on the banks of the Szczara

heavy rains and storms. A rabbi such as I should bring a flood, but since the Holy One promised mankind never to bring another flood, the sky remains clear and the sun shines."

The prankster of the town also confronted R. Aisel one day as he was returning from the synagogue. "I've heard it said by the scholars of Tiktin that the rabbi is not as great in Torah as he is supposed to be." "Perhaps the scholars said and perhaps they didn't say, so it's doubtful whether they should be punished. But you have definitely made this allegation, so you should surely be flogged," answered Aisel.

The death of Czar Nicholas I in 1855 was a great relief to Jews throughout Russia, and his successor Alexander II proved to be a much more liberal and tolerant man. The old decree of filling military quotas with the forced enlistment of young children was somewhat softened, and the fears of press gangs and kidnapping by unprincipled collaborators became a thing of the past. But it was not until 1874 that the status of the Jews regarding military service at the age of twenty-one became equal to that of other nationalities throughout Russia.

During the decree of the *"cantonistim"* which was in force between 1827 and 1855, many tens of youngsters from Slonim alone were abducted and spirited away to distant cantons where they worked on farms and subsequently become *Nikolaiski soldats* (Nikolai's soldiers). Boys of eighteen were taken directly to the army. These children were mainly orphans or the only sons of poor families. In the later years of this period, ways were found to circumvent these abductions, mainly by paying ransom, and this was to become one of the more important activities of R. Aisel. The Jews who carried out the abductions became outcasts in the community. They and their families found themselves beyond the pale of society even many years after the decree was suspended, and the daughters of such families sometimes remained unmarried as a result. The whole experience of the "*cantonistim*" left a deep impression on the Jewish consciousness for many generations, and was reflected in songs and literature of this and later periods. For there was not only pain aroused by the fate of the many children who vanished without a trace, but also by the fact that many "*cantonistim*" returned to their homes after twenty to thirty years' service in the army and kept the trauma alive.

In 1863 a second Polish rebellion by the citizens of the area was put down firmly by the Russians. In its wake the Russians began courting the Jews, who were an important element in Lithuania and had remained neutral during this episode. In this context, the minister of the army, who was in Slonim on the occasion of Czar Alexander's birthday, paid a formal visit to the Great Synagogue with his whole entourage. They were received by the heads of the community as well as the *shaliah tsibur* and his choir, who sang the national anthem and a selection from *Tehillim*. Refreshments were also offered to the civil guard who were stationed in the town, and the minister of the army made it clear to the invitees that they were enjoying the hospitality of the Jewish community.

I have found no reference to this occasion in R. Aisele's anecdotes. Perhaps he was away at the time, or simply thought it wiser to avoid comment. There is no doubt, however, that such occasions were part of Alexander II's quiet liberal policy of promoting the Russification of the Jews, and encouraging the *Haskalah* movement. Although, on the whole, the Jews withstood the policy, they nevertheless enjoyed the material and political benefits which came as a result.

Other reforms introduced by Alexander concerning compulsory military service included the suspension of the yearly draft for a period of eight years, and the introduction of the system of *kvitanziot,* which were receipts or authorizations. These papers were given to the families of volunteers who had fallen in the Crimean War, and the holders were freed from military service. Since these "bearer certificates" were transferable, they soon were in great demand, and their price rose from four hundred to a thousand rubles. Clearly only the very rich could afford to keep their sons out of the army, but R. Aisel, who viewed service in the Russian army as an evil to be resisted and fought against in every possible way, was determined to help the sons of poor Jews as well. R. Aisel became a big dealer in *kvitanziot,* and whenever he succeeded in acquiring them he would go in search of poor young men whom he could save from the dreaded army service. He placed himself in such jeopardy by his efforts to bribe doctors and officials in order to gain military exemptions that his family, concerned for his safety, tried to dissuade him from these activities. The danger was not only from the authorities but also from those Jews who, for various reasons, would have liked to see the rabbi exiled. But, due to his secretive methods and his habit of keeping his own counsel, no one could obtain any definite evidence against him, and he continued to raise large sums of money, which he spent on saving young men from Russian military duty.

R. Aisel had many other funds for his charitable work besides those for redeeming captives, including those for supporting established families that had fallen on bad times, for assistance to poor girls so that they could get married (*hahnasat kalla)* and, of course, for helping the sick. He kept no written records of these activities, but kept all the details in his head, never revealing who gave him money and certainly not those who received it. He became so well-known for his charitable work that the needy from other towns also came to him for help. Once the rabbi wanted to raise money for such a person, but was asked why he was concerning himself for a pauper who was not from Slonim. "I am the rabbi of Slonim, but I am a Jew everywhere," he replied.

During the reign of Alexander II, Slonim began enjoying an economic boom. The government was building railroads and fortresses for the army. A whole new railway network was being developed, together with access roads, and the new invention of the telegraph was also put into use, creating a demand for poles and cables. Much of the business went to Jewish contractors and sub-contractors, who made money for themselves and also helped others to make money. Since so many became wealthy and community funds were plentiful, the leaders offered R. Aisel a raise in pay so that he too would enjoy the benefits of the booming economy. R. Aisel, however, refused to accept more money, saying, "In Kalvariya I didn't get even three rubles a week and I was three rubles short. In Tiktin I received ten rubles and I was short five. Here in Slonim I already receive eighteen rubles and I am still a little short. So if I get any additional salary I will be even shorter, and who can bear so much suffering?"

In fact, R. Aisel did earn additional money from judging court cases of the newly rich, who contributed to what would today be called "The Rabbi's Discretionary Fund," but he never used any of this money for himself. It all went for the charitable works and other causes which he preferred not to publicize. The people of Slonim knew that their rabbi could have become a rich man if he had kept even part of the income for himself, but R. Aisel continued to maintain himself and his family on his regular salary, taking loans when necessary.

Now very careful about how he used his time, R. Aisel delegated as much of his work as possible. When asked why he placed so much responsibility on the *dayyanim*, he replied, "I didn't come to Slonim to make the acquaintance of the chickens which the housewives buy for Shabbat."

When he was asked why he had indeed come to Slonim if he refused to decide on day-to-day questions, leaving them to the *dayyan*, R. Shraga Feitel Feinstein, if he relied on Moshe Yitzhak the *maggid* to give sermons, and if he wouldn't teach in the yeshiva, where the lessons were given by R. Yudel, R. Aisel answered with a twinkle in his eye: "My job is to see that R. Yudel doesn't preach, that Moshe Yitzhak doesn't teach and that Dayyan Feitel doesn't declare them both unacceptable [not kosher]."

R. Feitel, one of the most famous *dayyanim* of his time, served in Slonim for more than fifty years. There is an amusing story which relates that R. Aisel once got so involved in a question that a woman brought to him that he spent hours searching out all the authorities, completely forgetting the lady, who was sitting patiently and waiting for his decision. When Aisel suddenly became aware that she was there, he asked what she wanted, and she replied that she was waiting for his answer. R. Aisel shook his head at his own behavior, apologized to the lady and sent her off to R. Feitel. After that, the story goes, he never again dealt with questions which individuals brought him.

R. Feitel would only consult with R. Aisel on serious problems which he didn't want to decide by himself. Once there was a question about a cow which had been slaughtered. Discussing the matter with R. Aisel, R. Feitel suggested taking a lenient stand, because the loss of a large amount of money was involved. But R. Aisel hesitated, saying, "A decision which is not in accordance with the *halakhah* involves an even greater loss." He was always in search of truth, and believed in honesty in all aspects of life.

On another occasion, during a *Din Torah* between two smugglers who were both known to be dishonest, R. Aisel whispered to R. Feitel, "How can we conclude this business?" "It's very clear, I see no difficulty," said R. Feitel in surprise. But Aisel insisted, "It is written that after you have passed judgment on them, they will be innocent in your eyes, and how can we ever see them as innocent?"

There was often a difference of opinion between R. Feitel and R. Aisel, the former sometimes finding it difficult to accept the latter's method of reasoning and decisions, especially since he himself was also a learned man and an excellent teacher. Once R. Aisel and R. Feitel discussed a certain *halakhah* about which they disagreed. Finally the *dayyan* said, "even the author of the 'Ba'er Heytev' agrees with my opinion." "Nevertheless," answered R. Aisel, "The 'Ba'er Heytev' was only a *dayyan* in Tiktin, and *I* was the rabbi."

But, after carefully studying the reasoning behind them, R. Feitel usually did accept Aisel's decisions, and he eventually became a good friend and supporter of the rabbi. Indeed, the scholars of Slonim generally enjoyed the atmosphere which R. Aisel brought with him, often keeping him in the Beit Midrash HaHoma (the Wall) after daily prayers, for intellectual and spiritual discussion.

Once, the well-known *maggid* Reb Zvi Dainow gave a sermon in the *Beit Midrash* when he was passing through Slonim. R. Aisel was amongst those present, and Dainow thanked him profusely for the honor the rabbi had done him. He then asked Aisel's opinion about what he had said. "Your 'saying' was excellent," replied R. Aisel, "but 'not saying' would have been even better."

Gradually, R. Aisel established his authority in the town and won over the community's twelve *parnassim*, who supported him and carried out the plans and projects which he initiated. Aisel wanted to build a new hospital, to refurnish the synagogue, and to re-activate old welfare and charitable institutions. He took no part in the daily conduct of these matters, relying on the officials to see that the work was done. His concern was mainly to collect the funds that made these projects possible.

R. Aisel did, however, find the time to visit the town shelter, which served vagrants and transients, in order to check the cleanliness of the linen on the beds and of the rooms in general. Unhappy with these unexpected inspections, the caretaker told him, "A rabbi should sit at home and decide problems of *halakhah*, and not waste time inspecting mattresses." To which R. Aisel retorted, "You had better be quiet or I will send R. Feitel the *dayyan* to check this *hekdesh* [shelter for the poor and elderly, with an older connotation of something dedicated to the Temple]. He is even stricter than I, and if he rules against you, you may find yourself without *parnassah!*"

All these activities involved much physical effort and emotional courage, for not everyone received the rabbi becomingly, especially when it was a matter of charity. Once one of the tight-fisted merchants shouted at him that he had not been selected as rabbi and given a good salary in order that he should knock on doors to solicit money. "I see the hunger of the poor, and you see my feet running back and forth for *zedaka*," R. Aisel told the miser. "But if your luck changes, I won't look at your feet when you have to knock on doors yourself seeking help."

It so happened that this man did lose his money within a short time, when one of his main debtors died and his sons left the country without paying his debts. In a desperate situation, the merchant had to request help from the public funds. But, when one of the *gabbaim* advised R. Aisel to withhold assistance in retaliation for the way the man had behaved towards him, Aisel ordered that not only should the merchant receive enough money to put him back on his feet, but that this should be done secretly in order to preserve the man's honor. "No, I did not predict that he would some day have to seek charity. I only said that I would not envy him if he ever came to such a condition."

During his time in Slonim, there was an extremely

severe winter which had a very bad effect on the poor and vulnerable. Children in particular suffered from lack of warm clothing and food, and were seen begging on the streets. Deeply disturbed by this situation, R. Aisel decided to advance the date of the annual charity appeal, which was normally held between Purim and Passover. In his usual way, the rabbi himself went from door to door asking for donations.

One of those he called upon was an extremely wealthy businessman who never gave money for any cause. But Aisel decided to call on him anyway due to the severity of the situation. Although the man was very surprised at the rabbi's visit, he showed him into his elegant living room. Once there, R. Aisel sat down and gazed steadily into the man's eyes without saying a word. Finally, the host said, "How is it that the rabbi does not tell me what has brought him here?" "You probably know what a serious situation there is this year," R. Aisel said sadly. "I am taking part in the special appeal to raise funds for the needy. Wherever I go I speak against the indifference of the population to their poor brethren. I came to ask you to participate in the great *mitzvah* we are doing, but then I remembered the words of our sages of blessed memory, who said: 'It is a good deed to refrain from saying that which will not be listened to' [Y'bamoth 65:b]. So I decided to take this opportunity to follow the advice of our wise men, and not to speak words to you which will not be heard. That is why I am sitting here in silence." The *gvir* understood the intention of R. Aisel and was sufficiently embarrassed to give him a generous donation.

The rabbi's house and the various public institutions

were situated in the *shulhof* or large square adjacent to the Great Synagogue. The *Batei Midrash* of the *Hevra Kadisha*, as well as those of the Tailors' and the Carpenters' Guilds were also there, and all came under the authority of R. Aisel.

R. Aisel had a particularly close working relationship and friendship with Reb Israel Kaplan, one of the twelve *parnassim* and a leading member of the community by virtue of both his upstanding character and his scholastic ability. Reb Israel and the rabbi used to meet daily to discuss community affairs. When people saw the two talking quietly in a corner, they would say "העיר מתייעצת" (The town is taking counsel) or "סלונים דנה במצבה" (Slonim is discussing its situation). This greatly strengthened Reb Israel's position, because everyone knew that if R. Aisel had complete confidence in him, he must be an honorable man.

R. Aisel's word was law in Slonim, and any wish of his was like a command. Not only was he regarded with love and esteem by (almost) all, but the entire community accepted his authority. However, compassionate as he was to the poor and suffering, he was as aggressive in his defense of religion and morality. This was demonstrated once when an "enlightened" gentleman and his mistress came to visit in the town. On the rabbi's orders they were invited to spend the night, under guard in separate rooms, in the community offices. In spite of their loud protests, R. Aisel would not relent, and the following morning they were expelled from the city.

In his deeds and in his decisions, he always tried to find the most humane, as well as the most just solution.

One year, a dealer brought a consignment of *etrogim* for the Succoth festival which were not of the best quality. R. Aisel found it difficult to tell those who inquired of him that the *etrogim* they had purchased were suitable for the blessings. So no one bought the *etrogim*. The dealer came to R. Aisel and complained that he would be ruined if he couldn't sell his stock. To which R. Aisel said, "I cannot lie in order to save your business." But the dealer continued to protest, and finally R. Aisel said, "You know what? If someone wants my opinion on one of your *etrogim*, give him two, and then I can say that one is better than the other."

One day a young woman came to R. Aisel's rooms crying bitterly. Her husband had deserted her and she was left without any means of support, like a rudderless ship on a stormy sea. R. Aisel immediately summoned the husband and tried to persuade him to return to his wife and repair the marriage. But the man refused, saying he could no longer bear to live with her. "If so, give her a divorce," demanded R. Aisel. After thinking for a moment, the husband declared that he was ready to give a divorce in return for a hundred rubles. Upon which, the wife, who was listening in the next room, burst into tears and cried out, "Where shall I get a hundred rubles! I haven't a kopek to my name!" "So you will remain an *aguna* [deserted wife]," said the husband. R. Aisel became very agitated at the woman's cry, got up from his desk and took the tractate *Kiddushin* from his book-case. Opening it at the first page, he said to the husband, "Read for yourself what the *Mishnah* has to say on the subject: 'A woman is married in three ways ..., and is released from marriage in two ways: by divorce or by the death of her husband.' So the choice is yours. In which way will you decide to release your wife from the bonds of marriage?" The astonished husband agreed to give his wife an unconditional divorce.

Once a rabbi from a neighboring town came to Slonim to raise money for a special project of his. R. Aisel allowed him to speak at the Great Synagogue, and a large crowd came to hear him. They listened attentively to the scholarly talk, but when the rabbi began his appeal for funds to support his cause, the audience gradually left the synagogue until only a few remained. The result was that the visiting rabbi took in very little money for his efforts. He came to R. Aisel to complain and voice his disappointment. R. Aisel heard him out, and then said, "Such things have happened before. When Moses gathered the children of Israel everyone came to listen — 'ויקהל משה את עדת ישראל' [Moses assembled all the congregation of the people of Israel; Ex. 35:1]. But when he appealed to them to donate silver and gold for the building of the Tabernacle 'ויצאו כל עדת ישראל מלפני משה' [Then all the congregation of the people of Israel departed from the presence of Moses; Ex. 35:20]. And if Moshe Rabenu didn't become angry, why should you?"

The Slonim Yeshiva

A large yeshiva had been established in Slonim in the early part of the nineteenth century, which gradually developed an excellent reputation. In 1830 R. Avraham Weinberg became the Rosh Yeshiva, but by the time R. Aisel arrived in Slonim, his place had been taken by R. Lima, apparently because R. Avraham had been too much of a *hassid* for the *mitnagdim* who made up the majority of the town.

R. Aisel devoted much of his time to developing and

strengthening the *yeshiva* financially, and also worried about the welfare of the students. He treated R. Lima with great respect but, although he visited the yeshiva often, and at times acted as examiner, he refused to teach there as long as R. Lima was *Rosh Yeshiva*. Over the years, other excellent rabbis followed R. Lima, the teaching staff was expanded and the yeshiva became R. Aisel's pride and joy. Aisel showed only affection, concern and encouragement towards the yeshiva students, with no trace of the deadly sarcasm of which others lived in dread. He was always in good humor with them and full of patience, even when he suffered one of his asthma attacks. The students returned Aisel's affection and esteem, always feeling free to approach him with their problems, whether scholarly or personal.

If he perceived an outstanding talent among the students, R. Aisel would take special interest in him. Orphans also received his special attention. Once a widow from a neighboring village came to R. Aisel with her young son to complain that the yeshiva would not accept the boy because none of the wealthy men in the town would undertake to support him. After Aisel examined the boy to ascertain that he was knowledgeable enough to learn in the yeshiva, he stomped off to the yeshiva, summoned the *gabbaim* and banged loudly on the table with his stick. "Because the rich landlords don't contribute to the yeshiva, you are making this widow and her orphan son suffer?" He then ordered that the boy be accepted into the yeshiva immediately and given a decent grant for his living expenses.

On other occasions R. Aisel quietly arranged monthly allowances for poorer boys, and he always took personal care of students who fell ill. When he met students whose mouths and teeth were darkened from eating blackberries, he would say, "So that's how we blacken the faces of those who study Torah!" a pun on the Yiddish expression *farshwartzed,* which means, being exhausted or depressed from hard work.

But not all the prodigies fulfilled their expectations. There was one young man who had been a brilliant scholar in his youth, but who left his books and sought less desirable society after his marriage. R. Aisel tried many times to get him to change his ways, but when all his pleas fell on deaf ears, he finally gave up and decided to ignore the young man. The latter, however, sought every opportunity to bother Aisel with vapid questions and to embarrass him. Once he asked the rabbi, "In *masechet Shabbat* it is written that the wife of Adam died because he did not fulfill his vows. But I have not fulfilled my vows for many years, and my wife's health has not been impaired."

R. Aisel replied, "It is a great sin not to fulfill one's vows, and such a person is liable to be punished by the untimely death of his wife. But you are such a sinner that you may be suspected of waiting for your wife to die in order to marry someone more beautiful. Do you really think the Almighty would award you such a prize for breaking your vows?"

In Aisel's time nearly five hundred students attended the yeshiva, which then consisted of seven departments, but they had to find their own lodgings and were dependent on the goodwill of the townsfolk for their meals. They "ate days" [essen teg] with various families in the town, who were happy to perform the *mitzvah* of promoting the learning of Torah, but R. Aisel found this old custom demeaning and embarrassing for the yeshiva boys.

Once Aisel was going to the bathhouse accompanied by a very thin young yeshiva student, who was carrying his *pekel*, or bundle, containing a towel, clean clothes, etc. On the way they met one of the rich men of the town, a very robust, well-rounded gentleman. After some conversation, R. Aisel said, "Tell me Reb Hillel, how many meals do you eat a day, that you are looking so well?" "At least three or four," replied Reb Hillel. "The luck of the rich!" exclaimed R. Aisel. "Look at this skinny young man. He eats 'whole days' and see how *he* looks."

R. Aisel sought a new solution to the problem, and when he heard that R. Israel Salanter of Kovno had asked his townsfolk to supply that town's *yeshivot* with food directly, in order to save the pride of the students, R. Aisel decided to inaugurate the same system in Slonim. Not only was a diningroom set aside for this purpose, but Aisel also worked hard to raise money to establish a kitchen so the boys could have regular meals in proper surroundings, without being dependent on the townsfolk. But he was not successful in this particular appeal.

R. Aisel had first met R. Israel when he visited Kovno to promote his first book, *Emek Yehoshua*. R. Israel came to pay his respects to Aisel on this occasion, even though according to protocol Aisel should have gone to him first, as he was a visitor to the town. (This act by R. Israel reflects the high esteem in which R. Aisel was already held at that time.) Aisel offered Salanter a copy of his book to peruse, but R. Israel refused it, apologetically explaining that it was not easy for him to grasp a book so quickly. Aisel was quite astonished by this answer, because Salanter, known by his book *Ohr Yisrael* (The Light of Israel), was one of the great men and original thinkers of the period. And indeed, after R. Aisel had been in Kovno for some weeks and had come to know him better, he expressed his amazement at Salanter's intellectual abilities. "Look what a creature The Holy One, Blessed Be He, has created in His world. Everyone tries hard to show the world what a great and wonderful person he is. Everyone worries lest their smallest utterance gets lost and might detract from their stature. But the *gaon* 'Ohr Israel' works equally hard to *hide* his greatness from the world." Although Aisel Harif was known as the one who towered over all the other geniuses of his generation because of his profundity and sharpness, he was a modest man. With particular regard to R. Israel he used to say, "I consider myself a scholar only up to the threshold of R. Israel's house, for when I am actually standing before him I am as nothing in the presence of his Torah."

In addition to overseeing the yeshiva and its students, R. Aisel kept an eye on the *hadarim* and their teachers, since his distaste for the way in which this early education was carried out stemmed from his own childhood experiences. He had much to say on the subject.

He was against the *melamed* receiving his fees directly from the parents, because he felt that this influenced the *melamed*'s attitude to the children of parents with higher status. R. Aisel was also against the *melamdim* holding classes in their own homes. He thought it was more important for the *heder* to be held in the spacious synagogues, and that the *minyanim* could be more easily held in private homes. For, "The Holy One, Blessed Be He, hears and listens everywhere, but it is doubtful if a child can hear and listen when he is learning in a kitchen or a bedroom."

R. Aisel also believed that little children should have proper study programs, and was much concerned that many of the teachers were not suited for the job of educating the young. He took strict measures to protect the young children from such *melamdim*. Once he forbade parents to send their children to a teacher by the name of Reb Isser. This man, although a *melamed* of long standing in Slonim, was a pedant with a bad temper which he vented on the children. Left without pupils, Reb Isser came to Aisel to complain. "My rabbi, how shall I make a living? I shall die of hunger." To which Aisel countered, "I shall lend you some money and you can start dealing in cattle." "But I know nothing about dealing in cattle!" cried Reb Isser. "You also know nothing about dealing with children, so go out and trade," was R. Aisel's final remark on the subject.

Similarly, when one of Slonim's slaughterers could not continue work because his hands had begun to tremble, he came to the rabbi with the suggestion that he become a teacher of small children. "No! No!" exclaimed R. Aisel. "Just as you are unfit for slaughtering cattle, you are also unfit to teach the young, and we cannot allow you to slaughter them."

But, try as he might, R. Aisel was not able to introduce reforms in this sphere because any change in the traditional form of education might be interpreted as giving in to the *maskilim*, followers of the Enlightenment movement, whom he felt were out to destroy the traditional roots of the Jewish people by introducing their new ideas. So, critical as he was of the ways the *hadarim* were being run, he was more critical of the Enlightenment or Reform approach. "Reform from within is a *mitzvah*," said Aisel, "but reform from without is an evil decree."

Nonetheless, the fact was that many young people in Slonim were quite influenced by the Enlightenment movement and wanted to introduce secular subjects into traditional Jewish education, but they were afraid to state their views publicly as this would bring down upon them the wrath of R. Aisel and his followers. This group secretly acquired secular and anti-religious literature from Vilna, and established an Enlightened *heder* (*heder metukan*) in Slonim in 1871. They also brought in a special teacher to teach the Russian language, but when this move provoked an outcry by both the public and R. Aisel, they were forced to dismiss the Russian teacher and close the *heder*.

The Reform group was surprised by R. Aisel's stand, as they knew of his opposition to the old *heder* system and had mistakenly thought he would not oppose the new venture. But they were afraid to challenge him for fear that they too would have to leave the town, or at least face the hostility of the townspeople. Immediately after R. Aisel's death in 1873, however, the *heder metukan* was reopened, this time under the pretext of a royal decree to keep from antagonizing those who revered R. Aisel's memory. (For more stories about R. Aisel's fight against the *Haskalah*, see the chapter, "Orthodoxy versus The *Haskalah*".)

As long as he lived, R. Aisel protected the strong foundations of Judaism in Slonim, preventing any cracks from appearing in it. Yet at the same time he refused to participate in meetings with rabbis who discussed ways to strengthen religion and prevent divisions within the ranks. "There are rabbis who are unable to protect the towns in which they live and who therefore turn to reforming the world. But I, who am unable to reform the whole world, will watch over the unity and purity of my own town."

During his first years in Slonim, R. Aisel worked hard to get the machinery of the community organized according to his own ideas, and eventually the affairs of the community ran smoothly with little intervention from him. He was then able to give much of his time to learning and writing, and was also able to spend time away from Slonim in order to oversee the printing of his books, which he usually had done in Vilna. Thus, he was able to publish his other nine works in rapid succession. *Ibbei HaNahal* and *Sefat HaNahal*, which deal with *drash* or homilies, were printed in Koenigberg in 1855 and 1859. But the work that won him the greatest acclaim was *Noam Yerushalmi*, his monumental work on the Jerusalem Talmud, which brought him accolades throughout the entire Jewish world.

The Jerusalem Talmud, of which only four sections survived, had long been neglected by scholars, because errors in printing and faulty setting had so corrupted the text over the years that it was not possible for even the best scholars to comprehend or evaluate its contents. R. Aisel's keen analysis and elucidation of the difficult passages, and his ability to re-arrange and set forth the text in its original clarity, restored the *Yerushalmi* to its proper glory. This he was able to do because of his profound knowledge of both Talmuds and their commentaries, and because of his deep conviction that the *Yerushalmi* was as important as the *Bavli*. He was one of the few scholars who held this belief.

Noam Yerushalmi caused a sensation upon its publication and it's still an important text today. It was as if R. Aisel had provided the key to a locked treasure chest, enabling new generations of scholars to study, interpret and comment on this little-known work. The work's publication brought honor and renown not only to Aisel himself but also to his town, Slonim. He well deserved the title חד בדרא (unique in his time) because of his great knowledge and wisdom.

The four parts of *Noam Yerushalmi* were published between 1863 and 1869. *Zera'im* (1863), *Mo'ed* (1866), *Nashim* (1868) and *Nezikin* (1869). In 1868 R. Aisel also published *Aizat Yehoshua*, a commentary on the questions asked by the "Sages of Athens."

In the preface to this work, Aisel alludes to the state of his health and prays that his eye problems will not hinder him from completing the last volume of the *Noam Yerushalmi*. In 1870, despite failing health, R. Aisel published *Marbeh Tevuna*, on Mussar, written according to the basic principles of the Babylonian and Jerusalem talmuds. Although he had plans for yet another book, his failing health prevented him from making much progress.

As R. Aisel grew older, his asthma began to trouble him more and more, and he felt the need for a change in climate during the summer months. He would leave for Vilna after Shavuoth, returning in time for the High Holy Days. But there is no doubt that the real reason he spent so much time in Vilna was that he liked to oversee the printing and proofreading of his works, not trusting anyone else with this important task. In addition, he also saw to the sale and distribution of his books.

R. Aisel was highly regarded in Vilna, where he was treated with honor and respect. He always stayed at the same lodgings, which were situated in the courtyard where the printing press of Avraham Yitzhak Dvorzatz stood. Aisel and Dvorzatz enjoyed a close friendship, as well as a good working relationship, during the period in which they cooperated on the publication of Aisel's works. Aisel had his own *minyan* in his rooms, which became a regular meeting place whenever he was there.

There are many anecdotes about these trips of R. Aisel's, so they must have occasioned much comment. Once some-one remarked, "Your honor sits here in Vilna, but receives his salary from Slonim?" "Yes," replied R. Aisel. "The peo-ple of Slonim are happy to pay me to stay in Vilna."

On the other hand, R. Aisel has also been recorded as saying, "It would really be a *mitzvah* if they would get rid of me. But they are afraid of this because, since one *mitzvah* brings on another, they can't be sure what may be in store for them if I am no longer their rabbi. So they let me be, and I am free to enjoy myself."

On another occasion Aisel observed that it was custom-ary for people to travel in the summer for a "change of air." This allowed people from various places to meet and, of course, to gossip. "And," he continued, "it is only natu-ral for them to gossip about their rabbi. I am afraid they will discover so many bad things about me that Slonim will want to dismiss me. Therefore I travel too, so that when they come to give me notice, they won't find me at home!"

Another story relates that R. Aisel claimed that, since the *maggid* Reb Moshe Yitzhak also traveled in the summer months, there was no one left in Slonim to tell the people of the faults and shortcomings of their rabbi who left them for such long periods. Thus, he could make his trips to Vilna with an untroubled mind.

During one of his visits to Vilna, R. Aisel was invited to a *Brith Mila* in a small village called Antakalia. Both rabbis of the place were also there. Said R. Aisel, "Such a small, dead little village and two rabbis! וגם את המת יחצון" (And also the dead one they shall divide; Ex. 21:35).

On another of his trips to Vilna, during the preparation of the *Noam Yerushalmi*, R. Aisel had to spend the night in a small village where a woman was having a very difficult labor. Since the doctor was at his wits' end, the husband, upon hearing that R. Aisel was in the village, came and asked for the rabbi's assistance. "But what can I do?" protested R. Aisel. "Pray for my wife," replied the worried husband. So R. Aisel raised his hands toward heaven and said, "*Rebono Shel Olam,* let my tribulations over the *Bavli* and *Yerushalmi* be credited to this poor woman to relieve her tribulations in childbirth." Within a few minutes, it is said, the woman delivered a healthy boy.

R. Aisel sometimes stayed overnight in a village called Zshetel. As soon as his presence became known, there was much excitement and a holiday was declared. The tradesmen closed their shops, the artisans put away their tools and everyone gathered at the home of the richest man in the village. A big *seuda* (meal) was prepared at which R. Aisel and the head of the Zshetel community would hold a Talmudic discussion, and people would sing and dance as if it were Simchat Torah. Once R. Aisel remonstrated that this practice involved a loss of work and business, but the villagers replied, "Rabbi, we want our children to see what כבוד התורה [honoring the Torah] is, so they might also be moved to want to study Torah."

During another Simchat Torah celebration in Slonim, R. Aisel was in very high spirits, and said laughingly, "Gentlemen, do not call me rabbi of Slonim, but rabbi of Warsaw!" When the company expressed surprise at these words, he explained: "Whoever calls me Slonimer Rav is lying, because I don't want Slonim, and Slonim doesn't want me. With regard to Warsaw, I would like very much to be rabbi there, but they don't want me either. So to call me rabbi of Warsaw is only a half-a-lie."

Fires were a common occurrence in small towns and villages because of the prevalence of wooden buildings, and the Beit Midrash HaHoma, where R. Aisel normally prayed, was rebuilt in masonry in 1790–1792 after the previous building burnt down. Although R. Aisel scoffed at the *hassidic* miracle-workers, there were many in Slonim who considered him to be a miracle-worker himself. He was supposed to have said once, "Where I am rabbi there will be no fires," and it was generally held that there were no serious fires in the town while R. Aisel served there. There is a story that a fire broke out one Shabbat morning not far from R. Aisel's home. A general panic ensued, but R. Aisel calmed the people who were then in his house; spreading out his arms toward his books, he declared, (perhaps commanded?) "There will be no more burning!" The fire died down and only one house was burnt on that occasion. The story goes on to tell of a rabbi, who tried the same technique on a similar occasion some years later, with disastrous results.

Although he was outspokenly critical of any undesirable behavior among his congregants, R. Aisel would not allow anyone from outside Slonim to do the same. "I am getting paid for what I say, but it is forbidden for anyone else to speak against these poor sinners free of charge."

But whatever his witticisms about the town, Aisel Harif could never disguise the fact that he loved Slonim and his congregation, and would not dream of exchanging them for any other. His years in the town were the finest and most productive of his life, but with his characteristic modesty, Aisel refused to take credit for his achievements there, neither for his own scholastic works, nor for his public activities as spiritual leader of the community.

The interior of the Great Synagogue before 1939

The interior of the Great Synagogue 2004

The almamer in Beit HaMidrash HaHoma, where R. Aisel prayed during the week

THE MEN WHO MADE SLONIM

The twenty years that R. Ariel spent in Slonim were the most fruitful not only of his own life, but in the life of the Slonimer Jewish community as well. R. Aisel and the men he gathered about him, some of the most outstanding scholars and educators produced by Lithuanian and Russian Jewry, brought the life of the community to its peak, so that the town became known as one of the most interesting centers of learning in Europe in those years. There were R. Aisel himself, in his public capacity as town rabbi and head of the *Beit Din*; his assistant, R. Feitel the *dayyan*; R. Moshe Yitzhak, the Maggid of Kelme; and R. Yehuda Vernikosky, the great Talmudic authority and author of *Pnei Yehuda*, who headed the yeshiva. And, of course, there was also R. Avraham Weinberg, who founded a new hassidic dynasty in 1858, "the Slonimer." Many currents were flowing in the spiritual life of the community.

Rabbi Avraham

R. Avraham had been head of the Slonim Yeshiva in 1830, many years before R. Aisel came to town. But as his interest in mysticism gradually drew him closer and closer towards Hassidism, people began to question whether a confirmed *hassid* should be heading the *mitnagdic* yeshiva in Slonim. However, this extremely learned man was apparently such an excellent teacher that he was able to keep his personal philosophy out of the classroom.

Nonetheless, by the middle of the 1840s, R. Avraham's

position became untenable, and he either resigned from his position or was asked to do so. He then opened a small *heder* where he could propound his views, as well as a *steibel* with his own *minyan*, where he could pray in the special style he had developed. Although his economic situation declined considerably, his influence and standing among the Kobryn *hassidim* gradually grew, as did his group of followers. Thus, in 1858, when the leader of the Kobryn sect Rabbi Moshe HaZaddik passed away, R. Avraham was the obvious successor. Since his "court" was already well-established in Slonim, it was there that he established his particular sect of Hassidism, which became known as the "Slonimer," thereby adding yet another facet to the already vibrant life of the Jewish community of Slonim as well as of Lithuanian Jewry in general. However, the Slonimer were not the first *hassidim* on the Lithuanian scene, this distinction belonged to the Karlin sect which had established itself in the town of Kobryn in the 1760s.

The distinguishing elements of R. Avraham's sect were his recognition of the personal nature of prayer and of worship of the Almighty; his emphasis on the kabbalistic philosophies of the hidden and the revealed; and his ongoing contact with Eretz Yisrael. This last he expressed by encouraging his followers and members of his own family to make aliya, and by providing assistance to those who chose to settle there in the Holy Land. In this respect, R. Avraham continued the tradition of the few hassidic leaders of the eighteenth century who actively supported aliya, and maintained their spiritual connection and authority with the faraway disciples. In fact, the aliya of Slonimer *hassidim* to Tiberias was one of the important *aliyot* of the last century.

The *mitnagdim* of Slonim looked with amazement at the phenomenon of this new hassidic sect in their midst. While there was no repetition of the violent opposition which had occurred in the past, there was much resentment and suspicion hidden below the surface.

On one occasion, shortly after R. Avraham was appointed leader of his sect, he and R. Aisel met at a social function. R. Aisel said, "Only yesterday, Reb Avraham was an ordinary man like everyone else, so how is it that he has suddenly become a *zaddik* and is called, 'Holy, Holy'?" "Why should that be so surprising?" replied R. Avraham. "It says in the Torah that if you take part of a sheaf of grain for an offering it becomes holy, forbidden to strangers and to the unclean, and is eaten in holiness and sanctity. So, too, is it with a simple man. If a whole community takes a man and dedicates him to G-d's service, and calls him 'Rabbi,' he indeed becomes holy." "If so," retorted R. Aisel in an oblique criticism of the unlearned masses who were attracted to the mysticism of the *hassidim*, "it is also written that if a deaf person, a fool or a minor makes an offering, it is not considered an offering."

Another time, R. Aisel's followers came to tell him that they had seen the *hassidim* carrying R. Avraham on their shoulders to the *Tashlich* ceremony, "Why are you so surprised?" said Aisel. "Isn't it written 'שקר אין לו רגלים' [that falsehood has no feet]?"

Nevertheless, in spite of the antagonism caused by their differing views, the two men lived and worked in the same town for a period of some fifteen years, together molding the religious and intellectual life of the community.

Both had strong personalities and were outstanding and creative in their own sphere, and both had achieved great renown in the Jewish world. Thus, although they occasionally crossed swords, they had great respect for each other's character, qualities and achievements.

Indeed, R. Aisel praised R. Avraham whenever possible. When people in distress came to Aisel to ask his intercession with the Holy One, Aisel often sent them to R. Avraham because: הוא מקורב לשכינה יותר ממני, ותפילתו מקובלת יותר מתפילתי. הוא כבן המחטא על אביו ועושה לו רצונו (He [R. Avraham] is closer to the Holy One than I, and his prayers are accepted more easily than mine. He is a son who want to please his Father, and therefore does all that he wishes). The personal glory of both these men was reflected in turn on the community of Slonim, raising the standard of learning and scholarship to new heights.

As a result, Slonim achieved great prominence as a town of sound Torah education and outstanding scholars. There was a very conservative attitude to religious observance on the part of all the spiritual leaders, who kept watch against the slightest change or suggestion of reform, for all of them were united in their fight against the threat of the *Haskalah* movement.

The house of the rabbi and the "court" of the *hassid* were centers of endless activity which drew followers and admirers from all over Poland, Lithuania and Russia. The townspeople thrived on the attention and adulation showered upon them, and enjoyed the fact that the intellectual activity made for a flourishing economic life as well. In short, this was a truly Golden Age for Slonim.

With his growing reputation as head of the *Beit Din*, R.

Aisel was called upon to deal with many of the important conflicts in the Jewish world. Once he was requested to arbitrate a serious problem between the rabbinate of Mir and the head of the Mir Yeshiva, R. Haim-Leib. On another occasion, he was asked to settle a case between R. Yosef Ber and R. Naftali Zvi Yehuda, the heads of the yeshiva in Wolozyn. As people came from far and wide with private and communal problems, R. Aisel gradually earned his second popular appellation, Reb Aisel Slonimer. Indeed, everyone knew that a reference to R. Aisele, or to Aisel Harif, or to R. Aisel Slonimer, was a reference to Rabbi Yehoshua Aisek Shapira of Slonim, and until today Aisel's name is connected mainly with that town.

The Maggid of Kelme

Not long after R. Aisel had settled into his new position in Slonim, he reminded the community leaders of one of the conditions of his appointment: that a permanent *maggid* be hired. The man he had in mind was R. Moshe Yitzhak, the Maggid of Kelme, one of the great preachers of his time. Although he was born and educated in the vicinity of Slonim, Moshe Yitzhak became known as the Maggid of Kelme after having spent a short but tempestuous time in that Lithuanian town during his various journeyings.

It is interesting that R. Aisel suggested R. Moshe Yitzhak for this position, in light of the fact that he had never liked preachers who would come to Slonim and accuse his congregants of all manner of sins of which they were innocent, but Moshe Yitzhak always managed to stir the hearts and conscience of his listeners to tears with his castigating sermons.

101

The two men were completely different from one another in style and temperament. R. Aisel was always full of energy and good humor, quick in movement and thought, using his wit to expose and criticize dishonesty in study as well as in private and public behavior. He did not suffer the company of fools gladly, and yet this hard and critical exterior concealed a good-natured soul who ached for the poor and suffering and worked tirelessly on their behalf as long as he lived.

Rabbi Moshe Yitzhak, on the other hand, was quiet and thoughtful in manner, and was always careful in his personal life not to hurt anyone's feelings. He had an excellent scholarly background, and enjoyed intellectual repartee as much as R. Aisel. But in his public life he was a fiery orator, scathing in his sermons. Instead of making use of *aggadot* or legends to make his point, he would tell parables which referred pointedly to a specific individual or group of people, of whose behavior he disapproved.

The following is a typical example: As a *mitnaged,* R. Moshe Yitzhak always used to pray in the appropriate synagogue while on his travels. Once, however, he came to a village where there was only one synagogue in which *hassidim* and *mitnagdim* prayed together. He was accustomed to hearing a *shiur* in *Mishnah,* or *Gemara* before prayers, but in this synagogue he heard no *Dvar Torah,* and in the midst of the prayers, he heard people chatting with their friends. Thus, when he came to give his sermon that afternoon, he told a story about a grocer who went to a neighboring town to buy his supplies, and amongst other goods bought a special brand of tobacco and a special brand of tea, which he placed together in his large bag.

One day a customer purchased tea in the grocer's shop, but returned it complaining that it tasted of tobacco, and another brought tobacco and returned it because it tasted of tea. "And so," said the Maggid of Kelme, "I, who have been used to praying with the *mitnagdim*, always see them studying Torah and not dragging out the prayers. And when I once prayed with the *hassidim*, I saw them praying with great fervor but did not hear the voice of Torah. Now here in this mixed synagogue, I see that each group has absorbed something of the other: the *hassidim* don't pray, and the *mitnagdim* don't learn Torah."

Once Moshe Yitzhak came to preach in Slonim and R. Aisel came to hear and meet the famous *Maggid* of Kelme. When R. Moshe saw R. Aisel he decided to quote from the sages instead of telling one of his parables. But he could not refrain from his usual attack against his listeners, accusing them of all kinds of sins and omissions in their relations to other people and to the Almighty. Hearing all the accusations against his congregants, R. Aisel's heart was filled with indignation.

When Moshe Yitzhak asked for Aisel's opinion at the end of his sermon, the latter replied: "I would like to tell you a story, as is your own custom. Once an angel came down to earth in order to see what the world of man was like. He came to a large town and saw beautiful houses, big shops and factories and all aspects of the good life in a town. It happened that a crowd of Jews gathered about him, and while he was telling them how much he enjoyed their city, a Russian policeman approached and asked for his passport. Not understanding, the angel asked the Jews what the Russian *goy* wanted from him. They explained that the policeman wanted his travel document so that he could see what the angel's name was, where he was born, where he lived, and so on. 'What business is it of his?' asked the angel. The Jews explained that there were many thieves and murderers in Russia, and one had to have a passport to prove one's honesty. 'And this simple fellow has the authority to do this?' asked the angel. 'Well, above him stands the minister of police, and above him the governor of the district, and the governor is appointed by the czar himself,' replied the Jews. 'And who is this czar who rules the country and appoints policemen to guard the honesty of the people? Is he wise and clever on the subject of justice and honesty?' the angel asked. 'Oh, the czar is a war hero. He killed tens of thousands of people until he conquered the state!' replied the Jews. At which the angel laughed and exclaimed, 'Foolish people! A man who has murdered tens of thousands of people appoints policemen to check whether every person in the country has a document proving he is not a thief or a murderer!'

"And you," continued R. Aisel, "who come here to preach morality and accuse the Jews of Slonim that they are guilty of slander, gossip and לשון הרע, you are yourself guilty of slander and gossip when you pour out your wrath on the congregation."

Nevertheless, when R. Aisel sought a permanent *maggid* for Slonim, he selected the same Moshe Yitzhak because, despite all the differences between them, both men were passionately devoted to the Truth and stood unafraid against the powerful community leaders whose interests were often opposed to those of the rabbi.

Each man moved independently in his own sphere, and

their meetings were always held away from the public eye. If there were any professional differences of opinion between them, they were never revealed. Indeed, they seemed to complement each other and worked together harmoniously for twenty years until R. Aisel's death. Thus, these two men, together with Admor (our master, teacher and rabbi) R. Avraham, worked to strengthen Orthodox Judaism in Slonim, while putting their extraordinary stamp on the town.

When Moshe Yitzhak first came to Slonim, R. Aisel said to him, "A rabbi without a *maggid* is like a wagon-driver without a whip, and a *maggid* without a rabbi is like a whip without a wagon-driver."

R. Aisel always spoke highly and with great respect of Moshe Yitzhak. "First he fills his own heart with his thoughts, and when his own heart overflows, his thoughts enter the hearts of his listeners and go deep into their souls." However, Aisel had not been so liberal towards itinerant preachers who used to speak in Slonim before Moshe Yitzhak's arrival. It is reported that he once approached a *maggid* who had spoken at great length, saying, "You are preferable to a dying man." "What do you mean?" asked the *maggid* with surprise. "Well, when a dying man finishes, everybody weeps, but when you finish, everyone is happy." Aisel asked another *maggid*, "The Lord visited so many plagues on the Egyptians before they let the Children of Israel out. Why didn't He put the plague of the preachers on them? Because, if He had, the *maggid* would still be preaching, and the Children of Israel would never have gotten out of Egypt."

But despite his criticism of their ways, R. Aisel always

allowed the itinerant preachers to speak because he didn't want to harm them financially. In addition, he established a special fund for them, so that even if they were too awed to speak before the Maggid of Kelme, they would still receive their remuneration.

As to Moshe Yitzhak himself, he was born in 1825 in a village called Ozranida, near Slonim, and was orphaned at the age of ten. His grandfather in Slonim, a scholarly and God-fearing man, took him in and saw to his education. Although considered a genius, Moshe Yitzhak, who had married at the age of eighteen, first turned to commerce as a source of livelihood, but he was unsuccessful as a businessman and returned to Slonim in search of other work. A gifted speaker, he was given a position as *maggid* for the Butchers' Guild, at a salary of half a ruble a week.

But Moshe Yitzhak did not see this as his life's career, and began wandering from town to town until he reached the home of R. Israel Salanter of Kovno, leader of the *Mussar* movement. He became Salanter's student, and spent some two years there, during which time his wife had to take over the responsibility of supporting the family.

After Moshe Yitzhak left Kovno, his first post was in Kelme, Lithuania, and although he remained there for only two years due to severe conflicts with the business people in that community, the appellation, "the Maggid of Kelme," remained with him for the rest of his life. What followed was not a happy period for Moshe Yitzhak, the pattern established in Kelme repeated itself over and over again: he would be acclaimed by the masses, but the traders and community leaders, outraged by his attacks on their dishonest behavior and practices, would either inform on him to the authorities or drive him from their town. Yet, Moshe Yitzhak was undeterred and continued to carry out what he saw as his task in life: to be a watchdog over the morals of the Jewish community and its Judaism. This was also the reason that Moshe Yitzhak preferred to speak in those towns where he saw that Orthodox Judaism was increasingly threatened by the growing influence of the *Haskalah.*

Once, when his travels brought him to Riga during the summer months, he was surprised to find almost the whole Jewish population away at the seaside. He decided to follow them to the resort of Dubeln where, to his amazement, he discovered that the men were praying on Shabbat without their prayer shawls.

That afternoon when he gave his sermon, Moshe Yitzhak told the following parable: He had come to Riga and found the town deserted, yet, as he walked down the street of the synagogue, he heard the sound of weeping. He followed the sound till he came to the house from whence the weeping came, but upon entering, he found no one at home. He went from room to room till finally he found the source of the crying: a tallis lying on the chest of drawers. "Little *tallis,* what is the trouble?" asked Moshe Yitzhak. "My owner has gone away for the summer. He took his wife, his family, his servant and all his valuables with him, but left me here alone in the empty house." The *maggid* said, "Don't cry. You'll see, the day will come when your owner will go on another long journey, and at that time he'll leave his family and all his possessions behind, and will take only you."

So important was his life work to him that R. Moshe Yitzhak refused to accept large fees even when they were offered to him. When he received the invitation from Aisel Harif to become permanent *maggid* of Slonim, Moshe Yitzhak accepted with alacrity because he knew R. Aisel's reputation. Later, when he realized with horror that the position carried the noble salary of eight rubles a week, Moshe Yitzhak declared: "The people of Slonim may think they can bribe me to keep my mouth shut, but they won't succeed." He also used to say, "A tailor who doesn't take the left over material for himself, a shoemaker who uses good leather and doesn't deceive the customer, and a shopkeeper who uses honest scales — they all have a greater share in the world-to-come than many of the rabbis."

Later on the *maskilim* and anti-Orthodox elements also became the objects of his fiery attacks, and they in turn saw in him their arch-enemy while at the same time acknowledging his talents and his powers. They wrote critical articles about him in an effort to enlist public support against "the Black Raven," as they called him, and demanded that he be expelled from their cities and handed over to the authorities. Yehuda Leib Gordon, the poet and writer, was the leader of the Reformists at this time, and the battle between the two men was carried on in the Jewish press by Gordon and in the synagogues by Moshe Yitzhak and his supporters. But Moshe Yitzhak would not be deflected from his cause. His popularity was unabated, and crowds still thronged to hear his sermons. One of his songs, "What Will Be When the Messiah Will Come?" (Vos vet sein ven der Mashiah vet kummin?), was sung by all and remains a popular folk song to this day.

The *maggid* remained in Slonim together with R. Aisel for nearly twenty years, refusing offers of positions which would have brought him much greater remuneration. But he preferred to stay with R. Aisel. Perhaps the bonds that tied Aisel and Moshe Yitzhak were their courage to stand up to the rich and influential, their demand for honesty, justice and care for the poor and needy, and their opposition to the *Haskalah* movement.

After R. Aisel died, the *maskilim* opened a secular library for young people, along with the *heder* they at last succeeded in opening. Moshe Yitzhak likened these activities to those of butterfly collectors, who store what they catch in bags where the butterflies die for lack of air. For, he said, the souls of young people caught in the trap of the Enlightenment also died because of the lack of Jewish atmosphere.

But eventually Moshe Yitzhak realized that he could not stem the tide of *Haskalah*. At the end of the year of mourning for R. Aisel, he resigned his position in Slonim and resumed his wandering life, even though he was now close to fifty. He never held a permanent position again and no one was ever appointed to fill the position he left vacant in Slonim. His travels took him as far as London, but he found the Jews there too phlegmatic and they found him too flamboyant. In the last years of his life, ill and a widower, Moshe Yitzhak was taken in by his son. He died in 1898, at the age of seventy-two. Even by today's standards of freedom of personal behavior, Moshe Yitzhak had been an unusual and highly colorful character.

HASSIDIM AND MITNAGDIM – BRIEFLY

The hassidic movement, which came into being in the early part of the eighteenth century, was founded in the Ukraine by R. Israel ben Eliezer, the *Baal Shem Tov* (i.e., Of the Good Name), who lived between 1700 and 1760. This was a time when the Jewish communities throughout Europe were still suffering from the aftermath of the collapse of Shabtai Zvi's messianic movement at the end of the seventeenth century. Shattered by the extraordinary finale of this popular movement, in which Shabtai Zvi, the false messiah, converted to Islam to save his life, a reaction of despair and disillusionment set in. The shock waves of Shabtai Zvi's apostasy, and the upheaval that followed, continued to demoralize Jewish life both materially and spiritually for many years thereafter.

This was a time when Jews of Europe were undergoing economic difficulties and were also being persecuted physically from time to time. Feeling helpless in the face of an antagonistic environment and an uncertain future, not everyone was capable, or even had the possibility, of finding solace in religion and in studying the Torah.

By stressing the importance of faith, enthusiasm and joy rather than of study, the *Baal Shem Tov* (Besht) brought to the masses a new emotional means of achieving spiritual fulfillment and maintaining an optimistic outlook. However, scholars today consider this to have been the second phase of Hassidism, while in the first phase the leaders (of whom the Besht was the foremost) were actually elitist scholars searching for new models of thought and personal mystical experience. These earlier *hassidim* were often in conflict with the establishment, which was essentially mitnagdic in style and character, and they split off to form new centers of learning, such as that formed by Shneor Zalman of Lyady in 1772. Even within this circle there were further philosophical and ideological difference which have been referred to in Chapter 1. It was the second generation of *hassidim* who expressed the ideas of the Besht in a more popular form, stressing feeling rather than intellect, and so capturing the hearts of the masses. It was only then that the movement began to spread quickly from the Ukraine to Poland and other Eastern European countries, and became a new means of unifying Jews of all classes and from all places in a common philosophy and way of life.

Although there were people called *"hassidim rishonim"* in ancient times, the title *"hassid"* was applied then to men of great piety and impeccable moral behavior.

In order to improve the level of *Yiddishkeit* and religious observance in even the smallest Jewish community, the *hassidim* established *shtieblach,* or small prayer-rooms, where prayers were conducted in a friendly, intimate style, with none of the more formal ritual, customary in larger urban synagogues. Each *rebbe,* as *hassidim* called their rabbis, played a key role in setting the style and character of his congregation, and therefore had an enormous influence on his followers. He acquired the virtues of a *zaddik* or righteous man, righteous in his relations with God and man, and was perceived to be the intermediary between the Almighty and his people. In the course of time, this led to the emergence of many different sects, each with its own charismatic leader, each sect further identifying itself by adopting a distinctive form of dress.

The Maggid of Mezerich, the successor to the Besht, inaugurated the custom of the *hatzer*, or court, which was adopted by all branches of Hassidim. Thus, the *rebbe* would "hold court" for his disciples, who would gather together to spend festivals and other special occasions at their *rebbe's tish*, or table. This meal, taken by the *rebbe* together with his followers, was held three times on Shabbat and twice a day on festivals, as well as on the yahrzeit days of zaddikim. At each meal the *rebbe* would give a *drasha* on the weekly *sedra* or an associated subject, and he would distribute *shirayin* or leavings of food from his plate to those around the table. Much time was devoted to singing, each sect often having its own traditional *niggunim* or melodies, depending on the musical talents of the disciples. The proceedings usually ended with dancing and chanting till the heights of ecstasy were reached.

However, maintaining that knowledge and understanding of the Torah and the sources was the supreme value, learned and scholarly rabbis quickly banded together to oppose the new development. This counter-movement was started by R. Eliahu ben Shlomo, the Vilna Gaon, who lived from 1720 to 1797. An outstanding rabbinical authority and an innovative educator, who opposed the pilpulistic learning of Poland and stressed instead a critical understanding of the texts, the Gaon drew his followers from the area surrounding Vilna and from Lithuania in general, which is one of the reasons why the *yeshivot* of Lithuania achieved such scholastic preeminence.

The followers of the Vilna Gaon were called *mitnagdim* or opponents. Although this is the Hebrew term used today, I always use the Yiddish term *misnagdim* when I speak because it arouses fond childhood memories. Since my father, who of course stemmed from the *mitnagdim*, married into a family of Gur Hassidim, I had much opportunity in my youth to hear arguments on both sides of the *hassidim-misnagdim* controversy.

The *mitnagdim* suspected the emphasis on emotion and intensity which displaced the traditional respect for logic and intellectual learning. After the catastrophe of Shabtai Zvi, they were suspicious of any new trends, especially abhorring the emergence of "personality cults" in which the *rebbes* were elevated to *zaddikim* who were said to do no wrong and were able to perform miracles. Both camps gradually developed completely different life styles.

As a leading *mitnaged,* R. Aisel was often asked how the son of a man who had been a devoted *hassid* and disciple of Schneor Zalman could have become such a strong opponent of the popular movement. But the fact is, that already as a young man, Aisel had followed the style of prayer of his grandfather, Mordecai, which was also that of the Vilna Gaon. When pressed further and queried if this did not make him guilty of dishonoring his father, he replied that the opposite was the case. For, since his grandfather had been a *mitnaged,* it was his father, if anyone, who had been guilty of not honoring *his* father. If he, Aisele, had also followed the *hassidic* way, he would have only deepened the blame on his father. But by returning to the ways of the previous generation, he had served to remove the stain of disloyalty from his father.

Someone once told R. Aisel that the true punishment of a *mitnaged* is to see his sons become *hassidim*. "And I bear witness to the fact that, although my father was a true *hassid*, I, his son, am a *misnaged*." He could not know that, two generations later, many of his descendants would either become *hassidim* or marry into hassidic families.

Yet, although R. Aisel chose a different path than that of his father, he always spoke of his father with great respect. Indeed, while never glossing over the fact that his father had been a fervent *hassid*, he acknowledged his debt to his father as teacher and mentor, and referred with admiration to R. Yehiel's chararacter, scholarship, devotion to Torah and worship of the Holy One. Once, when R. Aisel was speaking in memory of his father, the listeners were surprised to hear him praising R. Yehiel's Hassidism. "What has our rabbi to do with *Hassidut*?" they asked. "The honoring of one's father," replied Aisel. This only serves to show how crucial was the period that his father had devoted to studying with the young Aisele.

And when one of his sons asked him why he hadn't remained a *hassid*, R. Aisel made the following reply: "When I studied the early works as a child, I didn't find any new ideas and was more interested in the wit and sharpness of the later scholars. But as I grew older and wiser, I discovered that these "new" ideas were to be found in the earlier writers, and as I continued to mature, I realized that the best ideas were to be found in the *Germara*. Finally, I saw that I could find everything in the Torah, even the *Hassidut* that I needed. So what need had I to go and look any further?" When it was suggested to him that had he remained a *hassid* he could already have had the title of

Admor, R. Aisel laughed and said that he didn't believe that the *hassidim* were so foolish as to do him that honor.

Indeed, the *hassidut* which the young Aisele had seen in his own home did not arouse his antagonism, for his father had been a serious scholar, and there was no "court" in little Glovaki. It was only later, when he saw how the "court" of an *Admor* was conducted, with all the feasting round the *rebbe's tish*, and heard the stories of miraculous signs and wonders, that his opposition to *hassidim* and *hassidut* began to develop. And, as we have seen, he had to leave Kutno because of his incompatibility with the *hassidim* in that community. In this regard, it is related that when he first came to Kutno and held a *seuda* on Shabbat, some of the participants snatched the food from his plate before he had finished eating. Not used to such goings-on, Aisel smiled and asked whether they thought he was a greedy person who ate too much. Upon hearing their explanation that it is an honor to partake of "the leavings of the *zaddik*," he retorted that "A *zaddik* is one who leaves something and not one who is plundered."

In a similar vein, when he saw *hassidim* dancing on Simchat Torah, R. Aisel remarked, "True *hassidim*. They dance with the bride but do not know her." And again, when someone remarked that the *hassidim* liked to dance, he said, "Let them dance. It is very becoming because they have less in their heads than in their feet."

And, when during a Purim celebration someone proposed that a Purim rabbi be elected, R. Aisel declared, "At Purim everything is opposite, and therefore one must elect a *rebbe* and not a rabbi, for the *hassidim* turn everything upside down all the year round. Whereas every Jew should do all he can to help the poor and the sick, and leave the wonders to The Holy One, Blessed Be He, the *hassidim* do the opposite. They place the duty of help and charity on the Holy One and the wonders they keep for themselves."

R. Aisel was asked why the hassidic *rebbe* drove about in carriages with fine horses and *mitnagdim* rabbis always walked? "It very simple," he answered. "We have a saying that falsehood has no feet, so the *rebbe* must drive a carriage. But we *mitnagdim*, who stick to the truth, can go by foot."

R. Aisel found himself traveling with a hassidic *rebbe*, who made a great to-do about preparing for praying and finally prayed at a late hour. He noticed that R. Aisel was much displeased by his behavior and explained that he needed much time to prepare. "I think you are in need of much prayer to save you from the lengthy preparations," responded R. Aisel.

A similar anecdote is told of R. Aisel from when he still lived in Kutno. The rabbi reproached a *hassid* who always made lengthy preparations before he prayed or did any good deeds. "From the moment of law-giving at Mt. Sinai, when all the souls to be born in the future gathered together, you have been busy preparing yourself to enter the real world. If these centuries haven't been enough for you, this entire hour will not make any difference."

During a visit to Warsaw, a *hassid* handed R. Aisel a פתקא (note) in which he asked the rabbi to pray for him. R. Aisel returned the note and asked whether the *hassid* had the misfortune to be bereaved, that he couldn't pray for himself.

Another *hassid* once reproached R. Aisel for not wearing a *gartel,* or the tie-belt which it was their custom to wear. To which Aisel replied that he thought his trouser-belt served the same purpose (of separating the spiritual and physical aspects of the body). When the *hassid* kept nagging at him, R. Aisel finally said, "If a Sefer Torah is kosher the binder is tied underneath the mantle, but when it is not kosher, the binder is tied outside the mantle."

At first the conflict between the *hassidim* and *mitnagdim* was so violent that hassidic writings were sometimes burnt and each side even occasionally informed on the other to the authorities. However, with the emergence of the *Haskalah,* or Enlightenment movement, the antagonism between them waned somewhat as they took a common stand against the encroachment of the new philosophy. As he came to realize its contribution to protecting the traditional Judaism he loved, R. Aisel became more tolerant of *Hassidut* and its adherents, especially in view of the fact that the *maskilim* viewed *Hassidut* as their archenemy and as the greatest obstacle to reform. He was therefore always ready to help those *hassidim* who wanted to further their Torah studies, and admired learned *hassidim* whenever he found them. His friendship with R. Avraham Weinberg, whom he admired for both his scholarship and his personality, may also have played a role in Aisel's lessening his attacks on the movement, for he came to see in R. Avraham and his teachings a powerful bulwark in the battle against the *maskilim.*

When he finally gave up his attacks on *hassidim* this ·eventually led to an estrangement from his good friend, R. Yaakov Gesundheit. This occurred because he did not support R. Yaacov publicly in an argument that the latter had with the *hassidim* of Warsaw, when he was appointed rabbi of that town. The argument was whether to obey a Russian decree demanding the abolition of distinctive Jewish apparel. Gesundheit refused to condemn the decree and declared that it should not be seen as an anti-religious act, and that the clothing one wore was not a matter of importance. But the *hassidim* felt that their style of clothing was a principle worth dying for. Eventually the *hassidim* succeeded in having Gesundheit's appointment cancelled.

Later in his life R. Aisel said that the *hassidim* were real, God-fearing Jews, with deep faith and confidence in their beliefs: they had real Jewish beards and wore Jewish clothes, and by their external appearance kept guard over their inner souls. "To neglect the externals and preserve the internal, " he explained, would be like "שבור את החבית ושמור את היין" (breaking the barrel to protect the wine), which is, of course, impossible. Thus, when a *mitnaged* came to R. Aisel full of slander against the *hassidim*, he refused to listen, saying that an honest *hassid* was preferable to a *mitnaged* who lies.

ORTHODOXY VERSUS THE *HASKALAH*

The period from the seventeenth to the middle of the nineteenth century can be characterized as a time of great Torah scholarship, of piety and charity, and of the emergence of Hassidism. But the burgeoning *Haskalah* movement in the nineteenth century began to represent a serious challenge to Orthodoxy, which perceived the desire for reform and change as a serious threat to traditional Judaism and the very life style of the Jews of Poland, Russia and Lithuania. Even Hassidism, to which many of the masses were being drawn as an escape from the poverty and oppression of their lives, was perceived by the "purist" *mitnagdim* as a threat to "true" intellectual study and adherence to the Torah. Though R. Aisel was not as publicly active as R. Moshe Yitzhak in the war against Reform, he was known for his extreme opposition to any change in Orthodox Judaism. Thus, while the Reformists did not hesitate to engage in satirical attacks on religion and on the religious establishment, they were wary of tangling directly with Aisel, "the most dangerous amongst the rabbis, the shrewdest and sharpest of them all."

R. Aisel's basic philosophy was that a Jew can and should look to the Torah and to study of the Torah to fulfill all his needs, because it is the Torah that shapes a person's character, straightens his back, heals his thoughts, purifies his logic, helps him to overcome obstacles, teaches him to pray and keeps him close to The Holy One, Blessed Be He. In short, he felt that in and through the Torah, a man could achieve all that he needed to in this world. He therefore saw no reason to change the tradition of generations, which he viewed as proof of the unchanging truth of the Torah. Not interested in any form of secular knowledge, he belonged completely to the Torah, from which he drew all his knowledge and wisdom. While he did agree that specific external circumstances might necessitate change or modification, he viewed any such change as temporary, to be cancelled when the special situation had passed. (One can't help wondering what he would have achieved if he had been attracted to secular studies.)

Once Alexander Zederboim, who edited the paper *HaMelitz* and supported the *Haskalah* movement, came to Slonim in search of new subscribers. Besides being the first Hebrew paper to be printed in Russia (it appeared in 1860), *HaMelitz* became the mouthpiece of the *Haskalah* movement, and R. Aisel was naturally against his congregants reading it. (Another *maskil*, the poet Y. L. Gordon, became assistant editor in 1881.) The young people who were attracted by the new ideology complained to Zederboim, or *Erez* as he was known by the Hebrew translation of his name, that R. Aisel was constantly on the watch against them and repressed any attempts at Reform. Zederboim presented himself to R. Aisel to put forward his case. "How is it that the renowned rabbi, who is so shrewd and good-hearted, is so obstinate with people who wish to acquire knowledge? He doesn't allow newspapers, which aim to educate the public, to enter the town, and he registers every infringement in the community records. In my life I never expected to see the wise and clever one, he of cheerful temperament, standing at the city gates with a captain's staff in his hand!" "Let me tell you a story," replied R. Asiel with a smile, "Once there was a rabbi who sat studying by candlelight when the town's inhabitants were all fast asleep and deep silence lay over the village. Suddenly the rabbi heard a sound from his neighbor's house and went outside to investigate. Seeing that a wolf had penetrated into the neighbor's yard and was about to attack the calf, the rabbi took a heavy stick with which to chase the wolf away. The wolf set up a great cry, 'Shame! Shame! A rabbi whose faith is in the Torah goes about with a threatening stick in his hands!' The rabbi replied, 'Against a savage wolf who wants to penetrate into my village, a rabbi without a stick is no rabbi.'"

Regarding his attitude towards the *maskilim,* R. Aisel is reported to have told the following story about himself: He was walking alone late at night, when he was approached by one of Slonim's *maskilim.* "Rabbi," exclaimed the *maskil,* "isn't it written that a *talmid hakham* shouldn't go out at night alone for fear of evil spirits!" "In that case," replied Aisel Harif with a smile, "I have nothing to fear, for in this town the evil spirits [i.e., the *maskilim*] don't consider me a *talmid hakham.*"

To a *maskil* who asked him why he so disliked members of the Enlightenment, when "We are all children of the same Father, aren't we?" R. Aisel replied: "Yes, but not of the same mother (מותר, in Yiddish). What is permitted by you (מותר, in Hebrew) is forbidden (אסור) by us."

Another *maskil* once asked R. Aisel why the Jews "*shlug*" (beat) three times a year: on Purim (they beat Haman); on Yom Kippur (they "*shlug kapores*" and beat their breasts in repentance); and on Hoshana Rabbah they beat willow branches while enumerating the life-giving properties of water. R. Aisel told the *maskil,* "It is written הכה תכה [you will surely beat]. הכה represents the initials of Haman, *kapparoth, Hoshana,* and תכה means you shall beat." When the *maskil* then challenged Aisel further by asking him why kreplach are eaten on these three holidays, R. Aisel gave the following answer: Similarly, תכה means תאוכל [eat], כרפלך [kreplach] הרבה [a lot]."

Some other *maskilim,* angry at R. Aisel's negative attitude towards them, tried to bait him by remarking: "We see that you know everything. When you are amongst *maskilim* you are a *maskil.* And when you are amongst scholars you are a scholar. What are you when you come amongst dogs?" "This is the first time that I have ever found myself amongst dogs," replied Aisel Harif.

Yet another *maskil* asked R. Aisel "Why is it written in *Pirkei Avot* that there are seven qualities in a wise man and their opposites in a fool instead of the other way round: Seven qualities in a fool and their opposites in a wise man?" To which Aisel retorted: "But surely you should be able to understand the reason, because no matter how it is written, fools always ask why isn't it written the other way round."

During Aisele's later years the Jews began to abandon their traditional clothes and to wear modern short jackets. Aisele, who was of course against this trend, is said to have complained that the Jew had become very small. When asked to explain what he meant, he replied, "We have a saying, 'a Jew until his pocket.' And the pockets are worn so high nowadays that you can imagine how small the Jew has become."

Once R. Aisel was asked why he was so aggressive and sharp-tongued against his *maskil* opponents, while other Orthodox rabbis behaved much more politely and pleasantly. "The *maskilim* I know are simply unfortunate that they know me and not the other rabbis."

Asked why the *maskilim* usually behaved politely and with respect, while Orthodox Jews did not, R. Aisel quipped: "Well, such empty-headed people have to be endowed with some qualities, don't they?"

When the same question was put to R. Aisel on another occasion, he replied: "Well, when the Children of Israel came to receive the Torah, the *haredim* (Orthodox) rose early, as is their custom, and hurried to Sinai to receive the entire Torah, both the written and the oral. But, since the 'enlightened' rose late, as is *their* custom, and washed and dressed themselves leisurely, by the time they came to Mt. Sinai there was nothing left except tractates *Kalla* and *Derech Eretz!*" (tractates dealing with correct behavior in marital and personal relations).

In another variation on the same question, R. Aisel was asked, "If it is said that *Derech Eretz* came before the Torah, why don't we find it in the behavior of the *haredim?*" "Since the Torah completely supersedes *Derech Eretz,*" he answered, "the irreligious who didn't receive the Torah appear to be full of politeness. But, when there is nothing else there," he went on, "that too eventually disappears."

When the *maskilim* seeking reforms in education informed R. Aisel that in the future they would function with the assistance of the authorities, Aisel remarked, "Of course! On whom shall they lean if not on the wicked?"

Asked by an informer if it were really true that he could

find nothing positive to say about the Russian rule, R. Aisel laughingly replied: "Not at all! There is much 'good' in this rule. For example, it prevents arguments between scholars as to whether a certain czar was good or not, whether certain laws are good or not and whether the royal house is good or not. For the kingdom has proven without any doubt that there can be no arguments on these subjects."

The town's biggest *maskil*, the poet Yehezkel Feivel Rabinowitz, came to R. Aisel after prayers on the festival of Shavuoth to ask a question about the "אקדמות", the Aramaic poetry read on this holiday. "The rhymes and words in this passage — *r'shuta, n'kushta, tarushta,* and so on — are heavy and strange. What was the poet thinking of when he wrote this? I'm sure that if our *maskilim* would write verses, they would be so much better that even you would stop reciting the old *piyyutim*." "Let me explain to you," said R. Aisel indulgently. "Every object has a body and soul. For example, if you take a table, the wood is the body and the craftsmanship is the soul. If you take a book, the language is the body and the content is the soul. And if we value the work of the poets and keep reciting them, it is because we know they put their souls into their poetry. So, when your *maskilim* will put *their* souls into their verses, we will recite them as well."

Once a clean-shaven young man came to visit R. Aisel, who immediately asked whether he was a Kohen or a Levi. "What does the rabbi mean by such a question?" asked the young man. "Well," replied Aisel, "I asked because your face is certainly not the face of Israel!"

Another young "modern" complained to R. Aisel that the *haredim* concerned themselves with superficial things, often attacking him for wearing short jackets and for his gentile appearance. "Where is it written," the young man asked, "that Jews must wear long jackets and other strange garments?" "In *Parshat Bo* it is written 'And each woman asked of her neighbor vessels of silver and gold and dresses.' Why didn't the men ask for clothes? Because Jewish men didn't wear the short clothes of the Egyptians!"

Once a young man from Slonim had moved to Berlin, but did not succeed in establishing himself there. He returned to Slonim clean-shaven and in modern clothes and asked R. Aisel's permission to open a *heder* for children. Aisel refused. Asked to explain why, he said, "A *melamed* who does not appear to be what he is cannot be successful. For example, we read in the Torah, that 'Yosef recognized his brothers, but they did not recognize him.' Why? Because he was without a beard. With you it is the opposite. You left Slonim with a beard, the sign of a good Jew, but came back without one. Therefore, since you do not appear to be what you are, you cannot succeed as a *melamed*."

One evening when R. Aisel came to pray, there were only nine men present, and the *shamash* had to go and search for a tenth. He came back with a *maskil*, who was clean-shaven and wearing a short jacket. The others asked whether it was permissible for such a person to join the *minyan*, and R. Aisel answered with a quotation from Leviticus, 27: 32, 33. "Every tenth shall be holy to the Lord. A man shall not inquire whether it is good or bad."

A certain Doctor Levi in Slonim, who believed in the *Haskalah* and was not popular among the Jews, had to find most of his patients amongst the gentiles, including the Russian officials. Not liking doctors in general, R. Aisel surely didn't like this "modern" one, preferring to go to the local Polish doctor when necessary. When Dr. Levi threatened to leave the town after his young daughter had died in an epidemic, R. Aisel's only comment was, "There is some merit in the man after all, for he is trying to do a good deed on behalf of Slonim".

When the Enlightenment leader Dr. Mandelshtam was passing through Slonim in the period between Pesach and Shavuoth, he decided to pay a visit to R. Aisel. "Is it really possible," he asked Aisel, "that the learned rabbi opposes the opening of a modern *heder* where children can learn secular subjects like arithmetic. What can be wrong with that?" "Do you know arithmetic?" asked R. Aisel. "What day of the *Omer* is it?" The doctor could not answer the question. "You see," continued the rabbi, "if one learns counting according to your method, one forgets the counting of the *Omer*, and many other things as well!" (There is another version of the same story told about Yehezkel Latbolla, a mathematician from Slonim.)

R. Aisel was so aggressive in his attacks on the *maskilim* that friends once came to warn him he was in danger of being reported to the authorities by them and then being expelled from Slonim as a "fanatic." "Well," he replied, "if I am exiled, I will go. But it won't help the *Haskalah* movement much, because wherever I go my mouth will go with me, and all the officers of the czar will not prevent me from speaking my mind."

And from the following stories about R. Aisel's confrontations with *maskilim* in other cities where he happened to find himself, we can see that this most certainly was the case.

For example, on one of his visits to Vilna, R. Aisel met the writer and prominent Enlightenment leader Adam Hacohen Levinsohn, but he did not know with whom he was speaking. Realizing this, Levinsohn thought that he would use the opportunity to get the better of R. Aisel. Thus he asked, in a provocative tone, "I learned in the *midrash* of *Parshat VaYishlakh* that Jacob had sixty thousand dogs to guard his flock. Perhaps the rabbi can explain to me where the kennels of the dogs were, what Jacob gave them to eat and, finally, what happened to the descendants of those dogs?" But R. Aisel, immediately understanding what the leanings of the gentleman must be, answered, "In the *midrash* it is also told that Rabi (R. Yehuda HaNasi who lived from 132 to 220) spoke of a woman who gave birth to sixty thousand children. When he was asked how that was possible, Rabi replied that the woman was Yocheved, who gave birth to Moses, who was considered equal to sixty thousand men. Therefore we can also say that Jacob's dog was equal to sixty thousand dogs. And as to its descendants, one stands before me right now."

Then there was the doctor in Vilna who, although he was an observant Jew, was still influenced by *Haskalah* ideas. This doctor would often accost R. Aisel and ask him questions about things he had heard from his *maskil* friends. Once he asked Aisel "How is it that the great scholars of earlier times — the Rambam, the Ralbag and the Ramban — were also great in science, medicine and philosophy, whilst in recent generations the scholars are learned only in the Torah!" "I have often pondered the same question," Aisel replied, and one may better ask, Why is it that in olden times the great men of science were also great in Torah, while today the great men of science are otherwise ignorant."

During one of his trips to Vilna, R. Aisel sent a note to a well-known *maskil*, who also had a rather notorious reputation, asking him to come and discuss a certain matter. The latter sent back a message saying, "If the rabbi wished to see me, let him be good enough to come to my place." R. Aisel sent a message in return, "Are you discriminating against me because I am male rather than female?"

Another time in Vilna, R. Aisel was approached by a group of anti-religious young men. "We can understand that the old rabbis are against change and Reform because they no longer understand, but your honor is so great in knowledge and wisdom that we cannot understand why you oppose the forces of Enlightenment instead of joining them?" Aisel replied, "Yesterday, when I arrived in Vilna, a drunkard approached me in the street and asked why I, supposedly a wise man, didn't step into the public-house and enjoy a glass of *yash* in order to refresh my soul. I said to him, "When I see the condition you are in after enjoying a glass of *yash*, I lose my taste for the drink forever. Similarly, when I see you in your shame [i.e., shaven faces and short jackets], the taste of the Enlightenment is lost to me forever."

Again in Vilna, a *maskil* came to R. Aisel, clean-shaven and in modern clothes, to ask a provocative question. "It is said that if one sees a rabbi, one should stand still, and if one sees a dog one should sit down. What should one do if one sees a rabbi and a dog together?" "Well," retorted Aisel Harif, "why don't we go out into the street together? Then, we shall soon see!"

In accordance with his desire to thwart the encroachment of the *Haskalah,* R. Aisel never hesitated to show
his contempt for "modernizers" wherever and whenever he encountered them. Thus, when he was passing
through Bialystock and was visited by a gentleman named
Schottlander who was clean-shaven and was wearing
a short jacket, Aisel fixed the man with a critical gaze.
Hurrying to justify himself, Schottlander said: "The rabbi
should not consider me as a כלי ריק [empty vessel]. I am full
of both Torah and *Haskalah*. I am both *milchik* and *fleishik*,
a vessel full of both milk and meat." "In that case," scoffed
Aisel, "you really are *treif!*"

An unpleasant incident happened when a group of
maskilim in a Lithuanian town made fun of rabbis and of
religion. A delegation of observant Jews from the town
approached R. Aisel asking that he come to the defense
of the insulted rabbis, but in spite of his attitude to the
Haskalah Aisel refused. "During their lifetime rabbis experience both honor and humiliation. If I were ever asked to
rescue rabbis from the honors showered upon them, then I
would also come to their rescue when they are humiliated.
But if they know how to manage the honors on their own,
they should know also how to manage the insults."

THE STRICT BUT
COMPASSIONATE JUDGE

R. Aisel was well-known for his acute insight into the basic elements of human behavior and of quarrels brought to him for judgment. So wide was his experience as presiding judge in the towns where he served that he was often asked to sit on rabbinical courts outside of Slonim. His motto in court was ״באין אמת אין חסד, השקר אינו מסוגל לגמול טובה לאיש״ (Without truth there can be no loving kindness. Falsehood cannot bring good to anyone).

R. Aisel is said to have been able to detect when the plaintiffs who came before him were lying, and he would cross-examine them until the truth came out. Once, when two army contractors came before him, both of them dishonest and deceitful men, R. Aisel declared: "I think you should take your case to the gentile court, for it is there that you will find the kind of trial you are seeking." "What do you mean? Why should we go to the *goyim*?" the men asked. "The gentile judge is used to false law and will give you the judgment you seek," replied R. Aisel.

Another two wealthy army contractors, who were partners, came before R. Aisel, each suing the other for sixty thousand rubles. They had built extensions to the fortress at Brisk and had made a great deal of money through keeping three sets of books: the first a set of factual accounts, the second for the government and two third sets, one for each of them. When R. Aisel asked to have the books for one night so that he could check the material without passing judgment, the men laughed, saying that it would take weeks to look through all the material. But since he insisted, they brought their books in for his examination. The very next day the rabbi called in both men and asked them to supply missing receipts and to clarify certain other points. Not only had he absorbed all the facts and figures and understood the transactions fully, but he had already calculated, to the last kopek, just how much each side owed the other.

When R. Aisel had to deal with questionable characters such as these, he would sometimes say, "From the argument of the claimant I learn that the defendant is in the right, but from the defendant I learn that, in fact, it is the claimant who is in the right. So why should we call more witnesses? They will only prove that neither of you is in the right."

Once such a character appeared before him, warning R. Aisel that he would report the rabbi to the authorities if the case were not judged in his favor. Aisel castigated him as follows: "So, you are not only wicked, but stupid enough to threaten me as well. If I do as you wish, it is first of all doubtful whether the authorities will come to get me because of your informing, and if they do, it is doubtful that I would be found guilty. And, if by some chance I were found guilty, it is doubtful that I would not succeed in being freed. So do you think that you can influence my point of view by threatening to cast the shadow of a doubt against my certainty?"

Pitiless as he was towards liars, thieves and blackmailers, when those who appeared before him had genuine personal problems which required his evaluation, R. Aisel always endeavored to see both sides of the question. Reb Aisel once chided the Slonimer *dayyan*, who he felt was too severe in his interpretations of Jewish law: "it is not a problem to decide according to what's written in the law, but sometimes one has to know how to find in the law the decision one wants to make." In all cases brought before him, his wit never deserted him, and indeed often helped to bring a good-humored solution to the problem.

In a case brought to the Kutno *Beit Din* when R. Aisel was presiding, the fathers of a newly-married couple were arguing over which one should support the young people. The groom's father claimed that it should be the bride's father because his son was a scholar and had to sit and study all the time. But the bride's father said that, since it was a husband's duty to support his wife, his father should do so. After listening to both sides, R. Aisel asked the name of the bride, and upon being told that it was חיה, declared, "מאן דיהיב חיה יהיב מזונה" (He who gives life [Haya, the name of the bride, also means life] must also give nourishment). Therefore the father of the bride is responsible for supporting the couple."

Once a young couple came to the *Beit Din* to initiate divorce proceedings. R. Aisel made every effort to effect a reconciliation, but the woman refused all arguments, insisting that she must have a divorce. Finally R. Aisel asked her her name, and she replied, Rasha. At this the rabbi smiled and remarked, "I have often labored long and hard to resolve a difficult point in Rashi, but a 'Rasha' as difficult and obstinate as this one, I have never encountered." It is told that upon hearing these words, the wife relented and agreed to Aisel's advice.

R. Aisel's wit was not limited to those who came before him as plaintiffs or defendants. Once he and the rabbis of Kovno and Kobryn were sitting as a *Beit Din*. It was an extremely hot day and the other two rabbis complained constantly about the heat. R. Aisel remarked, "The *dayyan* should always see himself as if *gehenom* is opening before him. We are three *dayyanim* sitting here, so hell is opening from three sides and burning at our feet. Is it any wonder that it's so hot?"

A Polish judge once asked R. Aisel why it was said that יעוור השוחד, bribery causes blindness, rather than any other disability, R. Aisel replied, "Few *dayyanim* allow themselves to take visible bribes such as money, but many are not able to withstand bribery by tears or fulsome compliments. Since it is the eyes of the judge which register the tears, and flattery makes his eyes light up, it is therefore the eyes which have sinned [in acceding to such forms of bribery] and which must therefore be punished."

Sometimes those who appeared before him were rabbis or leading community figures with differences of opinion, and R. Aisel always attempted to find a solution that would be just and honorable to both sides. Thus, when he was invited to arbitrate in the case of a serious argument between R. Naftali Zvi Yehuda Berlin (הנצי"ב) and R. Yosef Ber, the two heads of the Wolozyn Yeshiva, he did much to calm the atmosphere, and persuaded both parties to submit their case to a *Beit Din* of rabbis and to accept the compromise advocated by them. But he himself refused to participate in such a court, for he preferred to work behind the scenes rather than be perceived as favoring one side against the other. R. Aisel was always careful not to cast doubt on any Torah scholar, or to embarrass him in public. He acted similarly in the disputes at the Mir Yeshiva. Seeing the personalities involved as gifted and righteous men, full of good qualities and studying and teaching Torah for its own sake, he did not want to weaken their standing in the eyes of either their students or of the public. But rabbis or *dayyanim* who were lacking in these qualities, or were weak or ineffectual, were not spared his scathing comments.

Once when R. Aisel was still in Tiktin, two Jews from a neighboring village came to him with a serious problem. "There is a base character in our town, an informer who makes everyone's life miserable. He blackmails and extorts money even from the poor, and then he informs on them anyway. What should we do with him?" "Why have you come to me?" asked R. Aisel. "You have a rabbi living in your own town." Upon hearing the reply "Our rabbi is afraid of the authorities," R. Aisel said, "And I am afraid for a rabbi who is afraid of the authorities and does not pass true judgment." On a later occasion the rabbi in question met with R. Aisel and said, "I am jealous of the rabbi of Tiktin for his courage and strength of character, for I am weak and cowardly." R. Aisel replied, "I think you should be more afraid of jealousy than of the authorities, for jealousy can remove a person from this world."

One day, two women came to R. Aisel with an argument about a ruble note. The first claimed that the other had stolen it from her, and the second claimed she had found it in the street. After a moment's consideration R. Aisel asked the claimants to wait in the hall, while he discussed the matter with the *dayyan*. As they were leaving the room,

R. Aisel said to R. Feitel, in a loud whisper, that it would be a good sign of ownership if one of the women knew that the note was slightly torn. Having heard this remark, one woman mentioned on returning to R. Aisel, that she could identify the note as one of the corners was torn. "In that case," declared R. Aisel, "the note is not yours because it is absolutely whole," and he gave it back to the rightful owner.

THE RABBI AGAINST THE RICH

The longer that R. Aisel sat as head of the Slonim *Beit Din*, the stronger became his prejudice against the rich. He said that he had become more and more acquainted with the devious and sordid methods by which people acquired wealth, but that what he objected to most was the vulgar display and the swaggering self-confidence which many people acquired together with their money. Because of the time he devoted to his charitable works, and his reluctant encounters with the niggardly and unscrupulous rich, these stories seem to make up the major part of R. Aisel's anecdotes. He really had ample opportunity to learn the truth of the Talmudic proverb, that one recognizes a man, "בכיסו, בכוסו, ובכעסו" (by his pocket, by his drinking and by his anger).

Once he was asked why he had such an aversion to the rich. What harm had they done to the rabbi? "Why do the rich hate the scholars?" he asked in return. "Because they know that they will never become scholars. And I suspect that I will never be rich, because I haven't the necessary deception or vulgarity."

R. Aisel used to say, "A rich man would rather give to a cripple than to a scholar. When he sees a cripple, he is afraid that he too might one day suffer some injury or lose a limb. But he is never afraid that he'll become a scholar!"

A boastful rich man once asked R. Aisel, "Why is a rabbi allowed to be proud of his knowledge of the Torah, while I am not permitted to be proud of my wealth?" "He who shows off his learning and teaches others increases learning in the world," answered R. Aisel. "But he who shows off his wealth, shows that he has nothing else to be proud of."

When R. Aisel first came to Slonim, he had much unpleasantness with one of the *parnassim*, a vulgar but well-connected man who had never been elected but had nevertheless held office from the days when the strong men of the town achieved such positions on their own initiative. There was even talk that the man was a *mamzer*, one born of an adulterous relationship between a married woman and a man other than her husband. R. Aisel tried to get rid of the man, but he refused to give up his position, declaring, "I am the congregation, and the congregation is me." Once, upon hearing that the leaders of the community had held a meeting in this man's home, R. Aisel told the following parable.

"Three parties came to The Holy One, Blessed Be He, with complaints: the prayer עלינו לשבח [*Alenu leShabeah*], the סעודה שלישית [*seuda shlishit*] and the ממזר [*mamzer*]. The first complained that her place was only at the end of the prayers, when people were in a hurry to leave the synagogue, and that they therefore did not pay her proper attention. The second complained that, while the first and second meals of Shabbat comprised both fish and meat, she, the third meal, had to make do with a piece of herring and some *Divrei Torah*. The third said, 'My parents sinned, but why must I be punished to such a degree that I am not even permitted to come into the congregation?' The Holy One, Blessed Be He, had a solution for each one. 'The prayer *Alenu leShabeach* will be compensated on the High

Holy Days, when it will be placed in the middle of Mussaf [the Additional Prayer], and the ark will be opened specially and the congregation will prostrate themselves while reciting it. The *seuda shlishit* will be compensated by the custom of the *hassidim*, who honor it with singing, Torah talk and cheerful spirits. And I will make the *mamzer* into a leader of the community. Thus, he will not have to come to the community, but the community will come to him, and he will be able to declare that he is in the congregation'."

There was a wealthy man in Slonim who rarely gave willingly to charity, but was always anxious to lead the prayer service, even though he was not a good *Baal Tefillah*. R. Aisel used to say of this man that he was doubly holy because, "The *Gemara* says ישראל קדושים הם, יש שיש לו ואינו רוצה ויש שרוצה ואין לו' [The Children of Israel are holy; there are those who have and do not want (to give) and there are those who want (to give) and have not]. This donor is therefore twice holy, because, insofar as charity, 'he has and he doesn't want,' and 'in prayer he wants and does not have.'"

In the same vein, there was a hunchback in Slonim who had become rich through contracting. When he began to show off his newly acquired wealth, R. Aisel remarked to him: "It seems to me that your hunchback has not become more beautiful, but perhaps is even a little more crooked because of the pile of money it is carrying."

During a Purim feast R. Aisel was asked why he attacked the rich, when they give to charity and did righteous deeds, usually in a good spirit. What would happen to the community if everyone was penniless and impoverished? Who would support the public institutions? R.

Aisel answered with a story from his past: "When I was a rabbi in Kalvariya, they did not have enough money to pay my salary. So they allowed me to run the bathhouse, and I employed an attendant. Once the bathhouse attendant came and complained bitterly about his fate. Part of his job was to beat the rich men in the steam room, with bundles of twigs. But since the men were very fat, the work was back-breaking, and the attendant was exhausted by the end of the day. So I said to him, 'Don't worry. We'll divide the work. You will beat them only on *Erev Shabbat,* and I will beat them all the other days of the year. "And thus I got into the habit!"

Once, when R. Aisel fell ill and was confined to his bed, the *parnassim* and other leading citizens came to visit him, amongst them a vulgar person who had little respect for the rabbi or for his scholarship. "I just happened to be in this street on some matter, and decided to do a *mitzvah* by paying the rabbi a visit," he declared as he came in. When the man rose to leave, R. Aisel got out of bed to accompany him to the door. When the visitor protested that this was not necessary, R. Aisel answered, "Never mind. I find that I must answer a call of nature, and that certain room is on the way to the front door."

One of the *parnassim* of Slonim, an extremely wealthy man and a very outspoken one, was not happy about the time that R. Aisel spent in Vilna overseeing the printing of his books. Once this *parnass* reproached Aisel about his long absences. "It is said that The Holy One, Blessed Be He, revealed to Moshe Rabenu 'each successive generation and its representatives, each generation and its teachers.' But how could the Holy One reveal our rabbi to Moshe

Rabenu if he is always on the road? Did he chase after him to Vilna?" "Well," replied Aisel, "after Moshe Rabenu saw that you would be a *parnass* of Slonim, he was not surprised that I ran away to Vilna!"

Once, Reb Aisel went to visit one of the wealthy men of the town to ask for money for a worthy cause. "By his coming here the rabbi proves that it is better to be a rich man than a rabbi. For I do not have to come to him," said the *parnass*. "The cow does not come to the owner to be milked either," remarked Aisel. "It does not mean that the cow is more important than its owner." On another occasion, in reply to the same statement that the *gvir* was more important than the rabbi, R. Aisel replied, "Does the sick person come to the doctor? No, the doctor comes to the patient, but that doesn't make the patient more important than the doctor."

R. Aisel called on one of the town's wealthy men for a small contribution to a charitable fund. When the man refused, he said, "I suppose you think that the tree of knowledge was a fig tree, and therefore you give a fig for *zedaka*!"

There is another story about an unnamed rabbi which definitely has the flavor of R. Aisel. A wealthy man refused to give charity to the rabbi, saying that he gave enough בסתר, secretly. "It's very interesting," replied the rabbi. "If you sin in secret, the whole town knows about it, but when you give *zedaka* in secret, no one knows about it."

There was a rich villager in the vicinity of Slonim, who came to settle in the town. Once, hearing a sermon about *Yehuda HaNasi* and how he honored the rich, he came to R. Aisel and asked why the rabbi didn't follow the example of the great leader, but instead treated the rich with scorn. "Tell me something," said Aisel. "How did Yehuda Hanasi honor the rich? With Torah? No, because they have no Torah. With wisdom? No, because the rich have no wisdom. With *mitzvoth* or good deeds? No, because the rich are not interested in good deeds. But he did honor them with silence, in that he did not reveal their shame, for in the early generations the rich protected their honor. But today the rich reveal their weakness before all, without even being asked to. So how can one respect them?"

Another one of Slonim's affluent men once appeared before R. Aisel at a *Din Torah*. After presenting his case he concluded by saying, "The rabbi can believe me. There is truth in what I say, and there is also firm support for my words." R. Aisel responded: "It is true that they say 'שקר אין לו רגלים' [Falsehood has no legs to stand on]. But it is also said that a man's fortune puts him on his feet. So I don't know whose feet are standing here, those of truth or of fortune."

As R. Aisel was returning from the synagogue one Shabbat, he passed the house of one of the town's misers, and the man himself happened to be standing on the balcony. He called out to the rabbi asking what *sedra* had been read that day. R. Aisel replied: "I am no longer young and cannot read the small print, but I saw that above [a reference to both "above" on the balcony and "above" or the top of the page] was written '*Korah*'" [This is a reference to the man who rebelled against Moses and was swallowed up by the earth, and who therefore had no place in the world to come.]

On Erev Pesach, R. Aisel used to make special efforts

to collect donations for the קמחא דפסחא (literally, flour for Pesach, or financial help for this festival), in accordance with estimates set by the *gabbaim*. When he asked one of the rich men for the donation which had been designated for him, the man protested violently. "Why do they always appraise my fortune at ten items more than it is worth?" "I will tell you," said R. Aisel. "Rich people are usually very secretive about their wealth, yet by their opulence they cannot help but reveal their vulgarity to all and sundry. When the *gabbai* comes to estimate their wealth, he measures their vulgarity since he has no other evidence. Thus, it is not his fault that a man's vulgarity is sometimes ten times greater than his wealth!"

In connection with the collection of קמחא דפסחא, the following story is told about R. Aisel: Once, on *Shabbat HaGadol*, the Shabbat before Pesach, the rabbi gave a lengthy and learned dissertation on the customs and traditions of Passover, and of the symbolic importance and ritual aspects of the baking of *matzot*. The scholars in the congregation were very impressed by his treatment of the subject, but as he left the synagogue a poor young man approached him and said, "What good is a lesson on *matza* and Pesach if I can't afford to buy any *matza*? The money I received from the *Kimhe dePascha* I had to use for other things because of my wife's illness." Upon which R. Aisel went back into the synagogue and commanded the attention of the congregation. "The real lesson of *Matza* is that no one in the community can be at ease until everyone has enough *matzot* for himself and his family. We cannot fulfill the *mitvah of Matza* until we achieve this goal."

Not long after another rich man had refused to give him

money for his funds, R. Aisel saw the *gvir* scrupulously cleaning out his pockets in preparation for Passover, in case any crumbs might be hidden there. "You don't have to worry about that," called out R. Aisel, "for you are a Jew only till your pocket!"

R. Aisel approached one of Slonim's wealthy merchants on a matter of charity, but the man told him in no uncertain terms: "I don't give even a kopek for charity, and that's that." R. Aisel signed and remarked, "What a pity that you didn't live in olden times. You would have made life easier for us." "What does the rabbi mean by that?" asked the miser. "It's simple. Why did our sages forbid the use of milk coming from non-believers? Because of the possibility that the gentile might take milk from an unclean animal and mix it with good milk. But if you had lived in those days, you would have proved the suspicion groundless since you are proof that an unclean animal cannot be milked."

R. Aisel came to the house of another skinflint who, upon perceiving who his visitor was, hid in the closet. But Aisel had noticed his act, and said loudly: "Now I understand the words of our sages, that "גדולה הכנסת אורחים מקבלת השכינה" [hospitality is more important than welcoming the *Shekhinah*], because when Moshe saw the שכינה in the burning bush, "ויסתר משה את פניו" [he hid his face]. But the gentleman of this house hides his whole body in the closet!"

On a similar occasion, the *baal habayit* fled to the kitchen and knelt down behind the stove, leaving on the table a book on *Mussar* open to the section on modesty. Seeing him crouched behind the stove, R. Asiel said: "What a pity he is not studying about pride, because then he wouldn't stoop so low."

A wealthy merchant declared himself bankrupt and refused to repay the loans he owed, saying he had lost all his money. But he soon took up his good life again, making it obvious that his fortune was really still intact. He even continued his extravagant way of life after he was expelled from the synagogue, boasting to R. Aisel that, although he no longer made the blessing over bread and honey on *Rosh HaShanah*, he was still enjoying a very good and sweet year. R. Asiel answered: "Nevertheless, your life will eventually be bitter. For blessed is he who maintains the custom of "מוציא עם דבש" [blessing over bread and honey], but cursed is he who only "מוציא מן החברים" [takes out from his friends]."

At a turbulent meeting with the *parnassim* R. Aisel answered a slighting remark against him by saying: "You say that it was you who made me rabbi of Slonim? Well, you are mistaken, for it is I who have made Slonim into a town and have made you into Slonimer *balei-batim*!"

Once R. Aisel was having a meeting about various matters with the community leaders. One of the men, by the name of Ze'ev (Wolf), had long borne a grudge against R. Aisel, and kept interrupting him whenever he spoke. Realising with whom he had to deal, R. Aisel remarked, "Today's meeting has helped me to understand a certain passage in the Talmud, which explains that one is permitted to say the *Shema* only when it is light enough to distinguish between a wolf and a dog. But, one may argue that it is possible to distinguish between them even in the dark, because a dog barks if he is disturbed and the wolf does not, and that it is therefore possible to say the *Shema* even while it is still dark. However, during today's meeting I have seen that even a Wolf can bark, and therefore it follows that it is indeed impossible to distinguish between them in the dark. Therefore our sages were correct in saying that one must wait till it is light enough in order to distinguish between a dog and a Wolf."

R. Aisel never made disparaging remarks about the weak or the helpless, treating the most tattered amongst them with respect and compassion. Once he was asked why he felt this way even towards those who were crippled or foolish. "If they ever become rich," said Aisel, "they will become honorable spokesmen of the community who will criticize and find fault with my deeds."

Thus, when a rich man and a poor man come to him for a *Din Torah,* and the former asked, "Why does the rabbi give my opponent preference? Because he is poor?" Aisel responded, "I ask the same question: Why is justice usually on the side of the poor?"

Once a wealthy man came to R. Aisel and asked, "Why does the Torah tell us "אל תגזול דל כי דל הוא" [Do not steal from the poor man because he is poor], but does not say anything about protecting the property of the rich?" "It is the way of the world to overestimate the property of the rich," commented R. Aisel. "If a man has ten thousand rubles, they say he has twenty; if he has twenty, they say he has fifty; and so on. But with the poor it is the opposite. If he has a few hundred rubles, they say he is penniless; if he has a hundred, they say he is a pauper. Therefore, what the Torah is really saying is: Do not steal from the poor with words. Do not make him less than he is because the rich will take his money anyway."

These anecdotes provide us with a brief sketch of some of the less noble citizens of Slonim, who by their selfish and uncharitable behavior provoked R. Aisel's biting and scornful remarks. Yet these unpleasant experiences did not deter him from his endeavors on behalf of the needy, and we can only guess at the frustration and anger aroused in him during his daily work.

For R. Aisel, the question of practical charity was the touchstone by which he measured all other qualities. Once there was a problem in the town of Lomza about deciding which of the two equally talented candidates should be selected to be the town rabbi. R. Aisel influenced the decision in favor of R. Eliahu Haim who had a better record of good deeds than the other.

On another occasion R. Aisel said, "A rabbi who is concerned only with Torah, and not with *zedaka*, is not worthy of his title. He may make new interpretations and discover new meanings, but eventually someone will destroy his arguments and nothing will be left of them. But when a rabbi gives clear directives about the importance of doing practical *mitzvoth*, his orders cannot be ignored or changed, and will always remain valid."

THE RABBI AS AUTHOR

Renowned as he was for his sharp wit, R. Aisel's eleven books were nevertheless the most important element of his life's work, the culmination of his years of original scholarship. As in other facets of his life, the anecdotes concerning his writing and publishing provide a wealth of information about his character and his perception of himself; about the attitude of others towards him; and about the social climate of the times.

When R. Aisel published his first book, *Emek Yehoshua*, he sent a copy to one of the wealthy men in Kalvariya. This fellow was quite incensed to receive a book he hadn't ordered and sent it back to the rabbi together with a five-ruble note. Some time later the *gvir* and R. Aisel were together at a wedding, and the former, thinking to make amends for his action, approached R. Aisel with the intention of apologizing. "No, no," interrupted the rabbi. "I was very pleased with your action. I was very reluctant to publish that book, but many people encouraged me, admired my Torah and my learning. So I published it, and many people bought the volume eagerly. There was a great demand for it. But I was worried, and saw it as a bad sign. For The Holy One, Blessed Be He, also tried to give away his Torah, but no one wanted to take it. So why should people accept my Torah? Maybe it is not true Torah? But then you came along and returned my book saying you don't want it. So, if people refuse to accept my Torah, it is a sign that it is true Torah."

ספר

נועם ירושלמי

והוא

ביאור על הירושלמי סדר נזיקין

וגם כמה כללים ועיקרים · ושיטות עמוקות · ובזה יתבאר גם
כמה ענינים והלכות עמוקות בהש"ס בבלי ·

אשר חברתי בעזה"י

אני הקטן יהושע אייזיק בא"א הרב מוהרי"ד יחיאל זצ"ל · החונה בקק סלאנימא · בעהמ"ח
ספר עמק יהושע · וספר נחלת יהושע · וספר אבי הנחל · וספר שפת הנחל ·
וספר עצת יהושע · וספר נועם ירושלמי · על סדר זרעים · ועל סדר מועד ·
ועל סדר נשים ·

ווילנא

בדפוס של ר' אברהם יצחק דווארזע

בשנת תרכ"ט לפ"ק

НОАМЪ ІЕРУШАЛМИ,
т. е.
Комментарій на Іерусалимскій талмудъ.

ВИЛЬНА.
Въ Типографіи А. Дворжеца на Николаевскомъ
переулкѣ въ домѣ Малиновскаго № 8.

1869 Г.

With further regard to *Emek Yehoshua,* there is an amusing story about Aisele's visit to Warsaw when he went there to promote the book. It seems that, just at that time, the well-known *hazan* from Vilna, Yoel David Shtrashonsky, had also come to Warsaw with the encouragement of his Polish teacher, to give a concert for the Polish nobility. Both he and R. Aisel stayed in the same lodging-house. The approaching concert caused much excitement, and a steady stream of visitors sent gifts or came to call on Shtrashonsky in his rooms. R. Aisel, on the other hand, sat alone in his room, not having yet made any friends in Warsaw. Not only was he disturbed by the noisy proceedings, but people constantly knocked on his door by mistake. By the day of the concert, the *hazan* had caught cold and became very ill. The concert was cancelled and he was not allowed any visitors. The *hazan* fell into a depression and passed away within a few months. In the meantime, Aisel had distributed his books in the town and the scholars and rabbis, greatly impressed with his learning, began to visit him, bringing gifts, holding study circles, eating and drinking and so on. To which R. Aisel is reported to have commented, in a sonorous tone, that unfortunately the feasting and drinking had moved from the *hazan's* room to his own. Perhaps the incident was even partly responsible for his later critical attitude to cantors.

R. Aisel once met a rabbi with whom he was not on friendly terms, and the latter began criticising his books, beginning with *Noam Yerushalmi,* then *Nahlat Yehoshua,* and finally *Emek Yehoshua.* R. Aisel answered as follows: "I began my work in the valley [*Emek Yehoshua*], then I ascended to the heights of Babylon [*Nahlat Yehoshua*], and

ספר

עמק יהושע

חלק ראשון

משו"ת המבארים כמה הלכות וענינים עמוקים בש"ס בבלי
וירושלמי בסברות עמוקות וישרות .

מכבוד הרב הגאון האמתי שר התורה רשכבה"ג צדיק יסוד עולם כקש"ת מוהר"ר
יהושע אייזיק זצללה"ה הגאבד"ק **קוטנא וסלאנים** .
בעהמ"ח ספרים יקרים **נחלת יהושע . אבי הנחל . שפת הנחל .** וארבעה ספרי
נועם ירושלמי על כל תלמוד ירושלמי **. עצת יהושע . מרבה עצה .**
מרבה תבונה .

הספר רב הערך הזה נדפס בשנת תר"ב וכבר ספו תמו ורבים מגדולי הדור משתוקקים אחריו .
לכן השתדלתי להדפיסו מחדש . וגם הוספתי נופך משלי מחידושי המתיחשים לדבריו הקדושים
נקוב בשם .

שפת העמק

אשר חנני החונן לאדם דעת בנו ותלמידו

הצעיר **משה שפירא** בעהמ"ח ספרי **פני משה** החונה פק"ק **ריגא.**

פיעטרקוב

שנת מים עמוקים דברי פי (משלי י"ח ד') לפ"ק .

וכעת בהוצאה רביעית

ע"י נין המחבר ר' זאב שפירא נ"י

פעיה"ק **ירושלים** תובב"א ,

שנת תשכ"ו לפ"ק

הכתובת : ר' זאב שפירא, רח' ז'בוטינסקי 75, תל אביב.
הרב מאיר קליימאן, רח' זכריה 5, ירושלים.

from there I went higher and higher to Jerusalem [*Noam Yerushalmi*], The good rabbi, however, began in Jerusalem, descended to Babylon and from there even deeper into the valley — but not the valley of Yehoshua, but into his valley, the vale of tears."

On another occasion, Aisel was having a conversation with a stranger who, not aware of Aisel's identity, quoted at length from *Nahlat Yehoshua* as if the ideas he was spouting were his own original thoughts. After listening for some time, R. Aisel commented: "A thief who steals from a thief is excused because he doesn't know to whom to return the stolen goods. But I would like to inform you that the author of the book from whom you have stolen is standing before you, and you may therefore return the ideas you have stolen from him."

When R. Aisel completed the printing of the *Noam Yerushalmi*, he returned to Slonim happy but much weakened and exhausted from this great effort. "It used to be," said R. Aisel, "that when a writer finally saw his work in print, he felt great happiness and waited for the opinions of great men. Today, it seems that everything has already been printed, the words of the great and not so great, of the good and not so good. During the time I have spent in printing my works I have seen how the wheel of fortune turns and how the letters דפוס [print] have been turned inside out and now spell ספוד [to eulogize]."

After he completed the printing of his work *Ibbei HaNahal* in Koenigsberg, he complained that he was utterly *farshwartzed* (blackened, but colloquially, worn out, exhausted) by the effort. When asked why, he replied that he had consumed large quantities of black coffee while

Isel Krinsky

ס פ ר

נועם ירושלמי

ו ה ו א

ביאור על הירושלמי סדר נשים

וגם כמה כללים ועיקרים · ושיטות עמוקות · ובזה יתבאר גם
כמה ענינים והלכות עמוקות בהש״ס בבלי ·

אשר חברתי בעזה״י

אני הקטן יהושע אייזיק בא״א הרב מוהר״ר יחיאל זצ״ל · החונה בק״ק סלאנימא
בעהמ״ח ספר עמק יהושע · וספר נחלת יהושע · וספר אבי הנחל · וספר שפת הנחל
וספר נועם ירושלמי · · על סדר זרעים · · ועל סדר מועד

ווילנא

בדפוס של ר' אברהם יצחק דוואָרזעץ ·

בשנת תרכ״ח לפ״ק

מהדורה שנייה

פעיה״ק **ירושלם** תובב״א
תשכ״ח

Jerusalem printing

seeing to the printing of his book, refusing milk for fear of transgressing the laws of *kashrut.*

On another of his trips, R. Aisel paid a visit to the rabbi of a town, and found two books lying on his table. One, of his own authorship, was simply bound in an inexpensive material, while the second, by another rabbi, was bound in very strong fabric. R. Aisel took both books in his hand as if weighing them, and said, "It seems that my book is not so *meshuga* as the second, which had to be bound as firmly as if it were in chains!"

Returning to Slonim from Vilna with a cartload of newly- printed books, R. Aisel stopped at an inn for some refreshment, leaving the books unattended. The innkeeper remarked on this and asked whether Aisel wasn't concerned that someone might steal his books. "No, I'm not worried," answered the rabbi. "I knock on many doors trying to sell my books and only occasionally find someone who is interested. And you think that here, in the middle of nowhere, someone will come and take a book on his own initiative? I doubt it."

On a similar occasion, a fellow traveller challenged the rabbi, "Once there were fewer books, but the people knew more Torah. Today there are more and more books and people know less and less Torah. How is that?" "I will explain it," answered R. Aisel. "Once men took more care of their faces and did not use razors. Each hair which fell from their beards was carefully placed in a *sefer.* Today there are many men who attack their faces like you do, and prefer to look like dogs rather than wear a handsome beard. So there are many hairs flying about which have to be placed in *seforim,* and so there is need for

ספר

פורת יוסף

סי ו ס ד

על פלפול עמוק בחקירות ודרישות עמוקות

אשר כוננתיו אני הצעיר

יוסף· בא"א· הוישיש·דהנכבד מוה' **צבי הירש** נ"י מדינאבורג·

החונה בק'ק· דרעטשין·

ווילנא

בדפוס ר' שמואל יוסף פין· ור' אברהם צבי ·ראזענקראנץ·

שנת **תרל"א** לפ"ק

СЕФЕРЪ ПОРЕСЪ ІОСЕФЪ

т. е.

вѣтвь Іосифа или толкованіе разныхъ мѣстъ изъ раввинской письменности.

Сочиненіе Гирша Шаупера изъ Динабурга.

ВИЛЬНА.

Въ Типографіи С. І. Фина и А. Г. Розенкранца. 1871

На Вилейской улицѣ въ домѣ № 711/94

many *seforim*."

In his later years, R. Aisel published a small work, prob-ably *Aizat Yehoshua*, simultaneously with one of his larger ones. When this was commented upon, he said, "What difference does it make? No one reads the books, whether they are short or long." Concerning these small books, the last three which he published, R. Aisel was asked why he wrote such small books. He replied that since he himself had to sell his books to the landlords, it was like a punish-ment for them when he came around. "So at least let it be a small punishment so that they won't suffer too much because of me."

Several important books were written in R. Aisel's life-time. In addition to his own *Emek Yehoshua*, there were "משרת משה," *The Servant of Moses*; "אילנא דחיי," *The Tree of Life*; "באר יצחק," *The Well of Isaac*; and "בית הלוי," *The House of Levi*. R. Aisel used to say of them, "Let the servant of Moses make a broom out of the tree of life, dip it into the well of Isaac, clean out the house of Halevi, and sweep everything into the valley of Yehoshua."

There is a story that when R. Aisel finished writing a book titled *Pnei Yehoshua* (The Face of Yehoshua), he found that his son Moshe had just completed a book on tractate *Pesahim* to which he had given the title *Pnei Moshe* (The Face of Moshe). The story continues that Aisel decided to change the name of his own book so that the public would not liken *Pnei Moshe* to the sun (son) and *Pnei Yehoshua* to the moon. Moshe asked his father why he wanted to do this in light of its being written that "One may be jealous of all men except of his son and of his pupil." "Nevertheless," replied R. Aisel, "the moon *is* jealous of the sun."

ספר

ברכת משה

יכלכל

ביאורי מקראי קדש מהנביאים וכתובים הבנוים על
יסודי הז"ל בבלי וירושלמי

אשר הברתי בעזה"י

הצעיר **משה שפירא** החונה **בריגא** בעהט"ה ספר **פני**
משה וספר **שפת העמק** וספר **דרשת מוהר"ם**

בן הגאון האמתי ציס"ע ורשכבה"ג נזר הקדש מאור הגולה
כקש"ת מו"ה **יהושע איזיק** זצ"ל האב"ד **בסלאנימא**.

הובא לבית הדפוס בהוצאות הגאון המחבר ע"י בית כ־חזר ספרים של הר' **יוסף צבי ליעו**
נ"י בווארשא (רחוב בילא 2 נ"א) בהרה"ג ר' **שמואל** זצ"ל שהיה אב"ד בק'
משנת תר"ט עד תר"ך ואחר כך כשנת כת"ר עד י"ט כסליו תר"ם היה ראב"ד
ופו"ץ במעזריטש יע"א ושם מנוחתו כבוד . תנצב"ה.

פיעטרקוב

בדפום של הרבני וכו' מו"ה **מרדכי צעדערבוים** ני"י.

שנת תרס"ט לפ"ק

БИРХАСЪ МОШЕ

т. е. Коментарь на нѣсколько мѣстъ въ Библіи,
Соч. Раввина Мовша Шпиро въ г. г. Ригѣ.

Типографія М. ЦЕДЕРБАУМА въ г. Петроковѣ. 1909.

I have tried to verify this story, charming though it is, because R. Aisel never published a book entitled *Pnei Yehoshua*. The book referred to may have really been *Aizat Yehoshua*, but this was published in 1868, while Pnei Moshe was not published until 1872, with a *haskamah* from R. Aisel. In fact R. Aisel himself suggested the title *Pnei Moshe*. Carrying on with my investigation, I eventually discovered that there was a book titled *Pnei Yehoshua*, but written by a different R. Yehoshua Shapira, so we can see how legends originate on the basis of a distorted interpretation of facts, or the combination of different events put together wrongly. In this regard, it is possible that some of the stories attributed to Aisel Harif originated with others, but became attached to him because of his reputation, and perhaps the opposite is also true, that others "borrowed" Aisel's stories and put their own names to them.

Even if some doubt arises as to the real source of some of these stories, all writers mention R. Aisel's pointed wit and humour as one of the outstanding elements of his personality, and it is not difficult to understand how, with constant repetition, the sayings and utterances attributed to him could pass into the realm of folklore and common knowledge, and acquire additional variations and embellishments.

הסכמה

מאמרי הרב הגאון הגדול אמתי עמוד התורה ושבכבהג בכ"ת מוהר"ד

יהושע אייזיק נ"י האבדק"ק סלאנימא ·

בעהמ"ח ספר עמק יהושע וספר נחלת יהושע וספ' אבי הנחל וספר שפת הנחל וספר עצת יהושע
וארבעה ספרי נעם ירושלמי על כל הש"ס יהשלמי וספר מרבה עצה וספר מרבה תבונה ·

לידידי חזי לי האי ספר **פני משה** אשר חיבר בני חביבי יקירי הרב הגאון המפורסם
חריף ובקי סיני ועוקר הרים כש"ת מוהר"ר **משה** נ"י על מסכת פסחים ·
ותזה בן חכם ישמח אב חכמת אדם תאיר פניו אפוי נהירין ונהירין שמעתתי
משה שפיר קאמר ושפירין שמעתתי חכם בני ישמח לבי גם אני · וברוך רחמנא דחזי
לי פירי כר וטוב פריו סודרוץ ומפז · חריף ומקשה מתן ומסתק דייק וגריס וגמר וסביר
ומראה פנים לפרש שיטת רש"י ותוס' בפנים מסבירות דכל חד למעמי' ולשיטתי' אזלי
ומסמיך לה מאתרין מניאין מעניין לענין באותו ענין ע"כ ראים הדברים לקובעם בדפוס וכל הני
מילי מעליתא יתאברן משמי' בשערי' הבצוינ'ם בהיכה והתית שמעתתי מברדן בעלמא
תן לחכם ויחכם עוד ישמע חכם ויוסף לקח :

דברי סכותב לכבוד התורה ולומדיה יוס א' כ"ב ימים לחודש תמח תרל"ב לפ"ק

נאום הק' **יהושע אייזיק** בלא"א הרב מוהר"ר **יחיאל** זצ"ל החונה פ"ק **סלאנימא**

R. Aisel's *haskamah* for Pnei Moshe, by his son, R. Moshe

דברי כבוד מרח הגאון הגדול יעמוד התורה מאור הגולה מק

יהושע אייזיק שליט"א האבדק סלאנים ·

לידידי חזי לי האי ספר **פורת יוסף** שחיבר חתני יקירי הרב הגאון המפורסם חו"ב
סיני ועוקר הרים כש"ת מוה' **יוסף** במחו' צב"י היר ש נ"י והוא מלא חכמה
וכליל יופי ושפירן שמעתתיה ותארבנה פארתיו והוא חורפא וחולי' רמי דיקלא וזקף
לי' חורז מענין לענין באותו ענין דולה מים סבורות עמוקים וספק חבל בחבל וניזמה
בנימה ומשיחה בשטחה וכמו דאיתא במדרש חזית דאמר ר' לוי אית דידע למיחרז
ןפי' לחבר ולסדרן ולא ידע למיקדח [פי' להיות בעמיק ונוקב לעומק של דברים]
ואית דידע למיקדח ולא ידע למיחרז כו' וחתני יקירי הרב הגאון נ"י בספרו **פורת**
יוסף הוא חרזא והוא קד'חא וידיו רב לו למישכל ולמיסורי בשמעתתא ולחבר
המאמרים בעומק של הלכות · ע"כ ראים הדברים לקובעם בדפוס וכל הני מילי
מעליתא יתאברן משמ' בשערי המצוינים בהלכה ולהיות שמעתתי מברדן בעלמא ·
ובסכו יראו ההכבים ויוסיפו לקח תן לחכם ויחכם עוד :

דברי סכותב לכבוד התורה ולומדיה יום ה' כ"ג מנחם אב תרל"א לפ"ק

נאום הק' **יהושע אייזיק** החונה פ"ק **סלאנימא**

R. Aisel's *haskamah* for Porath Yosef, by his son-in-law, R. Yosef Shluper

162

REFUSAL TO GIVE *HASKAMOT*

R. Aisel was often approached by would-be authors and scholars for a *haskamah* or endorsement of their works, or of their characters, because the endorsement of such an eminent and renowned scholar would enhance the person's professional, and even marital chances, and greatly increase the value of a book in the eyes of the public. But R. Aisel's extremely demanding and critical approach to scholarship meant that, to the great disappointment of most of the applicants, he almost never granted such *haskamot*. He did once endorse a book while in Kalvariya; however, it was not a rabbinical volume, but rather a secular book by Yosef Sheinhak, *The History of the Land,* (presumably the Land of Israel). There were a few other occasions when he was impressed enough by the logic or original thinking of a writer to give him his stamp of approval. He gave one for R. Moshe's book, *Pnei Moshe,* and for R. Yosef's book, *Porat Yosef,* copies of which are reproduced here.

When a group of rabbis had the idea of putting together a volume of *Divrei Torah* which would include new interpretations and commentaries by the great scholars of the time, including R. Aisel, the latter refused to participate. Surprised because they had believed he would approve of the enterprise, the rabbis asked Aisel for an explanation. "Well," he replied, "it's the way of the world. When a dancer is talented he dances whenever he wants to, whenever the spirit moves him. But those who cannot dance alone have to join a company and dance together."

It is therefore not surprising that there are almost as many anecdotes about Aisel Harif's scathing remarks to authors who sought his *haskamah* as there are about the rich who refused to give charity. R. Aisel was incensed against the writers who did not advance the cause of true Torah study, or whose material and ideas had been taken from others. Once he remarked, "Our sages said that if one has seen a *talmid hakham* transgress in the evening, one should not suspect him in one's heart the next day, because he might have repented. Of course he has repented," continued R. Aisel. "He has probably even written a תשובה [an answer; play on the word 'repentance' to prove that everything is permitted and that there never was any transgression."

Nonetheless, authors kept seeking R. Aisel's *haskamah* before printing their works, since his stamp of approval was a sure means of promoting their sale.

Once an author approached R. Asiel with a book which he had titled *New Interpretations by Redak* (the acronym of a famous rabbi of the thirteenth century, R. David Kimchi). When R. Aisel expressed surprise at the title, the author explained that in the customary way he had made use of his own and his father's initials: Rabbi David [son of] Kalman. "For the sake of honoring your father," said R. Aisel, "it would have been better to change the name to Durak, meaning David [son of] R. Kalman [and, in Russian, 'stupid']. Then your father will have the title and not you."

Looking through a book on another occasion, R. Aisel told the author: "This is obviously a sin of the printer, because not everything one thinks should be spoken, not everything one speaks should be written down and not everything written down should be printed."

Once when R. Aisel was asked to give a *haskamah* to a book, he took a large sheet of paper and wrote his *haskamah* in the top corner. Then he left a large space and signed his name at the very bottom of the page. When the author asked for an explanation of this unusual procedure, Aisel answered, "It is written, 'מדבר שקר תתרחק' (Put a distance between yourself and falsehood!)"

One writer who came to R. Aisel to ask for a *haskamah*, told the rabbi, by way of introduction, about his *yiches* (lineage). To which Aisel replied, "When King Solomon wrote the Song of Songs he didn't mention his lineage, but our sages of blessed memory liked the Song very much. When he wrote Ecclesiastes King Solomon began with his *yiches* "דברי קוהלת בן מלך ירושלים" — and in spite of this the sages wanted to exclude the book from the Canon because of its doubts and questionings. From this we learn that *yiches* is bad for a book."

Another scholar, the scion of a distinguished family, came to R. Aisel and, hoping to impress the rabbi, declared, "First I will tell the rabbi about my *yiches*, then I will show him my new interpretations." "If there is *yiches* from previous generations," nodded R. Aisel, "that is nothing new. And if there is something new, there is no need for *yiches*."

An author came to R. Aisel with a book entitled *Chen Tov* (Good Grace) on which R. Aisel commented, after looking through it: "I believe in King Solomon, who wrote in Proverbs that the good sense of man will bring him grace, but I doubt that this *Chen Tov* will bring much good sense."

In a similar vein, he said about an author that he "מחזיר עטרה ליושנה" (he restores the glory as in the past), that is, that he restored the paper to its origins which were rags, from which paper was made in those days.

Aisel once recommended that a writer name his book אז ירננו (Then They Will Rejoice). When the author asked him to explain why, he replied, "I have heard that they will soon stop using wood for heating and instead will burn books that are worthless and have no content. "אז ירננו כל העצים", then the trees will really rejoice, because they won't be used for burning. And you must give your book a title worthy of its future."

Another author who told R. Aisel that he had written his book because he was ill and needed money for medical treatment received the following reply: "An illness instead of a book, maybe, but a book instead of an illness — that is surprising." When asked to explain his remark, Aisel elaborated, "King Hizkiyahu refused to go to Yeshayahu the Prophet, and the prophet refused to go to the king. But when the king fell ill, Yeshayahu had to go to him to fulfill the *mitzvah* of visiting the sick. The question arises, if the illness came in order to bring the two men together, why didn't The Holy One, Blessed Be He, advise King Hizkiyahu to write a book so that he would have to go to the great prophet for a *haskamah*? From this we can understand that it is better to fall ill than to ask for a *haskamah*."

Another version of this story is as follows. Once R. Aisel came to visit a well-known rabbi who was indisposed, but the *rebbetzin* did not know Aisel and wouldn't let him in.

Only after R. Aisel sent a note to the rabbi asking to be received, was he invited into the house. "Now, suddenly I can understand a very difficult passage in the Talmud," said Aisel as he entered the rabbi's house. "We are told that King Hizkiyahu refused to go to Yeshayahu the Prophet, and the prophet refused to go to the king. The only solution was that The Holy One, Blessed Be He, caused the king to fall ill, and so Yeshayahu had to go to him to fulfill the *mitzvah* of visiting the sick. The question is, why did the king fall ill and not the prophet? Now I know the answer! The king was young and not yet married so there was no one to prevent the prophet from coming in. But if Yeshayahu had fallen ill, his wife, the rebbetzin would surely not have allowed him to receive Hizkiyahu!"

Once a rabbi came to R. Aisel and asked whether he should write a book on הלכה למעשה (the practical application of the *halakhah*), or whether to write a new interpretation of *halakhah*. "I suggest you write a book on the *Kabbalah*," he was advised. "But what have I to do with *Kabbalah*?" asked the rabbi. "And what have you to do with the *halakhah*?" was Aisel's reply.

Another rabbi came to R. Aisel with a book he had written on the *Kabbalah* and asked for a *haskamah*. "Today is *Erev Shabbat* and it is getting late. I suggest that you remain here over Shabbat and afterwards we will discuss your book," said Aisel. The next day the two men went to synagogue together and R. Aisel pressed his visitor to lead the afternoon prayers. Although the visitor was reluctant, he could not refuse. So he prayed, but with many mistakes, being extremely ill at ease. Afterwards the visitor asked Aisel why he had insisted that he lead the prayers when

"I have no pretensions to being a *Baal Tefillah*." "In the Gemara we are told that Rabbi Hanina ben Dossa used to say, that if his prayers for the sick flowed easily and fluently, he took that as a sign that they were מקובלים [received]. But if they did not, then he knew that the prayers were rejected. Since I know very little about the *Kabbalah*, the subject of your book, I asked you to pray so that I would know if you were a מקובל [a Kabbalist, and also "received"] or rejected."

An author who was axious to sell as many books as possible brought his book to R. Aisel for a *haskamah*. After leafing through the book and seeing that all the ideas therein had been taken from other sources without acknowledgement, R. Aisel realized that the writer was trying to pass off these ideas as his own, R. Aisel sent the man to someone else in order to get another opinion. This second gentleman burst into laughter when the writer showed him the book. "I am ignorant in these matters and have nothing to do with books, let alone with your book," said the man. The writer returned to R. Aisel in great anger and asked why he had made fun of him in this manner. "Well, I know for a fact that the man to whom I sent you deals in stolen goods, so I thought he could give you good advice about the book you are trying to sell."

R. Aisel told another author, who had written a commentary on Ecclesiastes that he was wiser than King Solomon. "What do you mean?" asked the writer in surprise. "It is written that Solomon was wiser than all the other men, but you have managed in your book to turn him into a fool. To succeed in this you must be wiser than he."

Another author brought his book, a commentary on

Proverbs, to get R. Aisel's opinion. After looking through the book, the rabbi said, "You know, I would advise you to write a commentary on the book of Job instead. He had so many troubles, one more wouldn't matter. But what have you got against King Solomon?"

After refusing a *haskamah* to an author, R. Aisel also warned him to make certain that he did not lose his book in Slonim that day. "Why does the rabbi give me such advice?" asked the man. Aisel smiled his usual smile, and explained: "Today is market day in Slonim, and the peasants come in from the villages round about. If you should lose your book some peasant may pick it up and try to sell it as his own."

A rabbi came to R. Aisel, to ask for a *haskamah.* "I cannot give you a *haskamah,*" said Aisel, "but I will give you a blessing. I hope your book will not be naked as it will not be hungry." The rabbi was very puzzled and asked R. Aisel to explain his words. "Your book will not be hungry because its pages will be used to wrap butter and cheese. But naked it will be, because I'm afraid no one will want to cover it."

An author once came to R. Aisel with a large volume full of new interpretations and pilpulistic arguments. The rabbi glanced through the book, reading a paragraph here and there, then laid it on his table and began to discuss other matters. After talking well into the night, the visitor got up to leave and asked Aisel to allow his *shamash* to accompany him, because it is written that a *talmid hakham* should not go alone at night for fear of evil spirits. R. Aisel handed him back his book and said, "Take this, and if the spirits come, let them look into it. They will know for sure that you are not a *talmid hakham* and will do you no harm."

An author who had written a commentary on the *Shas*, brought it to show R. Aisel. The rabbi leafed through the book and saw that it was full of nonsensical ideas. He returned it to the visitor saying, "I suggest that you leave the house as quickly as possible lest the *rebbetzin* do you some harm." The author paled and asked the rabbi what he meant. "Well, some time ago, a chicken flew onto my desk through the window and made a mess on my *Gemara*, which was lying open on the table. When the *rebbetzin* saw this she immediately caught the chicken and ran with it to the *shochet* who quickly put an end to his life. Now, what do you think the *rebbetzin* will do when she sees what a mess you made of the *Mishnah*?"

Once a scholar from the village of Dolny came to R. Aisel for a *haskamah*. After looking through the book, R. Aisel said, "You are really a סמוך [which means both ordained and near], but you are also אינו נראה [not seen, or not making a good impression]." This is a pun on the phrase "He who sits on the mountain is seen but not near; near but not seen is he who sits in the valley [i.e., the village of Dolny]."

A disappointed writer once asked R. Aisel why he refused to endorse his book when other important rabbis had agreed to do so. Smiling in his usual way, R. Aisel replied that he agreed and they agreed; he agreed to *Divrei Torah*, and they agreed to empty phrases (a pun on the Hebrew words מסכימים (agree) and משכימים [to rise early], which could sound the same with the Lithuanian lisp).

A scholar who brought his book to R. Aisel for a *haskamah* explained that in his title, *Mayyim Metukim* (Sweet Waters) meant that there is no lifegiving water other than the Torah, and that the new interpretations of Torah in his book were sweeter than honey. "The title certainly fits the contents," commented R. Aisel, "for it is written that stolen waters are the sweetest."

Another author brought a book to R. Aisel, entitled ויאמר יעקב (And Jacob said). R. Aisel leafed through the book and declared the title a good and appropriate one. "Why does his honor mention only the title!" asked the anxious author. "Come, I'll explain," replied R. Aisel. "It is written in the Torah 'And He said to him, What is your name; and he said Yaakov, without adding another word.' And you have named your book *VaYomer Yaakov*, also without adding another word."

Two young men came to R. Aisel with a book they had written together, with new interpretations of *Baba Kama*, the first section of tractate *Nezikin*. After looking through the volume and finding nothing of interest in it, R. Aisel asked the young men what title they had considered for the book. Upon hearing that they would like his opinion on this as well, Aisel's reply was brief and to the point: "השור והבור" [HaShor veHaBor]. In this quotation from *Baba Kama*, השור (the Ox) and הבור (the Pit) are mentioned as two of four factors which cause damage to humans and to property. (This could also be an intended pun on the Hebrew word for ignoramus, which is בור, or boor).

When another writer brought Reb Aisel a bible with wide margins, on which he had written his own interpretations, R. Aisel looked through the book and kept exclaiming "How interesting! How original," and so on, till the writer himself was so astonished that he asked R. Aisel if he really was so impressed with his ideas? "What

I'm mainly impressed with is your good sense in having written your comments around the Holy text. Otherwise I would surely have thrown your book out."

A variation of the story, if not a different one, is told about an author who brought R. Aisel a commentary on the Torah, which he had written in the margins around the text. In this case, R. Aisel is supposed to have said: "Yes, I like your commentary, for it is close to the truth!"

When R. Aisel was already well on in years, an elderly rabbi came to him for a *haskamah* and was refused in the usual way. But this rabbi was deeply offended and decided to attack R. Aisel in return. "Rabbi of Slonim, our sages wrote that תלמידי חכמים כל מה שמזקינין דעתם מתיישבת עליהם (great scholars become more balanced in their opinions as they grow older). So why is it that I find your honor's later works less good than his earlier ones?" R. Aisel replied to this insult with a smile on his face. "This saying is directed not only to writers but also to readers. And it is also said that, as ignorant men grow older, "דעתם מיטפשת עליהם" they become more and more foolish."

In a similar vein, one of his rivals once attacked R. Aisel by saying: "We have learnt that *talmidei hakhamim* grow wiser as they grow older, but in the case of your honor it is the opposite. If there was something of value in *Emek Yehoshua*, in your second book, *Nahlat Yehoshua*, there is nothing. Why such a diminution, rather than increase in your intellect?" "It is also written," replied Reb Aisel, "that ignorant men become more foolish as they grow older. When my first book was published you were younger and still capable of understanding something of it. But when the second one was published you were already older and more foolish and couldn't make head or tail of what was written there."

R. Aisel had great respect for his son-in-law, R. Yosef Shluper, yet he could not resist a joke at his expense. When R. Yossel brought his new book to R. Aisel, and complained that he could not go ahead with the printing as he could not think of a suitable title, Aisel said, "You know what? Just to be different, why don't you call it 'ישת חושך' [*Spreading Darkness*]. No one has ever used that title, and it will be really original."

But, with all his barbed remarks to other authors, R. Aisel also made fun of his own works. When it was pointed out to him that writers in early times had written briefly, yet he wrote at great length, he replied, "they knew what they wanted to say, so they could be brief, but I am not so sure of what I want to say, so it takes me longer."

In spite of R. Aisel's negative attitude towards giving *haskamah*, the stream of authors did not cease. Once someone remarked to him, "The rabbi so rarely gives a *haskamah* for his own books." "That's exactly why I never ask for one!" said R. Aisel.

It is ironic that Aisel's grandson, R. Avraham, son of Mordecai, who emigrated to America at the beginning of this century, felt it necessary, or desirable, to obtain a *haskamah* when he published the third edition of *Emek Yehoshua* in 1925. In fact, he was able to get three *haskamot* from then Chief Rabbi, R. Yitzhak HaCohen Kook ("The eleven stars of R. Aisel shine like sapphires in the sky"); from R. Avraham Cahane Shapira, head of the *Beit Din* in Kovno; and from R. Moshe Mordecai Epstein of Slobodka, head of Hebron yeshiva. I wonder what R. Aisel would have said about this, if he could have known.

R. Aisel reached the highest rung of Torah scholarship in his lifetime, and it seems that all his knowledge in the associated areas was always at his command; nothing was ever lost. Hence his impatience and intolerance of those less well-versed. He could also see the deterioration which had already set in with regard to the concept of the "Rabbi." In earlier periods, when Torah learning was the lifeblood of Jewish communities, the title "גדול בתורה" (Gadol b'Torah) had been synonymous with learning and scholarship; in addition the rabbi acted as a judge, as a *maggid*, as a teacher, and looked after the practical affairs of the community. Yet by the mid-nineteenth century, R. Aisel could see men who had not achieved an appropriate level of learning becoming rabbis. A giant amongst giants, he saw about him only dwarfs. Any "nobody" could become a rabbi, and every secretary an author. Certain that mediocrities could not build a strong Judaism or enhance *Torat Yisrael,* R. Aisel was therefore impatient with and critical of such "authors" and "rabbis." His heart ached, but he always tried to cloak his ridicule in a smile. He knew only too well that one must study hard and unceasingly to understand the Torah, and felt that those who took the Crown of Torah undeservedly were deserving of his wrath.

A Vilna teacher brought his son and son-in-law to R. Aisel to be examined for the rabbinate. He ordained the former but not the latter. When asked why he did this when both young men seemed to be of equal standing, R. Aisel replied: "You can't change the young man who is your son for a better one. But you can certainly find a better scholar for a son-in-law."

Another important man brought his son to R. Aisel to be tested on Rashi's commentary on that week's *parashah*, mentioning in passing that his son hoped to become a rabbi. After the examination R. Aisel told the father that his son was a *gaon*, a real genius. While the father was extremely delighted at this words, those sitting in R. Aisel's home were amazed to hear his opinion. "Don't be surprised," said R. Aisel smilingly. "You know that in each period the great rabbis and teachers were called by various names: *Tannaim, Amoraim, Gaonim*. Since Rashi lived after the period of the *Gaonim*, they did not know anything about him. And from this standpoint, that young man is really a *gaon*. But," he sadly concluded, "if he knows how to read, and his father is really one of the wealthy people in his town, I am sure he will one day be a rabbi."

A prominent man from another town brought his son to R. Aisel to be tested for the rabbinate. Finding the son to be unintelligent and not learned, R. Aisel did not authorize him as a rabbi. But he told the father that the son could be likened to a heavenly angel. The father returned to his town full of pride and boasted to his friends about the praise R. Aisel had lavished on his son. When Aisel was asked why he had been so generous to a young man who had no Torah and no wisdom, he replied, "It has been said that Torah was never given to the ministering angels."

A young man once came to R. Aisel for an examination to be approved as a teacher. Unimpressed with the young man's intellectual ability, Aisel asked him the meaning of the phrase "תנו רבנן". Quite insulted, the young man replied, "Any child knows that it means 'the rabbis learnt'. "No!

No!" R. Aisel exclaimed, "It is not written ,'רבנן תנו' but 'תנו רבנן,' First they 'learned,' and then they became rabbis, not the other way around."

There was a certain scholar in a town near Slonim, who liked to boast that he was more knowledgeable than R. Aisel. When this was mentioned to R. Aisel, he nodded his head. "Yes, it is so, but the difference between us is that he knows where it is written, and I know what is written. Therefore I agree with King David when he wrote in the Psalms, 'סעיפים שנאתי', I hate the 'verse quoters' — they only know where a certain verse can be found, but do not understand what is written there."

Two yeshiva boys came to R. Aisel to be tested for the rabbinate, one knowledgeable (בקי) and one sharp (חריף), who knew only a few sections of the Talmud. After examining them R. Aisel ordained the former, and remarked, "Now I understand the *Gemara* in *Horayoth* [a tractate in Nezikin] that "סיני" [knowledgeable] is better than "עוקר הרים" [sharp], because even if the sharp one wishes 'to move the mountain,' he won't succeed because he doesn't know where the mountain is."

Two other rabbinical students came to be tested for the rabbinate, one knowledgeable (בקי) and one sharp (חריף), R. Aisel ordained the first and not the second. When the student who failed to gain Aisel's recommendation said, "The Rabbi is himself 'sharp.' How is it that he does not ordain another who is sharp?" To which R. Aisel answered: "When someone is knowledgeable in his sharpness, that is good. And when one is sharp in his knowledge, that is also good. The one who is knowledgeable has a reserve to use at his discretion, but one who is only sharp, has none."

Once R. Aisel came to a village and was guest of the local rabbi. After some scholastic talk, Aisel realized that the rabbi knew little about *Halakhah* or *Aggadah*. "I'm very surprised," said R. Aisel, "that the rabbi lives in this village. The people here believe that they have a rabbi and depend on him. But you and I know that there is no rabbi here, and how can a Jew live in a place where there is no rabbi?"

Among the many factors which contributed to the deterioration or weakening of the rabbinate that so upset Reb Aisel was the custom of choosing a rabbi from another town, who would have more "glamour" than a local candidate. This experience also befell his own son-in-law, Yosef Shluper, in later years.

Once a *talmid hakham*, well-versed in Torah, came to R. Aisel complaining that he had grown up in his town and was well-thought of by the congregation, and yet when the rabbi passed away they did not even consider him for the position, but brought in a rabbi from elsewhere who hadn't nearly as much scholarship as himself. "You must realize," R. Aisel comforted him, "that this is the way of Israel and always has been. When Moses went up to Mt. Sinai and tarried there, the Children of Israel sought a replacement for him. So they made themselves a golden calf, when in fact, who could be more suitable to replace Moshe Rabenu than Aaron the priest? But the hooves of the calf from 'outside' were more attractive than Aaron the priest from 'inside'. And," Aisel added, "consider the difference between the early and the later generations. The Israelites in the desert took off their gold and silver in order to make themselves a god. But in our generation they take off their God in order to make silver and gold."

R. Aisel also detested the high-flown titles which were bestowed freely upon young scholars and rabbis, and was as loathe to make use of them as he was to giving *haskamot*. He wanted to see the rabbinate as representing the acme of scholarship, and he ridiculed those who embellished themselves to impress their congregation, for he believed that a rabbi should be a courageous fighter, leading his people and lighting the way for them, and not a puny fellow dependent on the whim of the *parnassim*.

In this respect, he once remarked that greatness had now come to the street of the cobblers; every rabbi was being addressed as *HaRav HaGaon*, (the rabbi the genius, or the great). "Soon we will see the prophecy of Isaiah also come true, that 'the fruit of the land will be great' and even a potato will be called great."

While R. Aisel lived in Slonim, a Rabbi Lieber, son of the author of *Afikei Yehuda*, R. Yehuda Lieber, also made his home there. The son always taught the wisdom of his father and nothing original of his own. Once R. Aisel said to him, "come and see how your character is *not* like that of the daughters of Lot." "What do you mean? What have I to do with the daughters of Lot?" asked the younger Lieber. "Well, it is clear. It is written that the daughters of Lot 'knew' and their father did not know. But with you it is the opposite: your father 'knew' and you, if you'll pardon me, don't know."

Once a young man came to R. Aisel with a diploma from another rabbi describing him as "האברך החו"ב" (the sharp and knowledgeable young man). He wanted a similar diploma from R. Aisel. But the latter, not finding any evidence of these qualities, refused. The insistent young man pointed to the diploma which said he was חריף ובקי. "Well, well, said R. Aisel. "I thought those [החוב] were the initials for 'החיה וכל בהמה' [the wild beast and other animals]!"

משרד החינוך והתרבות
המחלקה לתרבות תורנית

עירית תל-אביב-יפו
האגף לתרבות, לנוער ולספורט
המדור לתרבות תורנית

ב״ה

הזמנה

א. ג. נ.

כב׳ מוזמן לערב עיון במסגרת
„בימת הספר התורני"
שיוקדש לזכרו של

ר׳ אייזלה חריף (ר׳ יהושע אייזיק שפירא ז״ל)

רב ואב״ד בקהילות סלונים וטיקטין.
במלאת מאה שנה לפטירתו
ולרגל הוצאת המהדורה החדשה של כתביו וספריו.

דברי הערכה מפי כב׳ **הרב צבי מרקוביץ שליט״א**
יפתח וינחה: **מר א. גולדראט** (מנהל ספרית הרמב״ם).

התכנית תתקיים אי״ה ביום שלישי, ב׳ אדר ב׳ תשל״ג (6.3.73).
בשעה 8.00 בערב,
בספרית הרמב״ם, רחוב מזא״ה 22, תל-אביב.

נא לדייק !!!

Invitation to memorial evening on the centenary of R. Aisel's death, Tel Aviv, 1973

The Modest Genius

At times one is amazed at the sharpness of R. Aisel's tongue and his apparent disregard for the feelings of those he criticized. Surely he must have aroused great antagonism. Yet the evidence shows that he commanded great affection and respect from Jews and non-Jews alike wherever he went. And it was obvious that Slonim was very proud of its illustrious rabbi. The fact is that his was a complex character, with many contradictions, and while it is futile to try to "psychoanalyze" someone a hundred and twenty years after his death, it is nevertheless interesting to contemplate and try to understand how his formative years influenced his life and character. For example, was his caustic wit an expression of the anger and frustration he had felt as a young child when he saw his mother suffering in her poverty, while his father, albeit a loving parent, was away from home for long periods at the court of his *rebbe*? Or was it his frustration at having to be dependent on the community? Or personal unhappiness in his private life? Was his sarcasm always genuine, or did he feel he had to keep up his reputation as Aisel Harif? Did people purposely try to provoke him? The only thing we can be sure of is that Aisel had a quick mind and a sharp tongue from early childhood, and that his life experience made them even quicker and sharper, so that he always had an answer for every verbal and mental challenge.

On the other hand, although his books are full of original Torah interpretation and wisdom, depth and understanding and *pilpul,* he never preached morality in the customary style of fiery "accusation." He thought that a sharp rebuke cloaked in a humorous style was more effective than violent castigation. He therefore favored a fatherly, patriarchal approach. And although he was in the habit of giving his sermons in the sing-song style, with a *nigun,* which was then used by the preachers, R. Aisel never attacked his audience as they did. When asked to explain the reason for this, he replied that poetry was not like *Mussar,* or even like moral self-improvement. "When Solomon, the wisest man of all time, recited the Song of Songs, he did not mention his lineage, only his name, but the audience never the less enjoyed the poetry, responding 'Let him kiss me with the kisses of his mouth.' But when Solomon spoke morality in Ecclesiastes and mentioned that he was descended from David, King of Jerusalem, the audience responded 'Vanity, vanity, all is vanity says *Koheleth.*'"

R. Aisel loved truth and original thought, and was known as one who put all the *gaonim* of his generation to nought. Yet he was always embarrassed by the exaggerated and high-flown titles with which rabbis and *dayyanim* addressed him when they wrote asking for his advice or opinion. He always put these letters aside and did not read them. When one of his sons asked why he didn't read what people wrote about him, he replied: "What have I do with such untruths?" "But you should know what people say about you. What if they dishonor you?" continued the son. "If they really knew the truth about me," said Aisel, "they wouldn't be turning to me with their questions."

However, when he met R. Naftali Zvi Yehuda, a devoted scholar who was head of the Wolozyn Yeshiva, R. Aisel didn't react when R. Naftali complained that R. Aisel's witticisms and anecdotes were so eagerly sought after by the students in his yeshiva, that they were distracted from their Torah studies. And he only smiled when R. Naftali suggested that he confine his utterances to new commentaries on the Torah, so that the students would have to look there for his well-known humor. For R. Aisel had great respect for R. Naftali, even though Naftali was younger than he, and he didn't mind honest criticism. Although he knew his own intellectual worth, he never thought that he himself was suitable to be *Rosh Yeshiva*. Together with his great scholarliness and his sharp and witty mind, R. Aisel had the ability to laugh at himself. It was this, and his desire to be with and of his people, which endeared him to Jews everywhere and spread his fame far and wide. Indeed, A. Drouyanov, in his book *Sefer HaBdicha VeHaHidud*, which analyses the sources and development of Jewish humor, mentions R. Aisel as one of its fathers. Few of the great rabbis had terms of endearment or special nicknames added to their proper names, and if the term "Harif" was added to Aisel's, it was well-justified. But of this too he had something to say.

"חריף is nothing more than the initial of my father-in-law, חַתָן רַבִי יִצחק פַיין, the son-in-law of Reb Yitzhak Fine. And just as Reb Yitzhak made me *Harif*, so my mother-in-law made me *Baki*, because she made my life miserable at home, always chasing me out to spend as much time as possible in the *Beit Midrash*, studying day and night."

Another rabbi once asked R. Aisel why he was praised highly as being incorruptible when there were surely other rabbis who were at least as worthy if not more so. "And if people will say about you that you are not so great in learning," replied Aisel, "will you take any notice? Of course not! You will just ignore them. So please ignore what is said about me also."

In the same vein, R. Aisel told the following story about himself during a Purim celebration. "While I was in Minsk, my father-in-law begged me not to take on a position, but to devote myself to study. But I was deaf and did not listen to him. And so, I found myself in Kalvariya, where I discovered that I was foolish for having agreed to take on the rabbinate of that town. So now I was both deaf and foolish. Then, when I was in Tiktin, I received an invitation to become the rabbi of Nieswiez. But I thought to myself, I may be deaf and foolish, but I don't want to be small as well!" (In Hebrew 'small' is *katan*, which is also an acronym for the first letters of Kalvariya, Tiktin and Niewswiez.)

Another anecdote which illustrates R. Aisel's basic modesty, despite his great renown, tells of an incident in the bath-house, where he was washing in anticipation of the Sabbath. It seems that one of the townsmen, seeing Aisel only from the back, mistook him for an acquaintance and gave the rabbi a smart slap on the shoulder with his bundle of twigs. R. Aisel turned to see who had approached him in this manner, and the other fellow saw to his horror and embarrassment what a terrible mistake he had made. He began to apologize profusely and to explain how he hadn't recognized the rabbi. Aisel laughed and said, "Never mind, I'm not a rabbi from the rear!"

Once during the winter, R. Aisel was traveling together with one of the *gvirim* of the town. The carriage wheel struck an object on the road and overturned, throwing the two passengers onto the ground. "Look at us!" laughed R.

Aisel, "Now we are fulfilling the prophesy 'תורה וגדולה במקום אחד' (Torah and prominence together in one place)."

During one of his journeys R. Aisel stopped by the wayside for the afternoon prayers, and went to pray under a nearby tree. Watching him at prayer, the *baal-agalah* was surprised to see the rabbi weeping copiously. When he returned to the wagon, the astonished driver asked, "Has the rabbi sinned so greatly that he cries so much during his prayers?" "Just as you see," answered R. Aisel, "when one sins, one repents. But please guard my honor and don't reveal my secret to anyone."

His modesty notwithstanding, Aisel Harif would not put up with discourteous behavior, from anyone. During another journey he happened to stay at the same inn as a rabbi who was not well disposed towards him and always sought to belittle Aisel whenever possible. The rabbi pushed ahead to wash his hands first as if he were the more important. This man was therefore surprised when they sat down to eat and Aisel hastened to offer him the head of the herring which had been placed on the table, taking only the tail for himself. He asked why R. Aisel was being so generous. "Very simple," replied Aisel. "You and the head make one whole, while I and the tail make another."

When R. Aisel published his second book, *Nahlat Yehoshua*, one of his learned opponents pronounced the work so full of errors that it should have been called *Mahalat Yehoshua* (The Illness of Yehoshua). When this was told to R. Aisel, he answered, "According to this rabbi's understanding of the Torah, he should really be a doctor, and therefore his inclination to 'illness'. But is seems that his patients preferred to make him a rabbi."

185

And when he was asked why rabbis in earlier periods were great in Torah and earned little, while in his time they were less learned and earned much more, R. Aisel asked his questioner, "What does this remind you of? A man who is walking to his destination is overtaken by a cart that is going in the same direction. The driver picks him up and takes him along for a much smaller fee than if the man had ordered a special cart. Now, earlier rabbis studied for the sake of the Torah, and if they picked up a rabbinate along the way, well and good. Even at a small salary, the Torah was their only occupation. But in our day, the rabbis learn specially in order to become rabbis. Therefore they must have a higher salary!"

On the same subject, R. Aisel was once asked how it was possible that the "Sha'agat Aryeh," who had lived in Minsk in the middle of the eighteenth century, had received a salary of two or three rubles a month, plus two pairs of shoes a year, while now there were rabbis who received a hundred rubles a month. "It's very simple," replied R. Aisel. "How much does a chicken cost today! Fifteen to twenty kopeks. But if you want to buy a painting of a chicken, it will cost you a hundred rubles or more!

As modest as he was with regard to his own achievements R. Aisel was always more than ready to appreciate real learning in others. While he was still in Tiktin R. Aisel was told of a boy who had come to the yeshiva, and who claimed to have many questions about and criticism of the book *Emek Yehoshua*. The boy was thirteen years old, the son of a simple tailor. Aisel invited the boy to his home and listened to his points and criticisms, finding them just. "Well," asked R. Aisel, "have you nothing good to say about my book?" The boy then discussed other aspects of *Emek Yehoshua* and set about proving that R. Aisel's ideas and deductions with respect to those aspects of it were correct.

Although the boy's words impressed R. Aisel, he could not resist a little joke. "Well," he said, "I see that you are well-versed in many branches of Torah study, but I would like to hear some *Divrei Torah* of your father." The boy reddened but answered, "My father says it is better to sew a new garment than to repair an old one." R. Aisel smiled and said to the scholars who were seated around: "This boy will achieve greatness!" And his prophecy was true, because that young boy, Yeruham Yehuda Leib Perelman of Minsk, went on to become a rabbi and brilliant scholar and the author of *Ohr Gadol*.

Some years later, R. Yeruham had achieved fame in Minsk and in Kovno, and was known as "the great one of Minsk," but was still little-known in other places. Once he passed through Slonim, and decided to call on R. Aisel to hear some *Divrei Torah*. When he arrived at Aisel's home looking young and poorly dressed, no one recognized him. R. Aisel, who happened to be very busy at the time, told the visitor that he was not free for Torah discussions. But the young man was persistent and said, "We have both studied and learnt. We are neither tradesmen nor merchants. So what shall we discuss if not Torah?"

Impressed by the perseverance of his visitor, R. Aisel inquired if he had read *Emek Yehoshua*. "Yes, I have looked through it," said R. Yeruham. "And what do you think of it?" asked Aisel. "That it is not a valuable book for there are no new ideas in it," replied the young visitor. "Not a single new idea?" persevered R. Aisel. "Well," conceded the great one of Minsk, "there is something new, something wonderful on page such and such," and he proceeded to quote the entire passage by heart adding his own comments. Upon which R. Aisel hugged the young man in admiration and exclaimed, "That is the way to study!"

R. Yeruham was a follower of R. Israel Salanter, a supporter of the Hovevei Zion movement and rabbi of Minsk between 1883 and 1896. His great work, *Ohr Gadol*, was a widely respected collection of responsa.

Although R. Aisel's works made use of *pilpul*, he disliked the exaggerated use of it for the construction of devious arguments, his own interpretations being based instead on sheer logic and objective discussion. But, though extremely critical of others, he was also prepared to take criticism of his own work and change his point of view if it was proven wrong. In spite of his jokes and puns at the expense of others, there is no doubt that Aisel had great respect for genuine scholars and original thought. He used to say that between Minsk and Vilna was a לייב (lion, in Yiddish). When asked who that lion was, he replied, "R. Leibele Smorgoner [from the town of Smorgon]. Whatever clever innovations of Torah I wanted to discuss with him, he has always shown me that it had already been written by Rashi."

Nor did R. Aisel hesitate to be generous to his colleagues whenever possible. When the Crown Rabbi of Slonim (i.e., the one appointed by the government, for his knowledge of Russian rather than rabbinics) once complained to him that he couldn't understand why he was much less honored than R. Aisel even though they were both serving in the same town, Aisel replied: "We find many similar situations in life. On Pesach, for example, it is written 'על מצות ומרורים יאכלוהו' [they shall eat *matzot* and bitter herbs]. But the matzot are prepared far in advance, wrapped in clean white cloth and put away in a special place till needed, while the bitter herbs are prepared hastily on Erev Pesach, and put on the table without ceremony. However, even though the *maror* gets little attention, it is as important as the *matzot*, for we cannot make a *seder* without it."

One of the few stories that give us a glimpse into the private life of R. Aisel, and the only one that I have ever come across mentioning that he married a second time, is the following.

Commenting on the section of the *Gemara* which says that a man's first wife is in accordance with his merits and his second in accordance with his deeds, R. Aisel said, "This is quite a correct evaluation. With my first wife, whenever I returned from *shul* the house was in perfect order, everything in its place and the meals on time. According to my merits. But my second wife is really according to my deeds. Whatever I do she does too. I go to *shul*, so does she. I am busy with mitzvoth, so is she. We are both busy with the *Olam Habah*. And what is the result? Complete chaos in the home and in life in general!"

Perhaps here it is not amiss to pity the poor *rebbitzin*. For it seems that her home was always full of people, and travelers were often invited to spend the night. One wonders how she coped, especially if she still had young children. Did she have any help? Was her work ever appreciated or acknowledged, or was it simply taken for granted?

With the above story in mind, one can't help wondering whether the following ones too may not also be rooted in bitter personal experience.

It is reported that on one of the holidays the *rebbetzin* placed a bowl of hot *tzimmes* on the table, saying, "There is so much steam, Aisele, that I can hardly see you through it." To which R. Aisel nodded his head and replied, "Let us live another year continuing not to see each other."

R. Aisel was once asked about the custom of placing the *huppa* of a poor bride and her handicapped groom in the cemetery, at a time of plague or epidemic. "There is a theory," he replied. "that you treat like with like. Heat takes the heat from fever, and evil drugs defeat evil elements in the body. Since a bad wife is more bitter than death, the bride stands under the *huppa* in the cemetery in order that she will defeat the death of the plague." (The two "troubles" were pitted against each other in the hope that the more severe would drive out the lesser.) This story is one of the more enigmatic of the many anecdotes attributed to R. Aisel, and leads me to wonder whether it is the correct version, or whether, perhaps, the nuances of that period escape me today. It seems wrong to equate "poor" with "bad," yet in those days of no unemployment insurance or social security, to be poor was very bad and bitter indeed.

The whole question of the attitude towards women became rather aggravating. During my reading, it became clear that women were not considered as people in their own right, and were rarely mentioned by name. Men were known as the sons of, or the sons-in-law of, or the fathers-in-law of, but the wives and daughters remain anonymous. And if their first names are mentioned, the family name remains a secret. Beside other implications, this is a great obstacle to tracing back a family tree.

MORE STORIES

Wit

Aisel Harif did not confine his wit to remarks about any one group. True, some of his most caustic remarks and most telling parables were directed at the *hassidim*, the *maskilim* and the rich, but the objects of his wit were not always those he disagreed with. It seems that, no matter the situation, he always had an apt and pungent remark or comment.

———◦———

Thus, after a wealthy but unlearned man, with a very poor knowledge of Hebrew, had led the prayers in the *Beit Midrash* where R. Aisel used to pray, Aisel asked him, "Did you conduct the prayers to fulfill your obligation of observing a *yahrzeit* [anniversary of the death of a close relative], or because you simply wanted to contribute to the enjoyment of the congregation?" "Out of a desire to contribute," the man replied. "Well then, you must be one of the most generous people in this town, because in Slonim, there is a custom that if you don't have you don't give. Yet you, who haven't what to give, are giving anyway!"

———◦———

R. Aisel did not believe in prolonging prayer and was always the first to finish the silent *Amidah*, stepping backwards at *Oseh Shalom* before the congregation. When it was remarked to him that the *Baal Tefilla* usually has to wait for the rabbi, who generally finishes last, he said:

191

"What have I to do with other rabbis? They follow after the congregation, but I want the congregation to follow me!" In the original Yiddish version there is a nice pun here — taking the three steps backward is called *oisgehen* or "going out," which is synonymous with the verb "to yearn." So the other rabbis "yearn" for their congregations and are always trying to please them, but Aisel wants his congregation to "yearn" for him, and to try to please him.

———— ◦ ————

And when he was once asked why people are afraid of the truth and flee from it, he replied, "Because the truth is naked and will not be covered up. And, since people are basically modest, they flee it at any cost!"

———— ◦ ————

Against fools, R. Aisel is reported to have said: "I have sometimes seen a wise man commit a foolish act, but I have never seen a fool commit a wise act."

———— ◦ ————

Noticing that his *shamash* helped himself to a bottle of wine from the table, slipping it into his pocket, the rabbi asked the man what was in the bottle. "Only water," said the *shamash*. "So let me taste it," said Aisel. After ascertaining that the contents of the bottle were indeed sweet, R. Aisel commented, "King Solomon was right when he said that stolen waters were sweeter!"

———— ◦ ————

At a *Brith Mila*, where a variety of drinks had been placed on the table, the host offered R. Aisel two kinds of schnapps. "Actually, I prefer the better one," said Aisel, "because I believe in the expression 'הדיוט קופץ בראש' [the simpleton always jumps ahead], and therefore a simple schnapps goes straight to the head, and mixes up the mind."

At another *Brith Mila*, R. Aisel was honoured with the role of *sandak* (godfather). When the cantor began to intone the words, "And his name in Israel shall be...," the baby's father was struck dumb, and couldn't remember the name which he and his wife had decided on. R. Aisel whispered to him, "Avraham," and the young father gratefully announced the name to the *hazan*.

When the young man came to his wife later to congratulate her, he told her of the incident, and the wife confirmed that Avraham was indeed the name they had agreed on. The young man hurried back to the company to announce this miraculous deed of the rabbi. How had he known the name of the baby? But R. Aisel merely smiled and said, "No wonders and no miracles. When I saw the father standing there with his mouth open, like *Terach* [father of Abraham, and in Yiddish slang an old fool], I knew that the son should be called Avraham!"

Shmuel Yosef Fuenn was a well-known scholar and writer and editor of the newspaper *HaCarmel*. He was also the owner of a brick factory and a very wealthy man. He and R. Aisel met often and liked to banter, and once the latter said about him, "It is obvious that a brick-maker is judged by the hardness of his bricks, and a writer by the softness of his language. But with Fuenn it is the opposite: his bricks are soft and his language very hard [i.e., difficult]."

On one of his trips to Vilna, R. Aisel stayed at the home of Shmuel Yosef Fuenn. Although it was winter time, his host offered Aisel fresh cherries. "Please taste them, Reb Aisel. They will be a novelty for you." "Perhaps for you they are a novelty," retorted Aisel, "but we already had fresh cherries in Slonim six months ago."

———◦———

Asked why a midwife is called a wise woman in the Talmud, Aisel replied: "Because היא רואה את הנולד, she sees the newborn, of course!" (This is a pun on the expression, "to see the outcome," or future developments.)

———◦———

A young man came to R. Aisel to ask for advice on what he should name his newborn daughter. His previous six daughters had not survived, and he therefore felt it extremely important to give his newest child the right name. "Name her Bat Sheva, [the seventh daughter]," said the Harif, "and she will live for many years."

———◦———

R. Aisel was once asked about a passage in Tractate *Sota*, which relates that there was a town in which lived two scholars who did not get along with each other. One died, and the other was sent into exile. "How is it possible," asked the man, "that the town was left without a *talmid hakham*? And if one died, and there was no one for the second *talmid* to argue with, why couldn't he stay in the town rather than be sent into exile?" "That is a question you should ask the friends of the dead scholar," answered R. Aisel, "because they are the ones who saw to it that the other scholar was exiled."

———◦———

When asked why in the *Mishnah,* Rabi always used the words "חירש טיפש קטן" [deaf person, dolt, small] in that specific order, so that the fool always came between the deaf person and the child, Aisel Harif replied: "Very simple. That's how fools behave — wherever there are two people, they barge in between."

———————◇———————

A well-known Slonimer informer threatened that, unless he received three hundred rubles immediately, he would denounce the town to the authorities over improper book-keeping. As there was no possibility of paying such an enormous sum of money, the townsfolk called an extraordinary meeting to which they invited R. Aisel. After much consultation, the rabbi summoned the informer and asked him, "So, what is it you want?" "Three hundred rubles, rabbi," replied the blackmailer. "Such a *hutzpa,*" shouted R. Aisel. "If you aren't satisfied with fifty rubles, we'll find ourselves another informer who'll be happy to receive even half that amount."

———————◇———————

When he first began looking for a rabbinical situation, R. Aisel was interviewed by a *gabbai* who was a rough, uneducated man. When this synagogue official realized the calibre of R. Aisel as a scholar, he refused to take him on for fear that his own position would be weakened in the eyes of the community. Quickly taking stock of the situation, Aisel remarked: "As far as I can see, you are looking for a rabbi who has less learning than you, but you won't find such a person anywhere."

———————◇———————

"What is the difference between the earlier generations and the later?" R. Aisel once asked, and proceeded to answer his own question: "In early times, he who had brains became a rabbi; he who had money bought an estate; he who was honest and reliable manufactured goods. Today, a clever man becomes an agent and deals in cattle; an honest man refuses to give testimony; and one who has money buys a rabbinate."

———————— ‹◌› ————————

Once R. Aisel said that the invention of the sewing machine had stopped the study of Torah in Israel. "In the past, the tailor used to sew, the *hazan* used to sing, the *maggid* used to preach and the rabbi was busy with Torah. Since the invention of the sewing machine, the *hazan* took over the "sewing" from the tailor [i.e., putting together various elements in the prayers], the *maggid* took the melodies from the *hazan* [because he spoke in a sing-song voice] and the rabbi took over the sermons from the *maggid*. And thus the Torah is left neglected."

———————— ‹◌› ————————

A wealthy tax collector, whose son-in-law had been living with him on *kest* for many years, came to ask a question of R. Aisel. "It is written that one must study the Torah night and day, yet is it possible that the Holy One really expects someone to do only this throughout his entire life? After all, it is written that if one recites the *Shema* morning and night, it is 'as if he had fulfilled the requirement to study Torah night and day.' If this is so, why should I keep my son-in-law at my table and work so hard to support him in the evening of my life, in order to earn merit from his studies?"

R. Aisel answered as follows: "It is true that he who

reads the *Shema* morning and night, it is 'כאילו' [as if] he studies Torah day and night. But then his paradise is not a real *Gan Eden* but an 'as if' one. In other words, his reward is not a real one but an 'as if' reward. And you, a seasoned merchant, certainly know the difference between 'as if' and the real thing. So why should you question it?"

R. Aisel came to *shul* one cool summer day wearing his fur coat. One of the congregants remarked to him, "Rabbi, you know it is written that an *Aisel* [ass, in Yiddish] feels cold even in the month of *Tammuz*?" "Right," answered R. Aisel. "A man who sees that it is cool even in summer puts on a fur coat and feels warm. But the ass is he who is ashamed to put on a fur when he feels cold, so he freezes even in the midst of summer."

R. Aisel had a run-in with a rather common fellow who spoke to him in an insulting manner. "You are א גרובער יונג [a gross young man]," said R. Aisel, "like a loaf of bread." Puzzled, the man asked Aisel what kind of a comparison that was. "That is the point," answered the rabbi. "You are so vulgar that there is nothing with which to compare you."

R. Aisel once had a visitor who sat for hours and hours, talking incessantly. Whenever the rabbi wanted to say something, the man would interrupt him, not letting him finish a sentence. Finally getting ready to go, the man said, "I will leave you with a good word which I heard from a certain rabbi." "It is a lie," interjected R. Aisel. "What do you mean, Rabbi?" asked the man. "You haven't even heard what I'm going to say and you already say that it's a lie?" "Well," retorted R. Aisel, "I'll tell you. It must be a lie because you never hear what someone else is saying since you never let anyone finish a sentence!"

————◦————

R. Aisel once noticed that two young boys who had to share one *Gemara*, kept pulling the book from one direction to the other. "Tell me," he asked the boys with a smile, "do you perhaps think that the Torah will come from *tzien*?" (in Yiddish, to pull and a pun on the word Zion).

————◦————

Asked to explain the word אספסוף (rabble) in the weekly portion *Behaalotha*, R. Aisel said: "There are people who like to call meetings and gatherings, אסיפות, but don't do anything practical for the community. Of all their activity there remains only the words that they pronounce at the "Asefoth."

When asked "הלא תשוע ברוב יעוץ" (Is there not salvation in much consultation)?, he replied: "Yes, in much consultation, but not in much chatter."

Once, during Yom Kippur services, the man standing behind R. Aisel kept tapping him on the back unintentionally as he was saying the על חטא prayer (for the sins committed). After the *Shmoneh Esrei* prayer was concluded, R. Aisel turned to the man protesting: "What a *hutzpa*! A man sins and puts the guilt on me!"

————◦————

When a new *Sefer Torah* was brought to the *Beit Midrash* in Slonim, a great crowd filled the hall for the celebration. As R. Aisel worked his way through the throng, he noticed two young men who had taken off their hats because of the heat. Stopping, he said: "What's this? In the *Beit Midrash* without a hat?" "*Heis* [hot], Rabbi. *Heis,*" answered the young men, somewhat taken aback. "*Und ich 'heis'nit'* [And I say "No"]," answered the rabbi.

When the *shamash* in Slonim was too old to continue with his work, he was replaced with a younger man, a *melamed*'s assistant, who was known to be quite a foolish fellow. Once, when he was accompanying the rabbi on some errand, the *shamash* said, "They say in the *Beit Midrash* that the rabbi is not such a hard man as he appears, and that his humility is greater than his aggressiveness." "You shouldn't listen to what others say," replied R. Aisel, "for one day they might even say that you are stupid and have no sense. And would you really believe that?"

Another Jew in Slonim was in the habit of buying all his needs from the gentiles, refusing to give any business to Jews despite repeated entreaties to do so. One day, R. Aisel was walking down the street and saw this man passing the Jewish shops by and entering a gentile one. "Good morning Reb Pesach," shouted the rabbi in a loud voice. The fellow turned and answered, "I'm sorry R. Aisel, you are mistaken. My name is Haim." "No, I'm not mistaken," said the rabbi. "I remember very well! But your name *should* be Pesach, because it is written that *Pesach* is so called 'Because the Angel of Death passed over the houses of the Children of Israel.'"

Reb Aisel met one of the *baalei-batim* of the town in the street, and the latter began to complain to him about his *pekel* [bundle] of troubles. "Well," said R. Aisel comfortingly, "if a Jew only has one *pekel* it's not so bad. The trouble is that most Jews have many *pekelech*. Would you like me to prove this to you?" And he immediately called over a passerby and asked him where his *pekel* was. "Which *pekel*?" asked the man. "There," said R. Aisel to the man. "You see that this Jew has many *pekelech*!"

———————◦———————

A congregant complained to R. Aisel that he was suffering a period of bad luck and wished that he had the opportunity to ask The Holy One, Blessed Be He, what he had done to deserve it. "Come, come," replied Reb Aisel, "better not to disturb Him and not to ask Him any questions, because if you do, He will surely send for you to give you an explanation — and then you don't know what the outcome may be."

———————◦———————

Somebody once asked Aisele why preachers gave such poor sermons. They take their material from various books so why can't they select more interesting ideas instead of foolish ones? "Don't you realize," he answered, "that it is much easier to remember a foolish idea?"

Trips

During one of his visits to Warsaw, R. Aisel had to wait a long time at the inn till his meal was served. Before he left, the innkeeper apologized for the delay, saying that he had been attending to a distinguished person, the son of a very pious man, and that is why he had to let other people wait. "Indeed," replied Aisel, "to take away the fat left by the holy ones [reference to the sacrificial ceremony in the Temple in biblical times] was indeed a holy work (עבודה)."

———⟨◦⟩———

On another of his journeys, R. Aisel stopped at an inn for some refreshment, but whatever he asked for was not available. Finally he said to the woman of the house, "Your inn is really like the Garden of Eden." "But rabbi, you haven't eaten anything. What do you mean?" "I mean that, even in the Garden of Eden, you have to prepare in advance, otherwise there is also nothing to eat!"

———⟨◦⟩———

R. Aisel was coming home late at night from another of his journeys and stopped at an inn for refreshment. While he was drinking his coffee, the innkeeper came and asked how he liked it. "Your coffee has one fault and one merit," said the Harif. "Its merit is that it has no chicory in it, and its fault is that it also has no coffee!"

———⟨◦⟩———

R. Aisel's reputation grew with the years, and it was quite rare for him to go unrecognized and unacclaimed during his travels. Once he came to Ostrow to visit his son Berish, and it seemed that the whole town had turned out to greet him, even the women and children. "Nobody has ever had such a welcome in Ostrow," remarked one of the leaders to R. Aisel. "We reserve the greatest respect for the Torah." R. Aisel replied, "It is the way of the world that healthy people run after a crazy man and the unbalanced run after the famous. Since I am both a little bit crazy and a little bit famous, the whole town runs to greet me."

———⟨◦⟩———

During one of his many travels, R. Aisel came to a town that was deeply involved in factional arguments. When he arrived at the synagogue, there was such shouting and recrimination that the *gabbaim* were embarrassed that such a distinguished visitor should witness this scene. R. Aisel did his best to soothe them: "It is written of our father Yaakov, that when he came to Beit-El, 'he took of the stones of the place.' Our sages say that the stones quarrelled between themselves over which ones would be selected, but that Yaakov quieted them by saying, 'This must be the house of the Holy One.' So let us too say, that where the *baalei-batim* quarrel amongst themselves, like the stones, it is a sign that this must be the House of the Lord."

———————◦———————

There are many stories about the wagon drivers with whom R. Aisel rode on his journeys. They must have been a breed apart, rather like the cabbies of today. R. Aisel once explained why the drivers were called *ba'alei agalot* (*baale-golas*, in Yiddish). "Because if you fall into their hands, you suffer the weight of the *galut* or *golas* [exile]. If you want to go, they don't move, and if you want to rest, they force you to go on. When going uphill, they ask you to get out and push, and when going downhill, they ask you to walk because it is too dangerous. And there is also the possibility that they will turn over and drop you into the mud. They are impossible!"

———————◦———————

Once Reb Aisel was on a long journey and made a stop in order to say the morning prayers. He prayed from his *siddur*, but the *baalagolah* said his prayers from memory, and finished before the rabbi. Surprised, R. Aisel asked the driver how this was possible. "The rabbi probably learnt Hebrew in three or four months," said the man, "but I had to study for twelve years till I succeeded. So I know my Hebrew and can *daven* faster than the rabbi."

———————◇———————

On another occasion, R. Aisel was on a journey with a *baalagolah*, who was anxious to impress the rabbi with his interest in learning. Though R. Aisel was tired and wanted to rest and to concentrate his thoughts on his own affairs, the driver kept pestering him with quotations. Finally he asked, "Why did the *maggid* say in his last sermon that there would be two messiahs, one משיח בן דוד [son of David] and one משיח בן יוסף [son of Joseph]? Why do we need two? Wouldn't one be enough to redeem the Children of Israel?" By now R. Aisel was quite exasperated, and answered, "One is to redeem us from the גולם [exile], and the other is to redeem us from the בעלאגולם [wagon drivers]!"

Hevra Kadisha

The *Hevra Kadisha*, or Holy Society, is a unique feature of Jewish community life. Although originally there were holy societies devoted to various charitable works, the term gradually came to refer to that group of people who attended to the needs of the dead, in response to the religious injunction that the whole community was responsible for giving the dead a proper burial. Until modern times this was a voluntary activity. It was considered a great honour to belong to the *Hevra Kadisha*, but never the less, many stories were told at the expense of the members. For example, the old father of a wealthy villager died, and the man brought his father to Slonim to be buried, pretending to be a poor peasant. Thus, he paid the *Hevra Kadisha* a nominal sum. But the Burial Society eventually discovered that he was quite rich, and when the time came to set the tomb-stone, they demanded a large sum of money from him. The villager promised to pay but disappeared back to his village immediately after the stone-setting. When the members of the *Hevra Kadisha* came to complain to the rabbi, he said, "He is quite right. For, it is written, "הים ראה וינוס" [the sea saw and fled]. Our sages asked what was it that the sea saw? It saw the coffin of Joseph. But why should the sea be afraid of the coffin of Joseph? Because it saw that the coffin was being carried by members of the *Hevra Kadisha,* who are capable of draining a whole ocean [by their fees]. That is why the sea fled. And if the sea was afraid and fled, it is not surprising that this villager also fled."

Once R. Aisel met the members of the *Hevra Kadisha* in the street as they were coming back from the cemetery, and it was obvious that they could hardly stand on their feet because they had been drinking. "How strange," said R. Aisel, "they are coming from the world of truth [עולם האמת — the cemetery], but, like falsehood, they have no legs to stand on [לשקר אין רגליים]." (This is a play on the similarity between the Hebrew words for a drunk and a false-hood as well as juxtaposition of truth and falsehood.)

R. Aisel was once invited by the *Hevra Kadisha* to a festive meal. The wine flowed freely and many were soon tipsy. "Now I understand," he remarked, "why the name of Ephron the Hittite is usually written 'full' in the Torah, [that is with a *vav,* as in עפרון] and only once is it written 'short' [as in עפרן]. He was also a Hevra Kadisha man and we see that most of the time they are 'full.'"

When the body of a murdered Jew, an inhabitant of a nearby village, was found in the forest, the *Hevra Kadisha* of Slonim went to get the body and prepare it for burial. They came to R. Aisel to report the matter and told him of all they had done. "But what have you actually done?" he asked. Again they repeated how they had identified the body, questioned the wife and the neighbours, and so on. Again the rabbi asked what had been done, and again the delegation repeated the story. "You don't understand," said R. Aisel. "What I am asking is what have you done for the widow and the children? How will they live, how will they support themselves? They also have to eat!"

Cantors

R. Aisel was not unique in his aversion to cantors. Thus, he was simply giving voice to a popular expression when he said that the word "חזן" was merely an acronym for the Yiddish expression "חזונים זענען נערוניס," which means that cantors are fools. Perhaps it was their vanity and pride in their voices that led him to this opinion.

R. Aisel was asked why, on Shabbat, the *hazan* did not start at the beginning of the morning prayer, but only with the verse "שוכן עד"? "Well," replied Aisel, "most *hazanim* are quite foolish, and everyone knows that one shouldn't start up with a fool."

Asked what percentage of clever men there were amongst Jews, R. Aisel replied, "Ten percent, because it is written that Moshe Rabenu selected only the wisest men and made them 'officers of tens,' which means there was one wise man for every ten of the population." "Then how many fools are there?" he was asked. "Also ten percent, since every *minyan* [of ten] has a *hazan*."

———————◦———————

R. Aisel apparently did not enjoy *hazanut*, and sometimes made jokes about cantors. This may have been because he was not musical, or because he tended to pray quickly and cantors usually made an effort to lengthen prayers. Nonetheless, not wanting to interfere with the pleasure of others, and despite the objections of the older *gabbaim*, he allowed cantor Yisrael Shaulson to create a choir in the Slonim synagogue, which eventually played an important role in the local Jewish scene right up to World War II.

A *maggid* came to Slonim, but for some reason R. Aisel took a dislike to him, and did not allow him to speak on the grounds that he was not a God-fearing man. "Is it possible," asked the *parnassim*, "that a man can be a *maggid*, and not be God-fearing?" "It does not necessarily follow that a *maggid* must be God-fearing," answered R. Aisel. "In Rashi's commentary on *Parshat Vayehi*, it is said that a *maggid* came to tell Joseph his father was ill. Is it likely that there were *maggidim* then in Egypt? No, and therefore we can conclude that there are also preachers who are not even Jewish, much less God-fearing men."

Doctors

"Surgeons are like tradesmen," R. Aisel was known to have said. "Some are good and some are bad. Sometimes they help, sometimes not. Rabbi Avraham Ibn Ezra decided a long time ago that the Torah allows doctors to treat sick people, since it is written '*Verafoh yerapeh*,' and we learn from this that doctors are permitted to heal the sick — but only their bodily wounds; for their secret inner illnesses can only be healed by The Holy One, Blessed Be He."

———◦———

Once someone remarked to R. Aisel that since doctors help the sick, often saving them from death, he should not make jokes at their expense. "Doctors also help the Angel of Death in his work," replied the rabbi, "so he must be helpful to them as well by sparing some of their patients — otherwise the doctors would not continue to support him."

———◦———

"From doctors to death is just a question of time."

"Why are doctors called רופאים? Because they are like spirits [רפאים]. And, just as spirits know nothing, so the doctors know nothing. And that is also why the language they use, Latin, is called a dead language — because it is used by doctors who are partners with the Angel of Death."

———◦———

Another experience confirmed R. Aisel's opinion of doctors. It happened that once he fell ill while on a visit to Vilna, and the doctor gave a very pessimistic report on his chances of recovery, warning him that his end was near. Aisel recovered after only a few days. Going out to attend to his affairs, R. Aisel met the doctor in the street. The latter was astonished to see him and declared that a miracle had happened. "You are wrong on two counts," answered R. Aisel. "First of all, I didn't recover, I really died. And secondly, the miracle happened to you, not to me — because while I was in heaven I heard an edict that every doctor must go to Hell, including you. But I felt very sorry for you, so I quickly gave evidence that you are not a doctor at all, and they removed your name from that decree."

————————◆————————

During the wedding of his son Moshe, which took place in the town of Wakshne, the local doctor came to R. Aisel and claimed that he was more important than the rabbi — wherever he went, whether to a *simha* or to the synagogue, people made much of him and showered him with honors and attention. "Yes," commented R. Aisel, "in the Tractate *Baba Mezieh*, we learn that the loss of one's rabbi is greater than the loss of one's father, because a father brings one into this world, but a rabbi brings one into the world to come. Therefore we can say that a doctor is more important than a rabbi, because if a rabbi's teaching is at fault he may not succeed in bringing one to the world to come, but the doctor always brings one into the world to come!"

Zionism

Friends of R. Aisel came into his room one day, and saw a most unusual sight. The rabbi was standing with his head bent, before a simple fellow whose hands were placed on the rabbi's head, as if conferring a blessing. The friends quietly left the room, and when the other visitor came out, they asked him what had happened inside. "I am going to settle in Eretz Yisrael," said the man, "so I came to the rabbi to ask for his blessing. However, as soon as he heard that I was making aliyah, he said that I should be blessing him, because I am a greater *zaddik* than he. So what could I do? I placed my hands on his head and blessed him!"

————————◆————————

In the same vein, another Jew who was preparing to go to Palestine came to R. Aisel to ask for his blessing, the blessing of a great and holy man. "I think it is more fitting that I should ask your blessing," said the rabbi. For you are about to perform a great *mitzvah*, but I am still hesitant."

A Jew who returned from Palestine came to R. Aisel to bemoan the fact that he had lost all his money there. "Now I understand the saying of our sages that there is a man who prefers his fortune to his body," said Aisel. "For we see that you wanted to go to the Holy Land in order to have a preferred, respected burial for your body. But in the end you buried your money there and brought your body back here for a simple, ordinary burial. This is a case of preferring one's fortune to one's body!"

When R. Zvi Kalischer wrote his book proposing that the Jews themselves must rebuild Eretz Yisrael, without waiting for the messiah to come, many groups began to form with the purpose of settling the Holy Land. A group of wealthy Jews came to R. Aisel and asked his opinion on the matter. "In the *Shmoneh Esrei* there are three prayers following each other: "heal us and we will be healed"; "bless the coming year for us"; and "sound the great *shofar* for freedom and the ingathering of our exiles." Here you have prayers for health, prosperity and Redemption. But, if there is a sick person in a family, no one ever asks me whether to call a doctor or to wait for help from the Almighty. And, when business is poor, no one asks me what to do to improve the situation. However, when it comes to Redemption, they come to ask whether to do or to wait. Why? The answer is simple: health and prosperity are personal matters for everyone, so one must act and not depend on prayer alone. But since Redemption concerns all of Israel, they come to question and to complain, in order they should not have to give anything for others." This was R. Aisel's opinion regarding the duty of doing something real and practical for the rebuilding of Eretz Yisrael.

STILL MORE STORIES...

The sayings which appear below are taken from a manuscript entitled "Gliendige Koilen — Pereldige Sihot-Hulin un Harifutdige Hamtzaot fun R. Aisele Harif," (Glowing Coals — Pearl-like Conversations and Sharp Insights of R. Aisele Harif) by Shlomo Levadi, which is in the Yivo Library in New York. Shlomo Levadi was a Slonimer who left his town at the age of sixteen, probably about the turn of the century. After spending a few years in Palestine, he settled in the United States. In 1929 he visited the town of his birth, and made a home movie which shows the town and its Jewish inhabitants at that time. This movie was incorporated into the video film about Slonim, "HaAdama Teme'a — Hell on Earth," which was produced in 1992 by the Irgun Olei Slonim in Israel.

This book-draft about R. Aisel Harif and his sayings is written in Yiddish and bears no date. According to references mentioned, it must have been written in the thirties. Levadi mentions in his introduction that he collected a number of the stories from literary and other written sources, such as community records, registers of the Burial Society, private letters and so on, but the major part of the stories he heard directly from older inhabitants of Slonim, some of whom even knew R. Aisel personally.

I heard about the existence of this collection quite accidentally, from Mr. Zvi Shefet, chairman of the Irgun Olei Slonim, who saw the manuscript in the Yivo Library, and ordered a copy of it for his own use. When I contacted him to order a copy of the video film and tell him about my book on R. Aisel Harif, he told me about Levadi's work, and sent me the copy he had received. At that moment, the Hebrew version of my book was about to be printed, but having discovered the collection of stories I had not seen before, and alternate versions of stories I had used, I decided to delay the printing so that the additional stories could be included.

I subsequently translated these stories into English and printed them in this booklet, so that they can be added to my major work on R. Aisel.

E. Rafaeli

August 1993

One of the congregation of the beit midrash "HaHoma," where R. Aisele used to pray, was a respectable landlord, a scholarly man of pleasant manner, who was always eager to lead the prayers. He was a refined gentleman but had a weak voice, and when he led the prayers the assembled company could not follow his praying, because they couldn't hear him. The men were dissatisfied and grumbled amongst themselves, but no one had the courage to complain directly to the gentleman.

Once R. Aisele remarked to him: "Reb Dov-Ber, you know your wife is an aguna, a deserted wife?"

Dov-Ber looked at him with astonishment: "God be with you, rabbi, what are you saying, what do you mean?"

"I mean that one never hears anything from you!"

A scholarly yeshiva student came to R. Aisele to be examined for the rabbinate. The two held a wide-ranging discussion about halacha, about pilpul and the poskim. The young man was knowledgeable and had an open mind — a pearl! Suddenly R. Aisele asked him: "What happens if someone cuts his finger on Shabbat, and it bleeds?"

The young man replied: "Please excuse me for a moment rabbi, while I look up the *Shulhan Aruch.*"

Said R. Aisele: "No young man, you are not yet worthy to be a rabbi. Until you look up the *Shulhan Aruch,* a Jew can, Heaven forbid, die from loss of blood."

It was known that R. Aisele came from a poor family. His father was a watchmaker all his life, sustaining his family by the work of his hands. He was deeply religious, learned and an honest man [cf. with comments in chapter on Antecedents — E.R.].

Once R. Aisele took part in a festive gathering of rabbis, all renowned men who stemmed from important rabbinical families. Each one present contributed some saying or *dvar torah* of his father's or grandfather's. Amongst them was an eminent rabbi who was extremely jealous of Aisele, and saw an opportunity now to embarrass him. In a loud voice he interjected: "Slonimer Rav, what have you to tell of your father's wisdom?"

R. Aisele replied: "My father, may he rest in peace, used to say — one must never rely on another man's watch. A person must always know for himself his situation in time."

One winter's day, R. Aisele was returning from a *brith* in a *yishuv* (these were scattered settlements of Jews who lived amongst the Russian farmers — E.R.). On returning to Slonim the sled overturned and R. Aisele was thrown out and injured. Passers-by rushed to help him to his feet, and when they saw the blood on his face, cried out: "Oy Vei, rabbi, your face!"

R. Aisele nodded his head and answered: "Indeed, indeed, a fine face (a sheine ponim) the rabbi has amongst you" (i.e. cynically, what kind of an image does the rabbi have, is he respected by the people of Slonim? — E.R.).

———————◦———————

One of the *shohetim* of Slonim, a God-fearing man and a scholar, began to feel his age. His sight began to weaken and his hands became less sure. The leaders of the *kahal* looked for someone to take his place and found a young man who considered himself an expert and a good scholar, but it was rumored of him that he tended towards the ideas of the haskala, and was a little lax in observing the *mitzvot*. R. Aisele opposed the appointment: "No, I cannot allow such a thing in my town. I would rather have a man who is only ten parts *shohet* and ninety parts Jew, than one who is ninety parts *shohet* and only ten parts Jew."

———————◦———————

R. Aisele went forth one day to gather contributions for a particularly needy charity, and took with him his son-in-law, R. Yossele Shluper.

They entered the home of a certain landlord, who was a wealthy but very stingy man, one who coveted personal honor. He received the rabbis with great respect, they sat and talked about the matter which had brought them, but the *baaleboos* was in no mind to put his hand in his pocket. He behaved as if he didn't hear R. Aisele's pleas.

But R. Aisele was anxious to see some proceeds from

his visit. Time was getting short, and he began to flatter and compliment the man, to the skies. He in turn began to unbend and warm up, and finally came out with a sum of money.

As soon as they were out of the house, R. Yossele spoke up:

"Father-in-law, I am completely surprised by you. How could you lower yourself so before such an ignoramus?" "You must understand, Yosha my son-in-law, when it comes to milking a *behema* (beast) one must lower oneself a little to succeed."

————◦————

R. Aisele's son, R. Moshe, the Riga rabbi, used to quote his father: "It used to be, that when a Jew had a daughter to marry off, he would look for a Torah-scholar, a God-fearing man, for a son-in-law. But today, when a Jew looks for a match for his daughter he seeks a provider, and so he takes a son-in-law, a bread-giver, who will give his daughter bread even on Pesach."

————◦————

R. Aisele went to one of the wealthy skinflints of the town for a contribution. The man wanted to get off with a paltry sum of money, not in keeping with his station.

The rabbi remarked: "Reb Yid, one must not make a liar of the world!" "What do you mean," Rabbi, asked the man. "It is very simple," replied R. Aisele. "People call me *ha Rav ha Gaon* 'the rabbi the genius,' and so I try with all my might to show there is a little truth in what they say. I preside over the Beit Din, I decide questions which are brought before me, I write sermons, responsa, new insights to the Torah. I do what I can. And you, people call you a *gvir*, a wealthy man, so you too must show there is really some truth in that, and behave as a wealthy Jewish man should behave. If not, you make a liar of the world!"

A simple fellow once came into R. Aisele's house, and saw the rabbi's hat lying on a chair. He tried the hat on his head, and found it too small. He exclaimed to the rabbi. "See Rabbi, I have a bigger head than you!" "You mean a thicker one," answered R. Aisele (i.e. in Yiddish "grob" or vulgar — E.R.).

R. Aisele was travelling with a *baalegola* from Slonim to an outlying village. When it was time to pray, they stopped near an inn and stood aside to pray. R. Aisele prayed in his usual manner, but the cartdriver prayed more rapidly and finished before him.

Afterwards R. Aisele asked him: "How is it possible that you finished praying before I even reached the *Shmoneh-Esrei*?" "I'll tell you rabbi," answered the driver. "You probably learnt Hebrew only for a short time, so it takes you longer to struggle through. However, I studied with the rabbi for a long long time so my "Ivre" flows like water."

Replied R. Aisele: "What a pity your horses didn't study with the same rabbi — then they would perhaps have brought us to our destination more quickly!"

A husband and wife came to R. Aisele to get a divorce. At first he tried to reconcile them, to make peace and deter them from getting a divorce, but the husband had only one thing to say:

"Your efforts are for nothing, rabbi. I cannot get along

with my Rasha; my wife is obstinate and embittered, a 'mirsha'at' (bad-tempered)."

R Aisel answered: "Sometimes with me Rashi is also obstinate and difficult. So what? Should I divorce myself from him, Heaven forbid? No, we battle along, and eventually we come to some kind of understanding, and so continue to live in peace."

———◦———

R. Aisele was once asked which attribute had a higher value, Torah or wealth. "Torah, of course."

"In that case," continued the questioner, "why is it that Torah scholars and *talmidei hachamim* are always knocking on the doors of the rich, and not the other way round?"

"It is obvious," replied R. Aisele. "A man who is a *talmid hacham* or a student of the Bible appreciates the meaning of wealth, but a rich man cannot appreciate the words of the Torah or of wisdom."

———◦———

A young writer still living "on kest" with his father-in-law, came to R. Aisele for a *haskama* for his book, entitled *Yehene Hochma* (Wisdom Will Enjoy). R. Aisele read a passage here and there, and sent the author on his way without a *haskama*.

When the young man was already on the other side of the door, R. Aisele turned to those sitting in the room and remarked: "Did you ever see such a thing? A man calls his book '*Yehene Hochma*,' and "tzo ye-ane to niya hochma, y tzo hochma to niya ye-ane" (a pun in Polish, meaning: what is his is not wisdom, and what is wisdom is not his — E.R.).

———◦———

R. Aisele was known to be a very charitable man. Not to give, when a Jew asked for help, was for him unheard of. Even if he himself had no money at that moment, he would borrow or take from the benevolent funds and give away that money, and so it came about that he was often deep in debt.

Somebody once asked him how he could possibly extricate himself and pay off these debts.

R. Aisele replied: "*Baruch haShem*, there are enough rich men in Slonim who are in a position to pay back what I lay out for their poor."

R. Aisele was sitting in a meeting with the community leaders. There was a sharp disagreement between them about some matter, and the *parnassim* expressed themselves loudly and aggressively. Suddenly an old woman burst into the meeting room with a great cry: "Rebbinyu, save me!" "What is it my daughter, what has happened?"

The lady continued her sobbing and explained: "Oy Rebbinyu, my world has become dark. I had a bad dream. I dreamt that my only son became *meshuga* — it shouldn't happen to any Jew!"

R. Aisele cried out: "You should be happy and healthy my daughter. It is a sign of great wealth. Just take a look at these Jews, they should all be well. They are all rich men, very rich, may they be protected from the evil eye — yet just see what crazy pranks they are capable of carrying out."

Two upstanding *baale-batim*, from a small village near Slonim, came to R. Aisele and asked that he should find them a rabbi.

R. Aisele told them: "Be good enough and cross the bridge to the other side of the river, and ask there for Reb Hotcha the *melamed*. Tell him please, in my name, that I want him to take on the position of rabbi in your village."

The two Jews found Reb Hotcha while he was in the midst of a lesson. They greeted him with a *shalom aleichem*. "*Aleichem ha'shalom*," answered the melamed. "What good news do you bring?"

The two Jews explained that they came in the name of R. Aisele, and brought a message from him. Reb Hotcha pondered, made a grimace, cleared his throat, and then let out a deep sigh. "Nu, if R. Aisele says — if he really wants it — nu, if it is really so — then I accept. I will take on the rabbinate."

The *baale-batim* set out a bottle of brandy, and the three drank a *l'Haim*, wished each other *mazal tov*, and the two villagers went on their way. Reb Hotcha made his way with measured steps to R. Aisele. "R. Aisele, I have done as you wished, I accepted. Now I have come for your advice on what books I should buy."

R. Aisele smiled indulgently and said: "Foolish *melamed* — just take your psalm-book with you and go."

An affluent *hassid* once came to R. Aisele to ask his advice on a certain matter. The rabbi received him very courteously, they discussed the problem at great length, and finally R. Aisele gave him his advice on how to proceed.

When the *hassid* was taking his leave, he took an "imperiale" out of his pocket and pressed it into R. Aisele's hand.

R. Aisele looked at the coin in great astonishment,

and asked:

"A gold coin — what is this for?"

The hassid replied: "We hassidim have a custom, Rabbi, that when we come to a good Jew, we give him a *pidyon*" (a gift of money — E.R.).

"Is that so?" remarked R. Aisele. "By you a good Jew is one who takes money, and by us a good Jew is one who gives money."

―――――――――――

R. Aisele was once asked why renowned rabbis are referred to as *haRav haGaon*, the genius rabbi, while hassidic rabbis are referred to as *Botzina Kadisha*, the holy lamp.

R. Aisele replied: "It's like this. *HaRav haGaon* can be likened to a headache, and *Botzina Kadisha* to a stomachache. For example, when a boy doesn't want to go to *heder*, he will look for all kinds of excuses; he will even pretend to be sick. 'Mamme,' he says, 'my head is hurting.' So his mother touches his forehead — if it is hot, it is a sign he is really sick, and if not, she knows he is just pretending and sends him straight off to *heder*. But a more intelligent child will say, 'My stomach is hurting.' Now the mother doesn't know what to do, she may touch him from today until tomorrow, she must believe him. The same is with the subject you brought up. If someone calls himself *haRav haGaon*, you touch his head, that is you test his learning, and you find out immediately if he is a genius or not. But if someone calls himself a Holy Lamp — nu, be a smart man and go find out."

―――――――――――

A prosperous Slonimer wood-merchant came once to

R. Aisele in a state of anxiety."Rabbi, my situation is not good. I'm afraid I will soon become bankrupt. I have sent away a large shipment of wood on the river, but the border officials have stopped it and won't let it through the locks. If the officials, haters of Israel, won't let the wood through, I will lose a bundle, and will have to go knocking on doors" (i.e. to beg — E.R.).

R. Aisele tried to comfort him: "Don't worry so my dear fellow. We have a great God in the heavens, He will help."

A short time later the price of wood went up and the merchant made a great profit. In a happy frame of mind, he came again to visit R. Aisele. "Rabbi, now I can really see the watchfulness of the Creator." "That is the difference between a rich man and a poor man," declared R. Aisele. "The poor man sees the care of the Creator every day, but the rich man sees it once in a lifetime."

There was a young man in Slonim, of a fine family, who had an open, receptive mind, and was a good scholar. R. Aisele held him in high esteem and took a close interest in his progress. In the course of time this young man married into a wealthy family in Warsaw and became a successful businessman.

It happened that R. Aisele once had occasion to be in Warsaw, and he came to visit his former scholar. Naturally the latter received the rabbi with great respect and held a fine *seuda* in his honor, to which he invited scholars and important personalities of the town, who all came to welcome the genius of the generation and to enjoy a Torah discussion with him.

During the repast, R. Aisele turned to his host and

asked him:

"Tell me, my son, what do you do?"

"Blessed be the Name, Rabbi, I have nothing to complain about. I have an ample livelihood, and my family is well, thanks be to God."

R. Aisele did not comment, and returned to his conversation with the other guests. After a while, he turned again to the young man and asked him the same question. The young man replied: "I have nothing to complain about. I have *kein ayin'hara*, a plentiful income, a nice house, social standing in my community — all Jews should be in a similar situation."

R. Aisele remained quiet for a moment, then returned to his conversation with the guests, which ranged from scholarly subjects and pilpul, to matters of daily life. After a while, he turned again to the young man with the same question: "Tell me the truth my son, what do you do?"

The young Slonimer became a little flustered. "Excuse me Rabbi, please forgive me, but three times you have asked me the same question. I think I have already answered you. I have, thank God, income, health, *nahas* from my children."

"Yes, you have answered," said R. Aisele, "but not my question. Your health, prosperity and pleasure from your children, that is all given to us by the *Rebono-shel-Olam* (the Creator of the World). But I asked what do you do, you yourself? Do you have set times to study Torah, do you do proper acts of charity and loving-kindness? Do you cause others to do good deeds, and do you seek the company of wise scholars?"

A woman burst into R. Aisele's house, crying bitterly: "Rebbinyu. Save me! A great misfortune has befallen me!"

R. Aisele asked the lady who she was and what had happened to her. The woman explained that she was a widow with small children, who eked out a living by preparing goose *schmaltz* for Pesach for wealthy families. Now she had finished frying a pan of goose fat and had set it aside to cool. Then she put a cup of milk to heat on the primus for her sick child, and the milk pan overturned into the pot of *schmaltz*. Wringing her hands before R. Aisele, she implored him: "Oy Rebbinyu, have pity. If heaven forbid the *schmaltz* is *treif,* I will be ruined. I am deep in debt, mortgaged over my head because of buying these geese. I will never be able to repay these debts. Woe is me! If I cannot sell this *schmaltz,* I and my children will remain without a crust of bread, without a pillow for our heads."

R. Aisele looked thoughtfully at the milk pan, at the pot of *schmaltz,* measured their contents, and remained deep in thought. R. Feitel, the dayan, looked on and shrugged his shoulders. "Rabbi, what is there to ponder so much — the law is clear. Mixing milk and meat makes each treif."

Replied R. Aisele: "That is really the law — but for whom? For a wealthy lady! But when we are talking about a poor widow with orphaned children, one must make all efforts to find some kind of *heter* (permission). After all, the law is not a robber."

R. Aisele asked the woman where she bought her milk, and sent for that milk-woman and began to question her: "Tell me my daughter, from whom do you buy the milk which you bring to your customers?"

"From the village milkman, who brings the milk in early

in the morning."

"And do you take this milk straight to your customers, or perhaps you add a little water to it? Swear to me that you are telling the truth, the whole truth."

The frightened milk-woman admitted: "What to do Rabbinke? It is hard to make a living. Everything is expensive. In order to keep my customers, I must lower the price a little — so I add a little water to the milk."

"Is that so," exclaimed the rabbi. "And how much water do you add? Don't be afraid my daughter, I promise you, on my word, that it will remain a secret." "I don't know, a quarter or two to each container."

"No more than that?" "Sometimes more, sometimes less, depending on the price."

R. Aisele sighed: "Oy, livelihood, livelihood. The Creator of the World will surely forgive you, he has no option. But tomorrow morning, God willing, when he comes to town, please tell the milkman to come directly to me."

The milkman came. R. Aisele took him into another room, put the chain on the door, and said: "Shmuel, I command you with a rabbinical decree to tell me the situation as it is. How much water do you put into the milk?"

The milkman began to apologize: "You know rabbi, the cows don't always give the same amount of milk, so then one must add water. One can't come to town with half-empty cans!"

R. Aisele's voice became more severe: "I didn't ask why, I asked how much?"

The milkman answered: "Why to deny, rabbi; sometimes more and sometimes less."

"And in general?"

"More, rabbi."

And again R. Aisele asked: "How much milk do you bring into town each day?"

"About eight or nine bucketsful."

"And it is all from the same cows?"

"No rabbi, about half is from my own cows, and the rest I buy from the *yishuvim* nearby."

"Oh well that is understandable, but what about the milk that you buy? Do you add water to that too?"

"What is the difference rabbi? My milk or bought milk — if I add to one, I add to the other."

R. Aisele summoned the other people from the *yishuvim*, questioned and cross-examined each in turn. It was the same story; each one added a little water to his milk.

R. Aisele figured out the quantity of milk, the quantity of the water added to the milk, and the quantity of the *schmaltz*. Together with R. Feitel he summed up his conclusions and declared that the *schmaltz* was kosher. Then he turned to R. Feitel and said: "You see, Reb Feitel, instead of always bothering the *Shulhan Aruch* and the *Yoreh De'ah*, it is sometimes worthwhile for a man to put himself to a little extra bother. In the matter such as that before us, *batel be'shishim* (a sixtieth part cancels itself out — E.R.) is also a law."

JOURNEY'S END

The more we read about R. Aisel, the more enigmatic and full of contradictions he becomes. He was one of the greatest in his time in the sphere of Torah scholarship, yet he was modest about his achievements, considering his talent a divine gift. His whole existence and philosophy was rooted in the Torah and he was never tempted into the world of secular learning, yet he was wise in the ways of the world and understood human nature exceptionally well. He was an "original" in the sense that he always studied alone and found his own way in the vast sea of the Talmud, as he did in the practical aspects of daily life.

He knew that his intellectual abilities were unusual, but even in the years of his greatest achievements, when his leadership and genius were widely acclaimed, he retained his simple lifestyle and assumed none of the mannerisms and vanities of success. He continued to devote himself to education and charitable work for his community, and to his own private studies. Though one of the outstanding personalities of his time, he was ever ready to acknowledge greatness and original thought in others.

As we have seen, R. Aisel was courageous already in childhood, and as an adult he was never intimidated by officials or by the government. His motto was indeed, "אהוב את המלאכה ושנא הרבנות ואל תתודע לרשות" (Love work, hate lordship and seek no intimacy with the ruling power).

Though he served the community of Slonim and was in fact its employee, he was not in awe of the rich and powerful leaders, but treated all community members as equals, and the poor as more equal than the rest. He hated to be dependent on the *parnassim* and on the whim of the public, but was devoted to the public good, sparing no effort to achieve those objectives which he considered of prime importance. He was modest and reserved about his charitable work, about the causes he supported, the problems he solved and the people he helped. He was discreet about whose support enabled him to do what he did. Great amounts of money passed through his hands, some even intended for his own use, but it all went to those in greater need. Above all, he never used his authority for personal gain or to further family interests. He was incorruptible. Moreover, he seems to have been singularly uninterfering in the lives of his children, allowing them to make their own way in the world.

A great authoritarian where religious observance and community life were concerned, he tended to be more lenient in the area of practical problems. It was said of him by all, including his son R. Moshe, that he was always cheerful, always ready with a witticism, a joke or a good word. Yet there are stories of his weeping during prayers or at the sight of children suffering, a sure sign that he had a great capacity for feeling and probably many problems of his own, of which he never complained. He kept his moods under control with an iron discipline.

Although R. Aisel was as famous for his barbed wit as for his "sharp" scholarship, he never utilized either at the expense of his students or of the poor. He could not abide scholarly humbug and pretensions, and was ever ready to criticize the pompous in all walks of life. Yet he was prepared to accept valid criticisms of his work and was not above a joke at his own expense.

At times, he seems to have been cruel in his sarcasm, and there were probably some who resented him, yet the fact is that he was much loved by all those who came in contact with him. The poor and the rich, the scholarly and the simple, all found something to admire in this unusual man.

Though in the forefront of the battle against the Enlightenment, R. Aisel did not participate in the meetings called by rabbis to discuss this threat to traditional Judaism. He was suspicious of the protocol and formalities of such gatherings, perhaps even of the intentions of some of the rabbis. He did not have the patience to listen to the speeches and ramblings of others, and felt he could contribute more by practical deeds in his own sphere.

Thus R. Aisel lived out his active and useful life in Slonim in spite of his increasing frailty, characterized till the end by his greatness in Torah learning; by his strong leadership as a rabbi, by his "folksiness" and good humor; and by his devotion to charity and good deeds. Was his devotion to the poor also rooted in the deprivation and suffering of his childhood years? Obviously we cannot answer this with any great certainty, but it is certainly a possibility that we may consider.

During these last years, R. Aisel was once asked what his correct age was. "When a man is about to declare bankruptcy," he answered, "he does not reveal his balance sheet."

Towards the end of 1873, R. Aisel's health deteriorated rapidly, and his increasing suffering from asthma kept him largely in bed. His family and the townsfolk looked on with great anxiety as they saw his life drawing to its close. Once his older son, Berish, asked him to give vent to his discomfort and not to suffer in silence. "Will you all feel better if I moan and groan?" asked R. Aisel. "No, not at all," Berish replied. "Well then, what good will it do you or me?"

During this period, his family begged him to delegate some of his work to his son-in-law, R. Yosef, and thus lighten his responsibilities. But Aisel said, "He is still young and will have plenty of hard work ahead of him. He doesn't need the troubles of his father-in-law."

After some slight improvement, Aisel was again suddenly taken ill one Thursday night, the third day of *Tevet,* תרל"ג, 1873, as he sat in his chair with the *Gemara Ketubot* open in his hand. When he called for a doctor, pandemonium broke loose. Doctors were called, and they did all in their power to save the life of the great genius, but to no avail. Within a short time he passed away. He was seventy-two years old.

For the community, it was as if a disaster had struck. They congregated and wept in the streets, behaving as if each and every one had suffered a personal bereavement. The next day the whole town, from the most to the least important, attended R. Aisel's funeral. It is related that no one was permitted to come near the bier unless he had first immersed himself in the *mikveh,* and people donated large sums of money to the yeshiva for the honor of washing and dressing his body and bringing him to his last resting-place. Several thousand rubles were said to have been collected on this occasion.

The bier was carried into the Great Synagogue and placed near the spot where he had often delivered his sermons. Moshe Yitzhak, the *Maggid* of Kelme, gave a memorable הספד that was talked about for years to come. Everyone made a double קריעה, rending their clothes in mourning, as is customary when a Torah scroll has been torn or mutilated. At the cemetery, a second eulogy was given by the scholarly Zvi Arkin, one of the wealthy men of the town.

In addition, R. Aisel was mourned in all Jewish circles in Eastern Europe and throughout the Jewish world. Even his arch-enemies, the *maskilim,* paid tribute to him in their publications. In the Hebrew National Library at the Givat Ram Campus of Hebrew University in Jerusalem, there is a copy of the *hesped* "אבל כבד" which R. Benyamin of Novhardok delivered in Jerusalem in 1875. For many years after his death people in Slonim named their newborn sons after the beloved rabbi. Until the outbreak of the first World War, the *Hevra Kadisha* continued to pray at R. Aisel's grave every *Rosh Hodesh*. (As a *mitnaged,* he would not have approved of this custom.) His anecdotes became part of the local folklore, and the subjects of these stories achieved a measure of notoriety. The stories were published as collections in 1918 and 1931, thereby keeping his memory alive for many more years.

The following inscription appeared on his tombstone:

"פה מונחת כבוד אדמו"ר הגדול האמיתי,

מאור הגולה, גאון ישראל וקדושו, רשכבה"ג,

נר ישראל, עמוד הימיני, פטיש החזק כקש"ת

מדו כ"מ יהושע אייזיק זצק"ל בהרב ר' יחיאל ז"ל אב"ד דפה,

בעהמ"יח ספרי ----- נגנז ארון הקודש

ביום ערב שבת ד' לחדש טבת שנת תרל"ג לפ"ק תנצב"ה."

231

While it is very difficult to translate such flowery and metaphoric Hebrew into the prosaic language of today, the meaning is roughly as follows:

> Here lies his honor the *Admor* [our master, our teacher, our rabbi], the true great genius, the light of the diaspora, the genius and holy one of Israel, the rabbi of all the people of the diaspora [a title given only to rabbis great and famous in their generation], the Lamp of Israel, a pillar of strength [to those who lean on him], the great authority, may his holy name be glorified, our teacher His Excellency Yehoshua Aisek. May the memory of the righteous and holy one be for a blessing. Head of the *Beit Din* here [in Slonim] and author of the books.... The holy coffin was buried on the Eve of the holy Sabbath, the fourth day of the month of *Tevet* תרל"ג. May his soul be threaded into the chain of life.

(The expressions "Lamp of Israel, pillar of strength..." is a quotation from tractate *Brachot* 28. They were used by the disciples of Yohanan ben Zakkai when they addressed him.)

There were three cemeteries in Slonim. The first one was very, very old and situated in the outer suburbs near Zamot. It was here that the descendant of Rashi was said to be buried. The second one, over three hundred years old at the time, was situated within the town. Many *gaonim* and *zaddikim* were buried there. The third cemetery, called the "new cemetery," was about one hundred and fifty years old. The Admor Avraham Weinberg and R. Aisel were both buried there, as was eventually, R. Yosef Shluper.

R. Aisel's son R. Moshe once said of his father: "I doubt if my father ever said 'yes' unequivocally. He would say 'maybe' or 'perhaps' or 'possibly,' but he considered those non-committal phrases as obligating. If he didn't say a definitive 'no,' then it was like a promise one could build on, although according to the *halahkah* only a definite 'yes' is binding. He always did more than he was asked to do, and always fulfilled more than he promised. He was great in his words, but greater in his emotions and deeds."

THE NEXT GENERATIONS

R. Aisel Harif left two sons and a daughter. He had never tried to influence how his children should lead their lives, nor did he leave any instructions to the community or indication regarding whom they should appoint in his place. Indeed, it was due to this omission that Aisel's son-in-law, R. Yosef, "Yosha" or Yossele, Shluper, who was married to his youngest child, Nehama, had to wait some twelve years before receiving the appointment to Slonim, where he too eventually served some twenty years.

Berish, as Issachar Ber was commonly called, was R. Aisel's oldest son and my own great-grandfather. He married Zeesel Muntliak of Nowydwor, daughter of a well-to-do merchant. As was customary, Berish spent some years in his father-in-law's home, but unfortunately his wife died quite young. To the best of my knowledge, my grandfather Yehiel was the only child of this marriage.

Already a well-known scholar when he became a widower, having studied with his father for many years together with his brother Moshe, Berish's admirable *yiches* and good personality brought many offers of marriage his way. Eventually he moved to Ostrow Mazowieska in Poland, where he married into the Bromberg family. (Or perhaps he decided to marry into the Bromberg family and therefore moved to Ostrow.) I have no idea of what happened to the young Yehiel in all these events.

This is one of those chapters where, despite a wealth of information, there are few definite facts. For example,

R. Moshe Shapira

Isaac/Izak ben Yehiel Yosef
Shapira. Received from his son
Yosef

Yosef posing in his army uniform

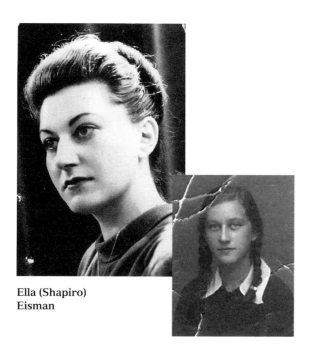

Ella (Shapiro)
Eisman

although the date of Berish's death is known (1902), I haven't been able to establish the exact date or place of his birth. Nor have I been able to provide the exact name of his second wife, the date of their marriage or the date of his wife's death.

Berish, although a rabbi, did not want to enter the rabbinate, nor did he wish to spend his time worrying about earning a living. He wanted to study, and he thought that a wife who could run a business and provide for him would be an ideal mate. And so it was. The Brombergs were a well-established merchant family, and they appointed Berish's wife as manageress of their textile shop, which was situated in the centre of Ostrow. Although Berish helped with the correspondence and the bookkeeping, it is said that he never actually set foot in the shop itself, devoting himself instead to Torah study and communal affairs. To the best of my knowledge there were no children from this union.

Before enlarging on the activities of Berish, I would like to make a small digression on the Bromberg family for those readers interested in the achievements of Jewish women in the nineteenth century. R. Avraham Yitzhak Bromberg was both a scholar and a businessman, whose wife, Feige Zeesal, worked together with him. R. Avraham died at an early age, leaving his wife and eight young children, six boys and two girls. After the mourning period, Feige Zeesal set herself seriously to managing the family business, at the same time bringing up her children in the proper traditional way and maintaining a large, hospitable and open-handed household. With acute business acumen, she succeeded in building up a flourishing enterprise with branches all over Poland. She became the richest woman in Ostrow and its surroundings, and she lived accordingly, gradually marrying off her children into the most respectable families of the cities of Warsaw, Biale, Kutno, Lodz, Pieterkov and Czestochowa. Many of them married into hassidic families or became *hassidim* (of Gur). One son, R. Yaakov, lived out his last years in Jerusalem, dying here in 1935.

I wish I could say that this was the lady my great-grandfather married, but the evidence is against it, for Feige Zeesal never remarried. She lived until the age of ninety-six, and died in the year 1923 in Warsaw, where most of her family had moved during or just after the First World War. Nor was it either of her daughters who married Berish, as the names of their husbands are known. I must therefore assume that there were other women in the Bromberg family, sisters or nieces, who were also good business-women, but who must remain nameless. In any event, Berish's second wife must have died in the early 1870s, because it was after that event that he made aliya to Palestine. However, with the outbreak of the Russo-Turkish war in 1876, some six months after his arrival in Jerusalem, he was advised to return to Poland because his Russian citizenship placed him in an awkward position. He returned to Ostrow, where he spent the rest of his life.

Following his original move to Ostrow, Berish soon became one of the outstanding personalities of the town. He was a spokesman of the *mitnagdim*, the defender of the Torah, a "power broker" in communal affairs, a perennial scholar and eventually, thanks to his wife, an independently wealthy man.

Ostrow came onto the map of Jewish settlement fairly late, because Jews were not given the right to build there until early in the nineteenth century. Although some Jews had lived in Ostrow before that, they did not become a majority in the town until after being granted these rights. Being close to the Lithuanian border, the town attracted a mixed population of Polish and Lituanian Jews, *mitnagdim* and *hassidim*. It was this that gave Ostrow its special character, because the rivalry between the two groups was very strong, continuing long after *mitnagdim* and *hassidim* had accommodated themselves to each other in other cities. But in Ostrow all communal matters continued to be affected by this rivalry. Finding a town rabbi who was acceptable to both sides was therefore always a difficult problem, demanding much diplomatic effort by the leaders of the two groups. Because of this reputation, some of the rabbis approached refused to even consider serving in the town.

At the time that Berish was leader of the scholars and the *mitnagdim* (his popularity being bolstered from time to time by the visits of his father), R. Benzion Rabinowitz was leader of the *hassidim*. Indeed, by closing ranks behind their leader and acting in a united fashion, the Ostrow *mitnagdim* were taking a lesson from the *hassidim*, who were always united and always did as their *rebbe* commanded.

Relations between R. Berish and R. Rabinowitz, while tense, were always correct, which was not always the case in other towns. Eventually they became good friends and worked together for the peaceful coexistence of the entire community. Did Berish recall his father's relationship with R. Avraham as an example for him to follow?

R. Aisel visited Ostrow many times, and each visit was a great occasion, not only for his son Berish, but also for the community at large. Anxious to be in the company of the great man, the scholars of the town filled the home of R. Berish day and night. And Aisel, in turn, delighted them with his commentaries and new interpretations. The *Beit Midrash* was always filled to overflowing when he spoke, and those who were unable to follow the close reasoning and the references to the various sources, which characterized R. Aisel's *drashot*, would later go to R. Berish for clarification and answers to their questions.

R. Berish was considered a moderate man in his private life, and easy to get on with. But in matters of Torah and learning he followed his father's ideas and teachings strictly. His greatest interest though was in *gematria*, the

Avram Shapiro, son of Mordecai, R. Aisel's third son, and Yeta Barg
Shapiro. Courtesy Stavisky family

Pauline Shapiro before marriage to Stavisky

numerical interpretation of Biblical verses and the matching of them with other verses of equal numerical value in order to reveal hidden mystical values. It was said that R. Berish could make such calculations within seconds. He wrote a book on this subject, but it was unfortunately neglected and eventually lost, so it was never published.

Berish belonged to a small group which called itself טו"ת, for "טלית (prayer shawl) and תפילין (phylacteries)", because the members would continue wearing their *tallitot* and *tefillen* after morning prayers, remaining in the synagogue to pray and study until noon.

After Berish's return to Ostrow from Jerusalem, he continued to devote himself completely to Torah study and to writing new interpretations that were later published in the second edition of *Emek Yehoshua*, which his brother, R. Moshe, published in 1896. By this time the *hassidim* had gained control of most of the town's communal institutions, and thus the traditional lifestyle lasted longer in Ostrow than in other towns influenced by the *Haskalah*.

R. Berish died on the tenth day of Adar תרס"ב, in the year 1902. I can't help wondering how the course of his life affected his son Yehiel. Was he a neglected orphan, or an indulged but lonely child? Did he take refuge with his Weinbaum cousins in Leczyca when his father left for Palestine (he was sixteen or seventeen years at the time), and thus contract an early marriage with Esther Leah?

Moshe, R. Aisel's second son, was born in 1835, probably in Kalvariya. He studied for many years with his father, absorbing much of his method and style, and then tried to establish himself in the field of commerce. When

this proved unsuccessful he decided to go into the rabbinate, and took his *smicha* at the age of thirty. He had married Feige Dvora, daughter of the wealthy R. Yosef Yaffe of
Wakshne, and his first position as rabbi was in that town.
(Feige's grandfather and his brother apparently came to
Palestine in the mid-nineteenth century and are buried
in Jerusalem). Then he moved to Willkomir, and in 1882
became Chief Rabbi of Riga, heading the congregation
Adath Yeshurun until his death in 1911. He seems to have
been a man of great style and charisma, who could accom-
modate himself to all sorts of people and ideas. He even
participated in special celebrations of the Habad *hassidim*.
Tradition has it that one could always meet leading personalities and scholars of disparate outlooks and interests
at his home.

When Moshe wrote his commentary on the tractate
Pesachim, he asked his father to suggest a title for the
book. "Call it *Pnei Moshe*," [The Face of Moshe] replied
Aisel, "because just as one could not look into the face of
Moshe, so no one can look into your book." It is a reflection
on his fine character that R. Moshe did title the book as
his father suggested. "One must follow the advice of one's
father, even when he is joking, because of the command-
ment to honor one's father."

R. Moshe continued his father's fight against the *maskilim*,
but unlike R. Aisel who contented himself with local community matters, he was very active in public affairs. Moshe
attended meetings of rabbis in St. Petersburg and was one
of the spokesmen of his time. He also had his problems
with the authorities, as we can see in the following story.

The governor of the district of Riga, a man called

Zinoviev, and Chief of Police Vilashiawsky, were both anti-semites. They were always seeking reasons to make trouble for the Jews, and often threatened to exile those to whom they took a dislike. However, since R. Moshe had managed to establish excellent relations with higher officials in St. Petersburg, he was often able to thwart their plans.

Deciding to revenge themselves for this challenge to their authority, Zinoviev and Vilashiawsky ordered the exile of R. Moshe on the pretext that he was interfering with their efforts to maintain law and order in the town. When the decree became known there was an outcry amongst the Jewish population, but, in characteristic fashion, Moshe chose to take action himself rather than to rely on others. He went to St. Petersburg for consultations with the influential Jews of that city, and his supporters decided that Baron Hertz Guinzberg, the most prominent member of the Jewish community, should give a large reception for the members of the czarist government, army officers and high officials, who were the superiors of the two trouble-makers in Riga. R. Moshe was of course invited to attend.

As invitations to the Baron's parties were eagerly sought, both for the delicious refreshments served and for the gifts the Baron bestowed on his guests, all those invited attended the reception, at which R. Moshe was presented with much ceremony. Of course, after being feted so sump-tuously, none of the officials felt able to refuse any request of the Baron. Thus on the following day, a message was received in Riga canceling R. Moshe's banishment.

R. Moshe was able to remain in his post in Riga for the rest of his life, despite being plagued by ill health for many of his later years, a fact which he mentions in the prefaces to his works *Pnei Moshe*, the Drashot that he published, and *Birkat Moshe*. From these prefaces we also know that Moshe underwent an emergency operation in 1899, and that he suffered a stroke some years before his death. Nonetheless, not only did he retain his positions as Chief Rabbi of Riga and rabbi of Adath Yeshurun, but he was able to find the time and the strength to continue his writing.

R. Moshe's first book, *Pnei Moshe*, was published in 1872, with a *haskamah* by R. Aisel. In 1895 he published a Haggadah together with the relevant parts of this commentary. Then, in 1896, he was finally able to fulfil his father's request that he publish a second edition of *Emek Yehoshua*. This edition of Aisel's work included R. Moshe's commentary on the original, under the title, *Sefat HaEmek* (The Language of the Valley), as well as some new interpretations of the original work by his brother Berish. In 1900 R. Moshe published a collection of his sermons for Sabbaths and festivals, titled *Drashot Maharam*. His last volume, *Birkat Moshe* (The Blessing of Moshe), was published in 1909, only two years before his death. The title was derived from Moshe's strong feeling that only a miracle had enabled him to survive all the illnesses and tribulations which had beset him, and that he must surely be blessed to have done so. In the foreword to his last work, R. Moshe expresses his thanks to his sons and to his congregation for their constant support in his work and in his illnesses. In all the prefaces he paid tribute to his wife and to the memory of his mother, as well as of his father. He died on the *yahrzeit* of his father in 1911.

Although they too were strong in learning, the sons

and son-in-law of R. Aisel were all quite different from him in temperament and personality. Considered clever and scholarly men, they were balanced, quiet and restrained in their behavior and maintained good relations with all, taking care not to hurt anyone's feelings. Although this may have been a reaction to the sharp and cutting remarks of R. Aisel Harif, they seem to have maintained good and close relations with him.

R. Moshe had three sons and two daughters. The oldest son, Shabtai Aharon, seems to have been an extremely gifted scholar, and we get the impression from the preface to *Birkat Moshe* that he was his father's pride and joy. Shabtai Aharon served as a rabbi in the small town of Gorzhd, near Kovno. The second son, Yehiel Yosef, is also mentioned by his father with much affection as being a great help and comfort to him. I believe he was also a rabbi and he had a son named Yitzhak, but there are no survivors of these two families. R. Moshe had a third son, Yisrael, who is never mentioned in the prefaces, and I only learned about him from one of Moshe's granddaughters, Fania Rolnitsky, who told me that he had become a painter. Although his portraits of family members hung in her parents' home in Vilna, she herself had never met him, and she knows nothing about his life or what became of him.

An interesting sidelight on the story of Yisrael turned up a few months ago, while I was in the throes of searching for material, a French art catalogue came into my hands, and in it I found the name Jacques Chapiro as well as photography of some of his paintings being offered for sale. Although I had never heard of any Shapiro relatives in France, in light of the fact that I now knew Yisrael Shapiro had been a painter, I felt that I had to find out who this gentleman might be. Beginning with the *Encyclopedia Judaica*, I discovered that Jacques Chapiro had been born in Dinnaburg (Dvinsk) in 1887and had shown a very early talent for drawing, using the holy books in the *heder* for his efforts. Jacques Chapiro moved to Moscow, where he painted and worked in the theater designing the sets for the Habimah Theater's production of *The Dybbuk*. In 1925 Chapiro emigrated to Paris, where he lived and worked for some thirty years, becoming an important member of the mainly Jewish group known as the Paris School. While it is not likely that Jacques was the son of R. Moshe of Riga, he might very well have been the son of Moshe's son Yisrael, the painter. I find the possibility quite provocative and hope somehow to elucidate the matter.

Moshe's younger daughter, Sheindel, married Shalom Mendel Avin, who succeeded his father-in-law as Chief Rabbi of Riga, a position he held until 1932. In 1915 he was one of ten leading citizens who were designated by the authorities as hostages, or guarantors, for the loyalty of the Jewish community. For a year these men lived under the threat of death sentence, in case of a treacherous act by a member of the community. Sheindel had no children, but her older sister Gittel, who married Eliezer Hanoch Kolpanitsky and lived in Vilna, had five children, two sons and three daughters. One son, Abba, was exiled to Siberia and never heard of again. The older son, Isaac, married a woman named Tanya and had one son, Moshe. Tanya and Moshe were in the Vilna Getto together with Fania Rolnitzky but Moshe, who was a student and worked as a

German translator, simply vanished one day and was never seen again. Tanya did not survive the camps to which they were eventually deported, but her husband Isaac did. He came to Israel in 1948, and lived in Tel Aviv till 1962.

Of Gittel's three daughters, Esther, the oldest, did not survive the War. Golda married Avraham Gordonowitz in Vilna, but he did not survive and she came alone to Israel in 1948. She had no children and never remarried. Now in her mid-eighties, she has recently entered an old-age home. One of her earliest recollections is of being taken to visit R. Moshe when he was old and very ill, and had expressed a wish to see his grandchildren. He was then under the care of a German professor.

Fania, the youngest of Gittel's children, survived the Vilna Ghetto and Kaiserwald labor camp. After the War she met and married Yaakov Rolnitsky, and the couple left for Israel with *Aliya Bet,* the illegal immigration, in 1948. Their ship was one of those intercepted by the British, and they were interned in Cyprus where they spent fourteen months living in a tent. Fania and Yaakov arrived in Israel in February 1949, and she gave birth to their only child, Gila, a month later. Today the Rolnitzkys live in Tel Aviv, where Gila, married to Amikam Preiss, has three sons — the only descendants of R. Moshe in this generation.

Little is known about R. Aisel's third son, Mordecai, and there are indications that he died at an early age, during his father's lifetime. But we do know that Mordecai lived long enough to get married and to have a child, Avraham. Mordechai's great-granddaughter in the United States, Martha Bernstein, relates that she had heard that

R. Yosef Shluper

Avraham, who was her grandfather, was raised by R. Aisel because Mordecai was not well enough to fulfill this duty. We don't know who his wife was, or what happened to her. As to Avraham, he emigrated to the U.S. in 1902, where he may have served as a rabbi in New York but his family remembers him as a business man, rather than a rabbi. He also reprinted R. Aisel's *Emek Yehoshua* in 1925 in Jerusalem. Avraham's son, Isaac Meyer, and daughter, Pauline Stavisky both produced large families who live today mainly in New York and Florida. Some of Pauline's descendants have close ties with my family and with Israel, which they visit quite often. (See genealogical tables).

R. Aisel's son-in-law, R. Yosef Shluper, was known in his youth as the "genius of Dinaburg," the German name for

Dvinsk, which was used in the German-speaking province of Kurland. He was the son of a wealthy family and his father, Zvi Hirsch, was a Lubavitcher *hassid.* A student of Naftali Zvi Yehuda Berlin, head of the Wolozyn yeshiva, Shluper was brought to the attention of R. Aisel as a desirable son-in-law when Aisel came to Wolozyn to mediate the famous dispute at the Yeshiva. Apparently, Yosef was a handsome fellow with a pleasing personality. According to the book *Talmidei Wolozyn,* he was one of the students called by the mediating committee which was trying to resolve the vital question as to who would run the yeshiva and how. Shluper declared that since he himself was "sharp," he would prefer a *rosh yeshiva* who was "knowledgeable." R. Aisel, one of the three rabbis conducting the hearing, was astonished that such a young fellow had the confidence to declare himself "harif," and challenged Shluper to prove it. R. Aisel's examination of the young man was so thorough that those listening thought he did not care for the prospective bridegroom. Thus they were surprised when — after cross-examining him and tearing apart his interpretations — Aisel returned to the question of the proposed match. "If he found favor in your eyes, why were you so severe with him?" asked the onlookers. "Just so that he should remember that I am not only capable of destroying his structures, but liable to do so," responded R. Aisel in his inimitable way.

Another version of this story relates that on the occasion of a visit to this same yeshiva, R. Aisel, who was always on the look-out for a *talmid hacham* suitable for his daughter, posed a difficult question to the students, but none of them could give the right answer. When R. Aisel was getting into his carriage after concluding his meeting, one of the boys ran after him and wanted to know the answer to the question. R. Aisel was impressed with this desire for knowledge and proclaimed that he would take this boy, Yossele Shluper, to be his son-in-law.

R. Aisel took Yossele into his household, where he looked after all his needs and made every effort to make him feel at home. Aisel never interfered in his affairs and treated him with great respect, as if he were as much master of the house as Aisel himself. Yossele married Aisel's daughter Nehama in 1860, and the couple remained in R. Aisel's house where Yosef was permitted to study undisturbed until he felt the need to become independent. He became a rabbi in 1867, and apparently assisted R. Aisel in some of his duties.

One day R. Aisel said to him, "Tell me Yossele, which one of us is rabbi of Slonim? On questions of *Heter* and *Issur* neither of us are needed because R. Feitel the *dayyan* deals with that. And we both sit in the *Beit Din* and both receive salaries. So tell me, who is the rabbi of Slonim?" "Please sir," smiled R. Yosef, "perhaps you can give me the answer?" "Well, I'll tell you — go out into the market place and listen. The person whom they are gossiping and complaining about, *he* is the rabbi of Slonim."

On another occasion, R. Aisel invited his son-in-law to give a חילוק on *Shabbat HaGadol* in the Slonim synagogue. This is a particular type of talmudic discourse requiring deep and thorough analysis of variations in concepts on particular subjects. R. Yosef delivered such a sharp *hiluk* that the congregation was overcome with delight at his intellectual capacities. Upon which R. Aisel remarked, "the custom of inviting the rabbi to give a חילוק on *Shabbat haGadol* was devised in order to test the learning of the rabbi to see whether one may sell him חמץ [food prohibited on the Passover] on *Erev Pesach.*"

Once there was a *siyyum* (conclusion of a study cycle) of tratate Gittin in the Hevrat Shas synagogue at which R. Aisel and R. Yosef were invited to say the *Hadran* (literally, repetition of the customary summing-up on concluding the study of a tractate). R. Aisel offered the honor to R. Yosef, who put the question, "Why did R. Yehuda HaNasi, compiler of the *Mishnah,* put the tractate on divorce before that on marriage, when we know that marriage comes first and divorce only later if the wife does not please the husband?" R. Yosef gave a brilliant pilpulistic argument in defense of this order and received a great ovation from the audience. But R. Aisel, who did not agree with this form of *pilpul,* said, "Why all this *pilpul*? Our sages have already said, "There is nothing as bad as a bad wife, and that whoever has such a deep trouble must be helped to find a solution. And, just as The Holy One, Blessed Be He, sends the cure before the plague, so our teacher, R. Yehuda HaNasi, put "divorce" before "marriage."

Yosef's first rabbinical position was in Dereczyn, a village near Slonim where he served for seven years. From there he moved to Wakshne, where he lived for about twelve years. In 1885–1886, twelve years after R. Aisel's death, he was invited to become rabbi of Slonim where he served until his death in 1905. He was buried close to the grave of R. Aisel in the "new" cemetery. When he took up his position in Slonim, R. Yosef had to work side-by-side with a government-appointed rabbi by the name of

Horowitz (רב מתעם — a rabbi on behalf of the government). Such men were appointed for their knowledge of Russian, to keep the civilian registers and records of the business life of the community, so that births and deaths were correctly listed, taxes were properly paid, military service fulfilled, etc.

It is said of R. Yosef that he disliked the rabbinate as much as his father-in-law. When his two daughters, Miriam and Hinda, were of marriageable age, he is reported to have said, "I am looking for a son-in-law, an *Am HaAretz,* because if he knows a little Hebrew, I'm afraid that he might become a rabbi."

In the same vein, R. Yossele was asked once why great rabbis received such small remuneration. He answered as follows, "London is the greatest town in the world, yet it has a terrible climate. Lodz is one of the greatest manufacturing towns but it has no water. Petersburg, capital of Russia and of the largest continent ruled by a king, is surrounded by rivers and seas, and has hardly any land. And that's how it is with great rabbis: much learning and little money."

During these years, there was a decline in the quality of Torah study in Slonim, and the town began to lose some of its luster. A group of worried Jews asked R. Yosef to follow in R. Aisel's footsteps and go forth in battle against the *Haskalah.* He replied, "I knew my father-in-law no less, and perhaps even more, than anyone else in Slonim. He was unique, and there is no other like him. Only he himself was able to do what R. Aisel did."

However, while he might not have been enamored of the rabbinate, Yossel was a popular rabbi and remained a dedicated scholar throughout his life. He published two works: *Porat Yosef* ("A Fruitful Bough is Yosef" — Gen. 49:22) and *Merkavat Yosef* (The Chariot of Yosef).

R. Yosef and Nehama had three children: Mordecai, Hinda, and Miriam. Miriam never married. Hinda became a dentist and married a pharmacist by the name of Pinchas Krynski. They lived in Nowygrodek and had two sons. At some time between the two world wars, Hinda's husband apparently left for the United States with both sons, leaving Hinda alone. She did not survive the Holocaust.

Mordecai, or Mottel as he was called, had a traditional Torah education, studying in Slobodka and then at the Rabbinical College of Odessa, where he took his *smicha*. An outstanding speaker, he was elected *rabbiner*, or Crown Rabbi, of Slonim in 1910–1911, after much internal politicking. R. Mordecai became a permanent and active factor in the public life of the town, representing the popular Zionist faction. Indeed, his election as Crown Rabbi was due to a deliberate plan of the Zionists to upgrade the status of Crown Rabbi from that of a purely "civil servant" status, to that of a suitable representative of the Jewish community vis-á-vis the government authorities, both Russian and Polish. He took an active part in the welfare programs of Slonim, for which there was a great need during and after the First World War, particularly in the care of orphans. I have seen photos of him, in uniform, in this capacity.

R. Mordecai continued in this position till 1929, when the Polish occupiers cancelled it and gave the job to the head of the *Beit Din*. But, due to his experience and the protests of the community, R. Mordecai was permitted to continue

Yehiel ben Issachar Dov Shapira **Esther Leah Weinbaum Shapira**

doing the work, albeit only as assistant to the head of the *Beit Din*. As representative of the Zionist synagogue, he had also been elected to the Jewish Council, which consisted of twelve representatives of the various synagogues and groupings in the community. He was an active contributor to the local Jewish press, writing a column called "לאהובי ורעי" (To My Friend and Beloved), in which he commented on community and Zionist affairs.

R. Mordecai maintained close ties with the Kolpanitzky family in Vilna. He married late in life and perished with his wife in the big massacre in Slonim in 1941.

My father, Ze'ev (Wolf), was the son of Yehiel, the son of Berish. As to Yehiel himself, he moved to the town of Leczyca (Lentshitz), where he lived out his life with his wife, Esther Leah (Weinbaum), and their eight children.

Leczyca (in Yiddish Lentchitz or Luntshits) in the Lodz province was one of the oldest Jewish communities in Poland. It is mentioned in royal decrees of 1453, during the reign of Casimir IV, which implies that Jews had been living there already for some time, possibly as early as the 11th century. In 1633 there was an incident of blood libel, and synagogue officials were executed, drawn and quartered and their body parts set on spikes in front of the synagogue, which was subsequently burnt down. Privileges given to the Jews were cancelled. In 1652 royal permission was given to rebuild homes and the synagogue. This new synagogue became one of a series of 'fortress' synagogues, which were built along the eastern and southern borders of Poland as part of the defense against invaders. During the Swedish wars against Poland in the 16th and 17th centuries, Jews from the surrounding areas took refuge in the Jewish quarter of Lentshitz. When the Poles attacked, believing that the Jews were helping the Swedes, an estimated 3,000 Jews were slaughtered and hundreds of Torah scrolls were burnt. A memorial tablet was dedicated to these Jews and existed until 1830, when it disappeared.

In 1676 King John Sobieski confirmed their rights and allowed the synagogue to be rebuilt, on the conditions that it not be taller or more beautiful than before. The Swedish Wars were over and Jews were allowed to engage in commerce. Excavations that were carried out in 1924 revealed a section of the outer wall of the synagogue, which had been part of the fortifications of the city. The wall was three and a half meters thick and was found to contain a corridor the width of a room. Remains of skeletons and wall inscriptions were found there, evidence that Jews and perhaps

Yehiel ben Moshe Shapira,
b. Lentshitz 1924–1940

Yosef ben Aisek Shapira, b.
Lentshitz 1911. My father's
nephew with daughter Zahava.

Ze'ev Shapiro (standing, middle) and his brother Moshe (seated, middle),
at a meeting of the Leczyca Zionist Society, 1917

other citizens had taken refuge there during the wars.

In 1939 there were 4,300 Jews in the city, including my father's immediate and extended family, making up about 30% of the general population. Gradually there were more and more persecutions and deportations started. They were eventually moved into a ghetto and before that was liquidated they were forced to destroy the cemetery and set fire to the synagogue. A heavy fine was imposed on these remaining Jews because of the vandalism they had supposedly committed. By 1942 the Jewish presence in the town was wiped out. When my brother visited the town in 1988, not a single trace of Jewish history was to be found.

Like his father Berish, Yehiel never wanted to be a rabbi or to be dependent on the community. Thus, despite his considerable scholarship, he made his living from a general store which was situated in the main square of the town. He was a very popular *Baal Tefillah* and, like R. Aisel, was against the unnecessary lengthening of prayers. Esther Leah's five nephews, sons of her brother, emigrated and established themselves in London. I am in contact with some of their descendants, the Stantons.

Yehiel's oldest daughter, Haya Zeesal, married a rabbi, Moshe Nathanson, but none of his four sons went into the rabbinate despite their learning. In old photographs in my possession, they are still wearing long coats even though they are clean-shaven. Although they adopted "modern" clothes soon after, they remained observant. Haya's second husband was also a rabbi.

My father was the seventh child and the youngest son. He hardly knew his oldest brother, Asher, partly because of the age difference and partly because Asher was sent to his grandfather's home to be educated. He eventually married into a hassidic family and lived in Lodz. That family did not survive the war. My father was very close to his brothers Isaac and Moshe, the former a scholar and teacher, the latter active in community affairs. All Zionists, they were members of the Hovevei Zion movement, spoke Hebrew and read Hebrew newspapers, poetry and literature, a fact which caused some sections of the community to disapprove of them.

Isaac's daughter from his first wife, Ita, married Leon Izbicki and came to Palestine in the early thirties. She died in 1954, and her husband died some years later. Their only son, Nahman, went to the United States to study and I have lost contact with him. Isaac's son from his second wife, Yosef, survived the war in Russia and came to Israel in 1949. He married a woman named Sarah Wohl and had two daughters, Zahava and Orly. Because of economic difficulties they moved many years ago to Buenos Aires, where the daughters eventually married. Yosef's sister Nehama and her family perished in the Holocaust.

Moshe, his wife and two children, named Yehiel and Esther, also perished in the Holocaust, as did my father's youngest sister Dvora Yehudit, as well as her husband and son. Another sister, Rasha, died of natural causes in 1930.

My father's sister, Bluma Nehama, married Eliahu Librach of Zgierz, and had five children. The families of the three sons perished. The younger daughter, Naomi, came to Palestine in the 1930s, married Yitzhak Tchernihowsky and had two children. The older daughter, Yehudit, married Leibish Weinstein from Zgierz, who was a textile expert. With their son Mayer they fled to Russia at the outbreak of

The Lentshitz synagogue, before 1939. From *Sefer Lentshitz,* published 1953

The synagogue on fire, 1942. From *Sefer Lentshitz,* published 1953

The Market Square in Leczycna. One of the the shops had belonged to my grandparents. The Street of the Jews at top right. A. Shapiro, 1988

the war and survived there in a labor camp. After the war they met up with cousin Yosef in Poland and came together to Israel. My brother and I met them in Paris, when we too were on our way here. Yehudit has survived her husband and lives in Tel Aviv, while her son and his wife Marilla live in Kfar Saba, and have two daughters. There were several marriages between the Librach, Weinbaum and Shapira families.

My father met my mother, Frymet (Fruma) Schultz while on a visit to Lodz in 1919. He always spoke of how he had seen her in the street and was immediately smitten. He asked his oldest brother to arrange a meeting, and they were married that same year, even though her father Avraham was a Gerrer Hassid. Previously a man of means, a sock manufacturer and an agent of a hassidic lottery, he had lost everything during World War I and the inflation which followed. Avraham and Rahel Leah Schultz had seven sons and one daughter (four other children not having survived infancy), and my mother was the third child.

After their wedding my parents lived in Leczyca for a couple of years, my brother Yehiel (known as Alec) being born a year after the wedding. Having come from the nearby city of Lodz, Frymet did not enjoy the restrictive style of close family life in a small town, but she did accept my father's plan to emigrate to Palestine and prepared herself to help support the family by learning to sew. It was apparently at this time that my father was so carried away by his Zionistic fervor that he donated the inherited family silver to the Jewish National Fund, and I remember that my mother would remind him of this incident from time to time. Although my youthful mind could never equate the small-town image that I had of my parents' life in Poland with beautiful silver heirlooms, it has become clear to me that the objects my father donated must have come from the household of the wealthy Berish. They had been passed to his son and grandchildren, and eventually, by my father's action, to the coffers of the Zionist movement. In 1921 my father made his way to Palestine, leaving Poland illegally because he had not served in the army. One of our favorite photographs shows him seated by Herzl's tomb in Vienna. My mother and brother followed him several months later. At first they lived in Herzliya, where my father worked bringing "zif-zif" (sea-sand) to building sites, and my mother ran a workers' dining-room. After I married, we eventually discovered that my father had worked on the house that was being built in Tel Aviv for my husband's uncle, Louis Kahn.

Pauline and Sam Stavinsky with some of their children on their trip to Palestine, 1925. Courtesy Ruth Levitz

Pauline and Sam Stavinsky celebrating their 58th wedding anniversary. Courtesy Ruth Levitz

One of my mother's brothers, Fishel, now known as Nomberg, also came to Palestine in the twenties and became a farmer in Herzliya. He married Zipora Rosenberg, who was much loved by all, and had two sons, Avraham and Pinhas. In 1936 they became founding members of Moshav Rishpon, where Pinhas still lives today with his wife Me'ira. They have four daughters and a number of grandchildren. Avraham died of a brain tumor when barely out of his teens.

Times were not easy in Palestine during the 1920s, and some time after my birth (I believe I was the first girl to increase the Herzliya population), the family moved to Jerusalem where my father worked on the construction of the Bikur Holim hospital. Of the stories I heard about the period, I was most impressed with those about the earthquake of 1927 and with the fact that I was a patient of the legendary Dr. Helena Kagan, a distinction I must have shared with several thousand other children! During that period there was also a visit from our American relatives, Pauline (Shapiro) and Sam Stavisky, who helped my father to acquire a camel, which unfortunately died. My brother and I renewed this acquaintance in Tel Aviv about 1951, when the Staviskys visited the country again, and have maintained contact with the family ever since (See genealogy charts).

The economic situation continued to be very difficult, and finally in 1927, influenced by the large emigration which occurred in those years, my parents decided to follow their friends to Australia. Thus, with no money, no knowledge of English and no relatives there to help them, my parents simply took off into the unknown with their two children. I presume that this was when the family name took on its present form.

After an initial spell at a Jewish farming area near Shepparton, they settled in Melbourne, as did a large majority of the Jewish émigrés, not only from Poland and Russia but also from Safed and Rosh Pina in Palestine. This group formed a vibrant club called the Ivriah, and an active Zionist organization which shaped the development and character of the Melbourne Jewish community, and was the focal point of its social life. My father traveled throughout the country selling clothing and linens and was therefore away from home for two or three weeks at a time. My mother utilized her knowledge of sewing by working in a clothing factory.

In 1935 my father received a certificate to enter Palestine and, although my mother opposed the move on the grounds that they were just getting on their feet in Australia, we packed up and made the journey by boat to Port Said (the S.S. Esperance Bay) and then took the train to Tel Aviv via El Kantara. But it turned out that my father's decision was a bad one and that my mother's caution had been correct. For the riots and atrocities of those years, and the bad economic situation, all of which I well remember, made it impossible to settle in. So within a year, we found ourselves back in Melbourne and shunned by the local Zionists for having betrayed their ideals. Indeed, it was many years before my parents could return to their rightful place in the community. However, they were fortunate enough to have good friends who stood by them, and only years later did my mother tell me what had transpired during those difficult times.

During the thirties, four other sons of Rahel and Avraham

Shultz dispersed themselves throughout the world; Yehiel and Yidel, the youngest, to South America, and Lipa and his wife Reine (Regina), with their two daughters, Hanna and Maida, came to Melbourne. Pinhas had already settled and married in London and during World War II sent his daughter Jean to us as an evacuee. Eventually they also settled in Melbourne, where Jean married Joe Salzman and produced three children, Mark, Daron and Ilana.

Avraham Schultz passed away in 1925, so that by September 1939 only Rahel and two of her sons were still in Lodz. She and her oldest son Simcha, and his family, remained and died in the ghetto, but Simcha's son Efraim fled to Russia with his uncle Herschel and survived the war there despite being conscripted into the Russian army. Eventually in Moscow, he married a girl named Sonia Berman and produced a son named Azriel. As Polish nationals they were able to return to Poland in 1956, and from there they immediately made aliya. Today they live in Herzliya. Rahel's other son, Herschel, joined Efraim in his flight to Russia. At first they contracted to work in a labor camp for a year. Efraim held out for the year and was subsequently conscripted into the Russian army. Herschel, however, anxious about the fate of his wife and two children, escaped from the camp in an attempt to reunite with them. He was taken prisoner by the Germans and spent the war years in various camps. His family perished in the Lodz Ghetto. After the War, Herschel got in touch with us, and my parents brought him out to Australia where he managed to rebuild his life and marry, but did not have any more children. He visited Israel many times, but now finds the trip too strenuous, so my brother and I have both visited him in Melbourne in recent years.

Despite their unsuccessful attempts to settle in Palestine, my parents never swerved from their Zionism, which was the lodestar of our lives, and it was always obvious to me that I would eventually make my home in Palestine. I was one of the original members of Habonim, but did not go on *hakhshara*. I took my B.A. degree at Melbourne University and then worked as a journalist on the local *Jewish Herald*. With the establishment of the State of Israel, I decided it was time for me to make aliya. My parents accepted this, their only stipulation being that my brother Alec should go with me, since it was not customary for young women to travel alone at that time. So, in August 1948, my brother and I left Melbourne on the *S.S. Maloja*, planning to see London and Europe and our relatives there, on our way to Israel. It was a six-week journey. We were fascinated by our encounter with Indian Jews in Bombay, both the merchants and those living in the Kadoorie School compound, awaiting aliya. In Aden the Jews told us of the recent pogroms (1948), and directed us to the desert camps outside the town, where those Yemenites who had walked for weeks from their homes in the mountain regions, were waiting to be transported to Israel, in what was subsequently called the Magic Carpet operation. This exciting encounter was one of the most unforgettable of my life.

There were two or three similar-minded Melbournites on the *Maloja*, one of them the painter Yosl Bergner. Only years later did I appreciate the generosity of my parents in sending their two children off together, not knowing when or if we would ever meet again. They were truly faithful to their ideals.

Alec and I arrived in Tel Aviv in February 1949, during the second truce of the Israel-Arab war, and we were taken in by my cousin Ita Izbicki whom I have already mentioned. Ita then lived in one room on Tel Aviv's Dizengoff Street with her husband, Leon, and son, Nachman, and shared the kitchen and bathroom with another family. Ita's half-brother, Yosef, was also there. Of course this arrangement was not very comfortable, and although the Izbickis soon moved into a two-room apartment, my brother and I decided not to impose on their kindness any longer, and to seek other accommodations. In the meantime we had re-established contact with our cousins, the Weinsteins, and with my uncle Fishel (my mother's brother) and aunt Zipora, in Rishpon.

Accommodations were hard to find and expensive, and I moved at least once a month, occasionally to a hotel, till I eventually found a comfortable solution. It was a very bohemian, adventurous and exciting period, in which I met all kinds of people who had come to help build the new Jewish State, although not all of them succeeded in establishing themselves.

I eventually found work in the publishing department of the World Wizo Organization, and was introduced to my husband Alexander Rafaeli, by a co-worker. He was born near Dvinsk and raised in Riga, Latvia, where the family name was Rafaelovitch. He had attended the Hebrew Gymnasia in Riga and had his first contact with Jabotinsky when the latter came there to organize the Betar movement in 1924. His father Boris (Dov Ber) was a businessman, and his mother Rosa had been active in the socialist revolutionary movement. He had a younger brother Yehezkel, who was known as Asya. Alex studied at the University of Heidelberg, taking his Ph.D. in Sociology, and had come to Palestine in 1933. He spent the initial period in Jerusalem where he came in contact with the group of young men who eventually formed the Irgun Zvai Leumi, or ETZEL. He worked as an economist and journalist, but after becoming a full-time member of the Irgun, he left his professional work, and was drafted for political work in Europe and for *Aliya Bet*.

Alex's father passed away in June 1940, just before the Nazis entered Latvia. His mother died in the infamous Rumboli Death March in Riga in December 1941, and his brother, who joined the partisans, was killed in an action in the nearby forests.

In 1940 Alex got out of Europe, and was sent by the Irgun to America to do public relations and to participate in the political and public campaign for the creation of a Jewish Army. In 1943 he was drafted into the American army and took part in the invasion of Europe, serving three years all told. After the war he continued his activities on behalf of the Irgun and *Aliya Bet*, which was done within the framework of the Bergson Group's Committee for a Free Palestine. But with the establishment of the State of Israel, he decided to leave politics and concentrate on his private life. He returned to Israel in 1949 to establish a plastics factory, and it was at this juncture that we met.

We were married in January 1950 and lived in Tel Aviv until 1954, during which time I gave birth to our two sons, Asi Dov and Aylon Yehoshua. We then moved to Jerusalem, where my husband was one of the founders of Jerusalem Pencils Ltd. Our two daughters, Varda Leah and Karni

Ella, were born subsequently at Bikur Holim, the hospital that my father had helped build in the 1920s. Today all four children live in Jerusalem. Asi is married to Nurit, an Arts graduate; Lonny to Yuli, Ph.D. and university lecturer; Varda to Amihai, an Egyptologist. So far they have blessed us with seven grandchildren. The boys look after the family business, Varda has specialized in Contemporary Jewish History and Karni is a social worker. (Fuller details are set out in the genealogical appendix.)

My parents, who made aliya for the third time in 1954, had the satisfaction of living another twenty-six years in the Jewish State and seeing their grandchildren grow to adulthood and serve their country, as they had always dreamt. During these years when already in his 70s, my father realized an old ambition: he reissued all the works of R. Aisel, and was also instrumental in having a street named for him in the area bordering between Bat Yam and Holon, a section where the streets are named after philosophers and scholars.

In the meantime my brother had married Aliza Blum, and they had two children, Jonathan and Naomi. The Blums were originally from Munich. In 1938 the oldest daughter Mady married and came with her husband Kurt to Haifa, where they are still living today. Aliza, with her sister Bobby, and her parents, managed to get to London at about the same time. Aliza came to Israel after the establishment of the State, served in the Israeli Air Force and subsequently met my brother and married him on January 1, 1952. Seeking to better his economic situation, Alec accepted a lucrative business proposition in Kenya in 1960, but due to the uprising there he had to move on to London, where he and Aliza are still living today. They make frequent trips to Israel, however, to visit their daughter Naomi, who married and settled here, and has a daughter called Netta. Their son Jonathan and his wife Linda, both doctors, have a practice in Warwickshire, and he has recently been appointed medical adviser to the regional National Health Authority. Since he and Linda have three daughters (Abigail, Elly and Jessica), it seems that our particular family name has now come to an end, and Jonathan is the last male Shapiro descending directly from R. Aisel Harif.

In Conclusion

My aim in setting out to write this book was to introduce an illustrious ancestor to his descendants before his image faded away. I thought it would be a simple matter to research and write a short biography and to gather and translate the stories of and about Rabbi Aisel Harif into English, to make them accessible to the family wherever they are located throughout the world. I soon discovered however, that it was not such a simple matter, and that I had unwittingly opened myself up to a multi-faceted experience.

First of all, although I found the search for material about R. Aisel fascinating, I was astonished by the amount of material that was available concerning other members of the family. There it was, all ready in the books, waiting for me to come along and find it. Yet, except for two or three articles which had come to our attention, neither my father nor myself had known of this treasure, and there may even be more that I have yet to discover. This information helped me to fill out the family background, and to give new dimensions to the shadowy figures of the past about whom my father had talked. As I worked, R. Aisel and other forebears gradually became real people to me, people with complicated characters who had lived lives of trial and tribulation, sorrow and joy. I came to feel quite sad for R. Aisel, who had fought so staunchly for his ideas, his standards and the world he loved, not knowing that the battle was, in fact, already lost.

Through my parents' anxieties, I was always aware of the European situation in the thirties and the reality of the Second World War and the Holocaust. The broad outline of the fate of our family does not differ essentially from that experienced by the majority of European Jewry. Yet to face it on a personal and individual basis brought home more strongly the tragedy and forlornness of the terrible devastation experienced by the Jews, with all its waste of lives and potential. Whole families were blotted out, preventing the continuation of millions of other families along with my own. Records of the Shapiro family had been kept for several hundred years, but now it has almost come to an end, for the Yehiels, Berishes and Esthers trapped in Leczyca were not permitted to mature, to reproduce or to make their contribution in life. This makes me feel very strongly that my own family is part of the *She'erit HaPleita,* the remnant that survived and returned to build anew in the Jewish homeland.

While writing this history I came to feel that I had closed many circles: the smaller one of fulfilling my father's Zionist dream by returning to live and raise my family in Israel and the larger one being the fulfillment of the attempted aliya of my great grandfather in 1876. Even the fact that my husband came from Riga, R. Moshe's town, seems significant for me, for there may have been contact between the two families already then. That I have been able to trace out the lives and fate of almost the entire family, saving them from complete anonymity, is a source of great satisfaction. Indeed, while doing so I was amazed to discover how strong had been the Zionist leanings in the family, with R. Aisel a strong supporter, if not an activist, in this field. For myself, to live with my family in Jerusalem satisfies a basic need that gives purpose and meaning to my life.

Jews have always stressed the importance of knowing and remembering and continuing, whether on the Festivals or on Holocaust Remembrance Day. I too want my children to know who their forebears were and to remember them, and to continue in their traditions, for we do not live in isolation; or as John Donne said many centuries ago, "No man is an island." We all carry within us our private and collective memories, which serve to influence our future. Thus my father sowed the seeds of this book with the stories he used to tell about his family. He also set an example for me, for I was terribly impressed that he began to reissue all of R. Aisel's works as perhaps the most important, most creative project of his life, when he was already in his seventies. This project breathed new life into my father and taught me that one can still find challenge and achievement in one's later years. And so I too, during a period of questioning and indecision, decided to carry out this project of my own, which I had been idly contemplating for some time. I could say that the memory of R. Aisel Harif has indeed been a blessing, both to my father and to myself. My next step is to bring out a Hebrew version of this story, for the benefit of my own children and grandchildren and *im yirze haShem*, their children and grandchildren to come. The books will mark the centenary of the birth of my father which fell on the sixth day of Hanukkah, in the Hebrew year תרנ"ב.

275

Jewish School, Riga, and home of R. Moshe Shapiro, son of R. Aisel. Photographed by me in 1991

POSTSCRIPT

Just as this book was ready to go to press, an unrelated letter of my brother's to a genealogy researcher in New York brought a response from a descendant of Nehama and R. Yosef Shluper, who was not listed in my brother's chart. It appears that the Shlupers had another daughter named Rasha, who was born in 1864–1865 and who married Zalman Kahn of Riga in 1881–1882. He emigrated to America in 1888, and she and their son followed in 1890, eventually settling in Belle Plain, Minnesota, where Rasha changed her name to Rosalia. Part of the family still lives in that state. Zalman Kahn died in August 1931, and Rosalia in April 1946. However, our correspondent, Bruce Kahn, Nehama's great grandson, tells us that the family was not aware of the connection to Aisel Harif until he began to correspond with my brother. This seems to indicate either that there was a rift in the family or that they became estranged as a result of distance and poor postal service.

I then decided to look for more information on the family in the prefaces to R. Yosef's books, in the National Library in Jerusalem. There I discovered, in his book *Merkavat Yosef* (1897), mention of another son, Alexander Yehiel, who financed the publishing of his father's book. When I contacted Fania Rolnitzky, she eventually recalled that her mother had occasionally mentioned another Shluper son, who had not been on good terms with the rest of the family. This means that the Shlupers had five children instead of the three we previously believed and that one branch is alive and well in the U.S. It seems that in endeavoring to tie up the loose ends of this story, we are discovering more and more loose ends.

For example, when the name Kahn of Riga cropped up, it provoked much curiosity in my husband and myself as it was his mother's family name, and we are now trying to clarify whether there is an inter-family connection here as well. I may even succeed in identifying the Rasha Shapiro who was my husband's great-grandmother, with the name Rasha that runs through my family, and discover that she too is somehow a relative of mine.

August 3, 1991

We (my husband Alex and I) have returned, exhausted, from our long-desired trip to Riga. The town was attractive and well cared for and the weather was beautiful — in strong contrast to our sad pilgrimages to the cemetery where Alex's father is buried, and to the mass grave in Rumboli, where we believe his mother is buried. While he looked for, and found, the apartments in which the family had lived and the schools he had attended, I decided to try and gather more information about my own great-uncle, R. Moshe Shapira.

The municipal archives were closed for the summer, so we could not pursue the possible link between the Kahn in my husband's family and the Shluper Kahn. At the offices of the Jewish community, situated in the elegant building of the Yiddish Theater, we were told that the Jewish archives had been destroyed during the war, but that there might be more material at Yad Vashem in Jerusalem than they had in Riga. No one could identify R. Moshe's synagogue, Adath

Yeshurun, since the synagogues were usually named after the streets in which they were situated, and no one had a listing of the synagogues by their Hebrew names. There had been sixty-three synagogues and *shtieblach* in Riga in 1939, but only one has remained, that in Piltivas Street.

The largest, most beautiful synagogue had been on Gogol Street. It was built in 1871, and was known as the Choral Synagogue because of the excellent cantors who served there. The *Beit Din* was situated in the *Beit Midrash*. The first action of the Nazis when they occupied Riga, was to cram this synagogue with Jews and burn it to the ground. Today, the large site is a park, with a memorial stone bearing a Magen David and an inscription in Yiddish, Russian and Latvian in memory of the "victims of Fascism." Of course, I couldn't help wondering if this had been R. Moshe's congregation.

We were sent to the Public Library where we asked for the year-books of 1896, 1900 and 1907. These books list the names and addresses of the citizens of Riga each year, and in all the books we checked R. Moses Shapira was recorded as living at 141 Romanov Street, along with his son-in-law R. Avin. The librarian did not know what the street is called today, but Alex deduced that it must be Lachpleshe Street. His conclusion was confirmed by others, including one couple who told us that they had been married by R. Avin in 1934. Apparently he was a handsome, personable man, much in demand for family celebrations. Our Riga friends were very impressed with my personal link to their city.

When Alex and I went to the above-mentioned address, we found a grand three-story building set in a large garden on a corner lot. The area had once been the Jewish section, and was known as the Moscow Forstadt, or Moscow Suburbs, because the road to Moscow went through there. The watchman told us that the building was over a hundred years old and was now a school. We looked for signs of a synagogue, but only the south-east wall suggested that there may have been a niche, or an extra section to the building, and decorative areas of concrete in the front may cover inscriptions. Unless the street numbers have been completely changed, it would appear that the synagogue, the office and the residence of the rabbi were all in this building.

When we visited the Jewish cemetery at Schmerli, I thought to inquire whether R. Moshe was buried there, but unfortunately it was Friday, and the office of the *Hevra Kadisha* was closed. However, we do have someone who will be able to make further enquires about this.

Now, with hindsight, I realize that I could have done more, but those enquiries were rather spontaneous and time was short. Perhaps I will still succeed in finding some of the answers to the questions which have arisen.

Some months later a letter arrived from our friend in Riga. She had learned that the cemetery in Schmerli was only established in 1914, which means that R. Moshe must have been buried in the old cemetery, no trace of which remains since it was turned into a park after the Second World War. Meanwhile, my husband recently discovered a book of historical documents on Riga, which shows that the building on Lachpleshe Street was acquired for a school by the Jewish community in the 1840s and belonged to the community till the German occupation when it was turned into the Nazi headquarters.

12 Years Later — 2003

The publication of my book in 1991 had the effect of a stone thrown into a pond. The ripples extended wider and wider, bringing us (my brother and I) new material, corrections of earlier misinformation, and discovery of previously unknown relatives. Much mail came in with acknowledgements and suggestions, and many people sent me additional stories or snippets of information about Reb Aisel and about Slonim. I received a tattered copy of Reitzeson's paperback 'Fun R. Aisele's Moil,' (1931) and a first edition of R. Moshe Shapira's Haggadah, 1895, which we subsequently reprinted and distributed. Later on, Mr. Zvi Shefet, chairman of the Irgun Olei Slonim, found a manuscript of the stories in Yiddish, in the YIVO library in N.Y., called 'Gliendiker Koilen' (Glowing Embers) by Shlomo Levadi, who returned to Slonim in the 1930's and made a home-movie there. He probably put the collection together at the same time. In this way I was able to double-check the stories and make what I think is the most comprehensive collection of all. Some of this information was incorporated in the Hebrew version of the book published in 1993, but as additional knowledge of the family increased, I felt it important to publish a second, updated edition of this family memoir, with more facts, more photographs and new personal anecdotes.

I would like to begin with some selections from the writings of Golda Gordonovitch. After reaching Israel in December 1948, she set down her experiences of the war in a booklet, together with some Yiddish poetry she had written. Her story reveals to us a little of the suffering which befell that branch of the family of whom so few survived to tell their story themselves.

Memoirs of an Extermination Camp
by Golda Gordonovitch

I was born in Vilna, "Yerushalaim deLita," and grew up in a home which was both traditional and Zionist. My paternal grandfather, R. Yosef Baruch Kolpanitzky, was one of the leaders of the Hovevei Zion movement in Vilna, and my mother was the daughter of the gaon Rabbi Moshe Shapira of Riga and the granddaughter of Reb "Aiseleh Harif" the rabbi of Slonim. We were three daughters and two sons. We were a warm and devoted family but all was destroyed and has vanished. The whole Gordonovich family was lost in the Holocaust except for one granddaughter who survived, by the name of Raya Kessel.

In August 1943 I left the Vilna Ghetto for the Vayvera camp in Estonia to which my husband had been taken in the big round-up (akzia) of Forobank. The Judenrat had announced that the families of those who had been taken could join them there. I remained there with my husband for one month. Each evening after the day's hard work we would meet and eat our supper together — a cold potato and a slice of dry bread, but we were together and that was the most important thing. The memory of that month was the only light which accompanied me during the seven stages of Hell which I experienced in those years.

Once again we were pushed into the freight cars with loaves of bread, each one to be divided amongst four passengers, thrown in after us. For several days the train was shunted back and forth and finally we arrived at the Kiwiauli camp in Estonia. The buildings were empty but there was straw on the floor and so we slept until the pallets were put up.

Together with us in the camp was a group of yeshiva boys from the well-known Radin Yeshiva of the Hafetz Haim, about thirty students together with their Rosh Yeshiva. They were very skinny and their appearance set them apart. They did not eat the daily soup portion because the meat in it was not kosher, so they subsisted solely on the ration of bread with margarine or jam. One day I was working in the kitchen and during a break in the work the Rosh Yeshiva approached me and introduced himself. He told me that he had heard I was from a religious home, and a granddaughter of Reb Aisel Harif, and therefore he wanted to ask if it would be possible for the women in the kitchen to cook potatoes for the students so that they could have some hot food each day. I said that of course I would be willing but I would have to get permission from the officer in charge. If he agreed, I would make the appropriate arrangements. The same evening I approached Czaplevitz and he said he would have to ask Koll, but thought that he would agree. The next morning Czaplevitz told me the matter was arranged on condition that it would be kept quiet, and that if it became known he would deny all knowledge of it. I accepted and went to speak to the women in the kitchen explaining to them the importance of the mitzvah they could do. They immediately agreed. Each day we cooked large portions of potatoes and the boys would come to a deserted room near the kitchen to eat while we stood watch outside. The Rosh Yeshiva told me that in reward for this good deed the Holy One would watch over me and keep me alive.

The men and women were housed in separate buildings a distance apart, and it was forbidden for a member of the opposite sex to enter. Nevertheless, couples did manage to meet and create ties of friendship, even sexual activity was known, for each person was alone, living in a void and needing some love and understanding, needing to belong to someone. Even great differences in intelligence and education did not matter, for every person wanted to escape from the terrible loneliness that was so difficult to endure.

Before the final liquidation of the camp our heads were shaved while the men's hair was shaved in the middle of the head, an obvious sign which would prevent people from trying to escape while being transferred to the next destination.

Again we were brought to a train and loaded into cars going to an unknown destination. We arrived in Tallin and boarded a boat. In the hold we found Russian prisoners… We were transferred to small boats which brought us to Stufhof, a very large camp. We entered a large hall where all our clothes were taken from us. They were then placed in a heap on the floor and re-distributed. The tall women were given short dresses and the short were given long dresses. This was a deliberate act in order to humiliate us.

Every morning the commander of the camp held a parade where we stood in rows of five and attendance was checked. After the count we were marched to the train accompanied by the "Blitz Girls", who carried whips with rubber thongs with which they would lash us. They were extremely cruel. The camp commander stood near the gate observing us scornfully and would announce: "This load of garbage can move on." Every time I heard this I wept silent tears.

The Strelentin camp was high in the mountains, and in the past had been a holiday resort. It was March 1945 and the snow was beginning to melt and water flowed down the hills. One night I woke with high fever and extremely thirsty. I didn't have the strength to get up, and crawled out the door on hands and knees to drink some cold water, and then crawled back.

Every night someone would die. Once I lay next to a young girl who was suffering from dysentery, who passed away late in the night. In the morning the guards would come round and carry out the dead. Thus passed the days and nights in that cowshed. Sick, miserable, lonely, without hope of salvation but with the hope and belief that it would end soon.

Suddenly we heard the sound of marching feet and became panicky. Perhaps it was the Germans coming back to finish us off? We could hear orders in German – "raise your hands!" I knew this was the end, but in a moment discovered that they were Russian soldiers. They shone bright torches in our faces and were shocked at our appearance. I was the only person who spoke Russian and acted as the interpreter.

The soldiers told me to tell the landlady (in whose house we had taken refuge) that we three women were to stay in her house and she would be responsible for our welfare. They ordered her to prepare warm baths, clean clothes and warm beds, and added that they would kill her if she did

not obey. I translated word for word. The woman undertook to fulfill all the orders, adding that they hadn't known
and hadn't heard about the liquidation of the Jews. She
immediately began to prepare food for everyone and the
table was soon filled with all kinds of dishes. The soldiers
were tired and hungry and ate and drank with great appe-
tite, but they only allowed us to drink and to eat some toast
so that we would not be sick. The landlady took the three
of us to another room, took away our lice-infested clothes
and burnt them. Then we had hot showers and were given
clean warm beds to sleep in. The soldiers came upstairs
to check if everything was done as they ordered and then
left, promising to come back the next day. At this stage I
weighed 38 kilo.

I must add here that this was the time of the big Russian
offensive on Berlin and many units of the Red army passed
through our village. There were many cases of rape in the
nearby villages, of German and sometimes Jewish women,
who happened to be there. We were aware of this and took
great care not to open the door without checking who was
outside. One day the reply was "effent kinderlech" (open,
dear children) and when we opened the door a Russian
officer walked in and introduced himself as a doctor and a
Jew, who had come to help us. My feelings at that moment
were indescribable — a Russian officer speaking Yiddish
had come to help me!

I received the necessary treatment but I remained bed-
ridden for six weeks before I was able to walk again. The
German landlady treated us very well as she was afraid we
would complain if we were not satisfied — every morning
she would bring each of us a bowl of nourishing porridge,

as if we were in a first-class nursing-home and thus we were able slowly to regain our strength.

During this period, after the release from the camps, nearly everyone congregated in Lodz, Poland, in order to search for survivors and for news of their families. Many women from our village also went, and a few even managed some business transactions. One day one of the ladies came running to me and told me the following story: she was on the way back from Lodz, and at the station where she had to change trains she met a group of women. One of them approached her and asked what town she was from and what camp she had been in. The woman replied that she was with a group who had been in Estonian camps and were presently in Strelentin. The lady with the questions asked whether she had come across a woman by the name of Golda Gordonovitch. "Yes," my friend answered, "we have been together all the time." The stranger was very happy and said that her name was Marianna and she was the sister-in-law of Fania, Golda's sister. They had been together in the Kaiserwald camp and were now in the town of Slopeck, and she gave my friend their address.

It is impossible to describe the feelings that swept over me when I heard this news. It was unbelievable. When I calmed down I began to consider how I could possibly get to Slopeck. I approached the head of the village, a Pole, and told him the story, adding that I must get to Slopeck as quickly as possible. He arranged for someone to take me to the train, which in turn brought me to the town, where I was reunited with my sister and her sister-in-law in a very emotional meeting. We talked for hours and hours, each of us telling her experiences, a collection of very sad stories.

Later on I found my brother Isaac who had survived Dachau, and then the three of us remained together. Many others joined up with us and we became a group of one hundred survivors. We organized a committee that provided many activities – cultural, sport and health, aliya and preparation for army service. I worked in the UNWRA offices as a secretary, and my brother as a bookkeeper until December '48 when we made aliya in the ship "Negba," and arrived at our final destination and safe haven. My sister Fania and her husband Ya'akov had left in February 1947 in an illegal attempt, but upon reaching Haifa they were taken by the British to Cyprus where they remained, in tents, for fourteen months. They arrived in Israel in February 1948.

N.B. Golda passed away on June 16, 1993.

Bruce Kahn

The contact that was established with Bruce Kahn in 1991 grew into a close friendship. He visited my family in Jerusalem on several occasions and he shared a common interest in genealogy, computers, and photography with my brother Alec. He visited Alec in London, and in 1995 they traveled together to Lithuania to meet a newly-found relative in Vilna of whom I will write later. They attended genealogy conferences, and Bruce managed to gain access to city archives in Lithuania and Riga before such access became a lucrative profession for the local populace. Alec also visited him in Rochester, N.Y. one year, and took the opportunity to meet his parents, Carrie and Joe Kahn in St. Paul, Minnesota.

When my daughter Varda spent a year at Harvard in

From left to right: Bruce Kahn, Yosef Shapiro, Alec Shapiro. Vilna 1995

2000, I visited her to attend the graduation ceremony. Bruce and his wife Amy came from Rochester and we spent a very pleasant evening altogether. They now have two children. In 1995, on the fiftieth anniversary of the end of World War II, my husband, who had served in the American army, was invited to Maastricht for a reunion

Rosalia Shluper Kahn, daughter of Nehama, with daughter-in-law and grandchildren Joseph, James and Sylvia. C. 1942. Courtesy Bruce Kahn

of his unit. (Old Hickory), which had liberated the city. Bruce's brother Robert, who is based in Europe, came to meet us and make our acquaintance. He subsequently married Cecile Lardry of Paris. I was unable to attend the wedding, but my brother and sister-in-law did. They now live in Geneva and we maintain e-mail correspondence and share greetings for holidays and announcements of new offspring of which they now have two.

Incidentally, the excitement caused by the discovery that Bruce's grandfather Kahn had been born in Riga and

The grave of Rosalie (Rasha) Shluper Kahn, Belle Plain, Minn. U.S.A.

might be a relative of my husband, led to nothing since Bruce revealed that Kahn was not the original family name but he did not know what was.

Recently (February 2003) my brother's attention was directed to an entry in Otzar haRabbanim, 1904, concerning a committee of Lithuanian rabbis who in 1900 drew up the *Takkanot,* or procedural rules, for the ordaining of rabbis. R. Yosef Shluper, Bruce's great-grandfather, served on this committee. These *Takkanot* had to be presented to the Russian Government for approval and presumably to

291

help them in their selection of Crown rabbis, who were also known as Rav MeTa'am (the rabbi on behalf of the government) and held the title 'Rabiner." These *Takkanot* show how careful the rabbis were in their selection of the committees, in order to achieve objectivity and avoid favoritism.

Yosef Shapiro (Josifas Sapiro), Vilna

After the publication of the first edition of my book, I noticed an advertisement in the paper by the Slonimer Landsmanshaft, Irgun Olei Slonim b'Yisrael in Tel Aviv about a video they had produced concerning the events in Slonim during the Second World War. I was interested in seeing this video and I contacted Mr. Zvi Shefet, the chairman, to make inquiries. He in turn wanted to know who I was and why I was interested in Slonim. After I told him about my connection to Reb Aisel and that I had written a book about him, he was very cooperative, acquired several copies, and publicized my book in the organization's journal. In the summer of 1994, some of the members made a visit to Slonim. Unfortunately I wasn't able to participate because of my husband's poor health. After their return in August, Mr. Shefet wrote to me that the group had also visited Vilna where he discovered a gentleman in the Jewish Museum by the name of Yosifas Sapiro, who claimed to be a descendent of Reb Aisel Harif. He was very surprised when Mr. Shefet told him that there was a branch of the family in Israel and that a book had been written about R. Aisel. I soon received a letter from Yosef and it turned out that he was indeed a grandson of Yehiel Yosef, third son of R. Moshe of Riga and therefore a great-great-grandson of R. Aisel, the same relationship as myself. My brother and I had presumed that there were no survivors of this family, as previously mentioned, and were happy with this discovery, as was Yosef, and so both our families expanded a little.

In the first letter, which Yosef wrote to me in September 1994, written in Russian and translated by my husband, he told me what he remembered of his family. He recalled that his father Izak/Isaac spoke much about the family background, about his great-grandfather R. Moshe (haRav haGaon HaGadol HaMefursam) and about R. Aisel Harif. I smiled upon seeing that in spite of the long years under Communism, Yosef still remembered the traditional rabbinic phraseology, and even wrote a Hebrew word here and there. He also knew a little of Jewish history. There had been many documents and religious tomes in the home, he wrote, in Hebrew and in Yiddish, and in one of them a record had been kept of those generations that had passed on. Of course nothing remained of those after the German occupation.

Izak, born in 1895, grew up in the Vekshne (Vicksniai) district of Shavli (Siauliai), in the town where his grandfather Moshe had served as rabbi, and where his grandmother's family, the Yaffes, originated. Yosef remembered there had been contact with members of this family. He also mentioned that his father, amongst many other activities, had been a writer.

It was noted in the Riga city records, which Bruce Kahn had procured, that in December 1908 there were some male Shapiros living in R. Moshe's apartment whom I had not been able to identify with certainty. Laser-Idel (Yidel or Yudel) Josselev, born in December 1890 and citizen of Vekshne, came there in 1908 and was due to be called up to the army in October 1910, but left earlier for an unknown destination. In these same records, it was interesting to note that R. Shabtai Aharon had come from Shavli to visit his sick father in May 1909 and stayed there ten days. It was also noted that in 1914 a Shapira named Yisrael-Natan had come from Vekshne with his wife Esther, a photographer. Was this the son of Yisrael who had been disowned by R. Moshe or perhaps a descendant? Was Esther the second daughter of R. Shabtai Aharon, a cousin, or a member of the extended Shapiro family? It seems that this apartment, number 7, at 141 Romanov Street (now called Lachpleshe St.), was used by the family over an extended period, even till the 1930's, when R. Avin, son-in-law of R. Moshe, and his successor, lived there.

Izak left Riga in 1909, preferring to enroll in the Military Academy in Lithuania where he graduated before the beginning of the First World War. He was drafted into the Russian army and in the summer of 1915 was taken prisoner by the Germans. Because he could speak many languages, he worked as a translator in the camp and had much freedom of movement. He and his fellow prisoners made two attempts at escaping. The first attempt ended tragically — the Germans caught the prisoners, lined them up and shot every tenth man. The second attempted escape took place in September 1917 on the eve of Yom Kippur. After they plied the guards with liquor, the group escaped and crossed the Nemunas River into Lithuania.

On November 23, 1918, the Lithuanian Government issued a proclamation urging Lithuanian nationals to join

volunteer regiments in order to defend the country's independence. On that day Izak, whom Yosef refers to as Papa,
being a great nationalist, joined the ranks of the volunteers
and worked actively to promote the volunteer regiments.
I have a copy of a Yiddish article he wrote on this subject
in a paper called *Der Schild* (The Shield). In the Lithuanian
State Archives, there is a document which declares that in
early 1919 there were over 500 Jewish volunteers in the
Lithuanian Army. Conscription was announced only in
March 1919. In 1923, Izak was discharged from the army
and settled in Yonishkis (Joniskis), a town 40 km. north
of Shavli and 10 km. from the Latvian border. In 1930 he
began to realize an ambition to organize a Jewish Fighter's
Union and in June 1933 it was officially registered. Izak
was elected chairman, a position he held until August 1940
when the Union was of course disbanded. In 1993, the
sixtieth anniversary of the founding of the Union of the
Jewish Soldiers who fought in the battle for independence
was celebrated.

Izak was much decorated for his war service. In later
years he was very active in the Jewish ex-soldiers association and published their journal *Frontkampfer* (Front-Line
Fighters). After a prolonged break in their relations, Izak
visited his mother in Riga after the war, in about 1922-23.
His father, R. Yehiel Yosef, had passed away in 1912 and
his mother, subsequently, married Meir Kissin of Riga, a
bank manager.

After Lithuania achieved independence in 1918, the
Jews were granted autonomy, and a committee of nine that
included Izak, ran the community affairs. It is interesting to
note the election results, which gave the Zionist party 323

votes against 91 for the religious and 4 for the Democrats. In municipal elections in 1934, Izak and another Jew named Pinsker were elected together with the other seven Lithuanians. Izak also served later as vice-mayor. When the Germans arrived in 1941, he was amongst the first to be arrested and hung.

Eventually my brother and Bruce visited Vilna in 1995. When they visited Yosef's museum, they saw the special display Yosef had set up dedicated to the memory of his father and the other Jewish soldiers of the Lithuanian army.

In March 1996, my brother invited Yosef to London and my husband and I made the trip to meet him. We found a tall, good-looking man who had been a captain in the Russian army and was still suffering from shrapnel in his legs. He and I had to speak Yiddish, but my husband was able to converse with him in Russian. Incidentally, our correspondence is also carried out in Yiddish and we actually manage to understand each other although I have never learned to write it. At that first meeting, we were surprised at Yosef's height, knowing as we did that R. Aisel had been slight in stature, and we had seen that those genes are still active in some branches of the family.

Yosef was born in Kovna (Kaunas) and grew up in Yonishkis. In 1932, at the age of twelve, he was sent to study in Shavli where he had cousins, the Kolpanitzky family. He then went on to Kovna and came to Vilna in 1938 and entered the Military Academy. He served in the Soviet army in the Lithuanian Division and rose to the rank of captain. He was wounded four times and received eighteen decorations. He was at the battle of Stalingrad and also in the campaign that liberated Ukraine and Poland. What would R. Aisel, who fought so strongly against the Russian conscription of Jews, have said of this desire of his descendants to serve in the Russian army?

After the war, Yosef worked as a senior engineer in a printing company and began his career as a "collector." He amassed a very large collection of Jewish ExLibris and established what he claims to be the only museum of its kind, which is part of the Jewish Museum he established in the Jewish Community Center in Vilna. This collection is his pride and joy. He is also very active as a stamp collector, and was at one point chairman of the Philately Society, holding official positions that enabled him to go to international congresses, and to maintain a long list of correspondents, which he can no longer afford to do. He also has an interesting collection of seashells and minerals.

Yosef also has some artistic talent and likes to design ExLibris for his friends and family. He did not have any formal art training but his designs left me wondering what he might have achieved had he had the opportunity to study art, although in the Communist world in which he grew up, this was not an option. Nevertheless, this ability reminded me of the story that R. Moshe had had a son Yisrael who became a painter, and was disowned by his father. It seems that there is an artistic streak in the family, as I learned that his sister Ella had been musically gifted and loved to sing. Her hobby, I later found out, was compiling an encyclopedia on music. As for my own descendants, in the families of each of my children there is at least one child with a marked artistic bent.

A grandson of Yosef, Eugene, came to Jerusalem on a

student program for teenagers (Na'aleh) in 1994. We met several times, but after his graduation we lost contact. It is possible that he returned to Vilna.

Yosef's connection with the Community Center proved to be a vital element in our family research since many Jews from all over the world visited the Jewish Center in Vilna and he was only too happy to discuss his *yichus* with them and to reveal his family connections. That was how we had discovered him and how later on we also discovered the Krinsky family, the "missing" descendants of R. Aisel's daughter Nehama. Today Yosef lives mainly on his military pension and both he and his wife are beset by ill health. He still undergoes operations for the removal of shrapnel from his legs. Unfortunately, I have not yet had the opportunity of visiting them, but hope to do so this summer.

Ella Shapira Eisman

In his first letter to me in September 1994, Yosef mentioned he had a sister in Tel Aviv, Ella Eisman, but he had not heard from her for seven years. He gave me her address and phone number and asked me to get in touch with her and let him know how she was. This was rather surprising to me, as I would have thought a brother and sister who had survived the Shoah would maintain close contact. He felt that Ella would remember more about the family than he, since she remained at home whereas he had left at an early age. I then got in touch with Fania Rolnitzky and told her about my letter from Yosef. This news awakened a flood of memories in her and also confirmed the fact that Yosef had a sister living in Tel Aviv with whom she was in occasional contact. There had been close contact between all the Shapira families in Lithuania before 1939, and later on they were even together in the Vilna ghetto. Ella had come to Israel in the early 1950s. She was divorced and had no children, and was in a rather unhappy situation. I couldn't help wondering how Fania had overlooked this fact in all our talks and meetings, but I presumed that there was probably some 'unfinished business' between the cousins. This incident also warned me that one could not rely completely on people's memories or intentions, and I found also on other occasions that it was very difficult to establish the exact sequence or reality of events that occurred during the war period. It was also disappointing to find errors and factual mistakes in some of the reference books that I used, which fortunately I could detect because of my own knowledge, but which will confuse others.

I haven't mentioned that my father discovered his relatives Fania Rolnitzky and her sister Golda Gordonovitz when they attended the memorial evening for Reb Aisel that he arranged in 1973. Or perhaps more correctly, they discovered him, because, having come out of curiosity to find out who was the Shapiro who had initiated the evening, they introduced themselves to this unknown relative. They maintained contact till my father passed away in November 1979.

I telephoned Ella and made an appointment to visit her in her apartment in Herzliya. It was December 26, 1994. She was very excited at my arrival and about my book, which I had of course already sent her. It was obvious that she had been an extremely beautiful woman, but was now very lonely and sad concerning her personal situation. She told me what she remembered about her family. Her father Izak had studied medicine in Riga, and on a visit to his Kolpanitzky cousins in Vilna, he met and fell in love with Malka (Manya) Lieder. However, since his mother did not approve of this marriage, he left Riga and he and Malka settled in Yonishkis, near Shavli. By 1940, the population of the town had increased from 23,000 in 1914, to 31,641, but the Jewish population decreased from 10,000 to 6,600, largely because of emigration, the majority making aliya. Izak's brother Ilya, who was an engineer and named for his maternal grandfather Eliahu, left Riga for Leningrad and married there, but there were no children from this marriage. Yosef told me that this uncle came once to visit him in Vilna in 1964, but he never heard from him again.

Ella told me she was in fact also named after this same grandfather. Both sons were not on good terms with their mother Fira and many years elapsed before there was another meeting between them. Ella herself had been on good terms with this aristocratic grandmother and often visited her in Riga, which was only a few kilometers away across the border, but she told me that Yosef also had not been on friendly terms with her because as a youth he had been a fervent communist and was critical of her capitalistic lifestyle.

Izak left medicine and became a pharmacist. He later became an inspector of pharmacies and apparently at some stage visited the pharmacy of his relatives the Krynskis in Nowygrodek. He also pursued other occupations, among them writing, bookkeeping and local politics. He was a member of the Municipality and at one stage served as vice-mayor. Ella spoke of her father as being a member of parliament, adviser on Jewish affairs to the then President, and also his speechwriter, but this I was unable to verify. Like Yosef, she remembered the books and *seforim* that had been in her home; she knew all about R. Moshe of Riga, but was not aware of the connection to R. Aisel. Ella spoke of Izak as being an astute and wise person whose advice was sought by many.

In the years 1937–38 many Jewish refugees from various countries passed through Yonishkis, which was close to the border. Izak used to go out at night to bring false passports to the refugees and Ella recalled that many such strangers stayed with them for a day or so on their journeys. Her mother busied herself with charitable activities, and Ella's duty was to assist in distributing food to elderly people for Shabbat. The family, however, who was observant only to a minor degree, was not Zionist-oriented and did not consider aliya. Even when Yosef, who had entered the military academy in Vilna, warned his father that war was imminent, Izak did not want to leave, saying "whatever will be, will be." Perhaps he felt his position in public life protected him.

In 1940 Lithuania became a Soviet Republic and the Lithuanian nationalists, traditionally anti-semitic, began their harassment of the Jews. When the Germans came in June 1941 they deligated to them the task of dealing with the "Jewish problem," which the Lithuanians did with great enthusiasm. Izak was one of the first group arrested by the Nazis and was publicly hanged.

Ella told me there had been very close relations with her cousins the Kolpanitzkys, especially with the cousin by marriage, Tanya, wife of Isaac K. who lived in Shavli. At some point Ella lived with them when she was sent to the Jewish Gymnasium there, but her homesickness got the better of her and she returned to her parents in Yonishkis. There was also the family of Shabtai Aharon, R. Moshe's oldest son, who was the highly respected rabbi of Gorzhd (Gruzd, Gruszdziai) and who had four daughters. The Gorzhd Yizkor Book mentions that R. Shabtai was treated with great respect even by the Lithuanians. If they met him walking in 'The Garden' on Shabbat afternoon, the only park in the town, they greeted him very politely. The Jewish community in Gorzhd was very devout and the synagogue and many *'klois'* (prayer-halls) were always full on the Sabbath and Holydays. There was also a Talmud Tora, a yeshiva and Beit Midrash with a large library. Festive religious occasions, such as a *siyyum* of the 'Shas,' were celebrated with lavish banquets.

Even before the Germans came, the Lithuanians were extremely anti-semitic and committed acts of great atrocity. When their household was confiscated, Ella fought to keep her piano, but was told that since they were being moved to the ghetto she would not need it. She told me that they had previously given some of their valuables to their friendly postman who promised to return them after the war. When hunger set in in the ghetto, Ella was able to meet with the postman to procure money and food, but the second time she did this he betrayed her and she was taken by the Lithuanian SS for interrogation. She was released because of her youth, and warned against leaving the ghetto again without permission. Later she was in the Vilna ghetto with her mother and with her cousins Fania and Tanya. Tanya had a son called Moshe who was then a university student, talented in languages and also an achiever in sport. He worked as a translator but was betrayed one day and simply disappeared, not to be heard of again.

On one occasion of an 'action,' Ella escaped detection by hiding in a wardrobe, but when it was announced that the ghetto would be liquidated, she and her mother assembled with the rest of the Jews. During the ensuing march, a German officer, impressed by her Aryan appearance and her unusual blue eyes, plucked Ella from the ranks, asking in surprise how she had gotten there, and she was returned to the ghetto where she was employed in some protected work. Altogether some 80,000 Jews were murdered in Ponar, the killing fields of Vilna. When the ghetto was liquidated, Ella was sent to the Kaiserwald camp. She did not talk much about her experiences, and I did not want to question her too closely as I saw that the whole subject was painful for her, but she told me that after the war she had been briefly married and had come to Paris where she underwent some medical treatment, which left her unable to have children. She came to Israel in the early 1950's and eventually married again, but when I met her she was again divorced.

It is probable that the narrative of this period is not in correct chronological order, but I believe the various incidents to be true.

Our conversation on that first meeting covered a wide range of subjects. She recalled, as did Yosef, that there were many *Seforim* in her home but of course nothing remained and she did not remember exactly what they were. After I gave Ella title pages of R. Aisel's books, which my father had reprinted, and R. Moshe's books which the Kolpanitzky family had reprinted, she had them framed and hung on the wall. She developed a relationship to them as if they were her living family.

I kept in touch with Ella and visited her as often as I could. My daughter Karni and my niece Naomi, the daughter of Alec, both of whom lived nearby in Ra'anana, also took an interest and cared for her as her health began to deteriorate. In 1997, she fell and broke her hip, had an operation, but never made a complete recovery. She spent much time in hospital and passed away at the end of 1999. Sad to say, I never knew why she was never reconciled with her brother Yosef. In spite of her loneliness Ella was not one to compromise.

Isel Krinsky

In September 1997 I received the following letter:

> *Dear Esther,*
>
> *I am presently visiting Vilna, having been to Slonim to see if the tombstones of my grandfather R. Yossele Charif (Szluper) and my great grandfather R. Aisel Charif (Shapiro) were intact. All I found was a monument in Hebrew commemorating the extermination of thirty-five thousand Jews in Slonim and its environs and the wreath from "תושבי סלונים בישראל". The cemetery is now a green field. On my visit to the local Jewish Community Center I met up with your cousin Yosef and he established that our great-grandfathers were brothers. Yosef has*

304

Isel Krinsky

*a complete family genealogical record and he
is giving me copies. He showed me a book in
English published by you with family photos.
I would love to get copies of the book. Let me
know how much I must remit to you in dollars.
Some 20 years ago I got some books in Hebrew
published by Levine in Jersualem.*

אבל העברית שלי לא כל כך.

Many thanks, (Isel) ביידות, אייזל

This letter came as a great surprise. I had learned from
Fania Rolnitzky something about the unhappy life of Hinda
Shluper, who had been abandoned by her husband in the
late twenties, and we had understood that he had taken
his two sons to America. Alec and I had given up hope of
ever tracing them, but now it appeared that the family had

actually gone to South Africa where most of Isel's brother's family still resides. Isel himself was presently living in Canada. I was surprised by the spelling of his name, which varied from my version (Aisel), but perhaps this was due to our differing transliterations of the Yiddish.

In his next letter of October 1997, Isel told me the whole family story under the title:

My Family – Past And Present

> I am the grandson of R. Yossele Charif (wife Nachama) and the great-grandson of R. Isel Charif (wife Chaya) after whom I am named. My mother Hinda, born Shluper (Szluper in Polish), in Slonim around 1876 qualified as a dentist in Tropa University in Warsaw early in the 20th century. She settled and practiced in Nowogrodek (then in Poland or Russia, now in Belarus).
>
> My father Pinchas (Phillip) Krynski (changed the spelling in South Africa) was born in Nowogrodek, I think in 1888, and qualified as a pharmacist in Kiev. He went to the U.S.A. in 1908 and came back after three years. He was the only one in Nowogrodek with a knowledge of English. His parents and nine uncles and aunts went to California in 1913–1923. My father had a pharmacy (Yosef Shapiro mentioned in his first letter that his father Izak had visited this pharmacy in his work as an inspector, and knew that the owners were Shapiro relatives — ER) which he sold, and around 1923 my parents moved to Zhetl where my father bought a pharmacy and

Presumably Nehama Shluper,
daughter of R. Aisel. Courtesy
Isel Krynski

Hinda (Shluper) and Pinchas
Krynski, 1914. Courtesy Isel
Krynski

Yossel and Isel Krynski as
children, 1924. Courtesy Isel
Krynski

my mother practiced as a dentist. My brother Yosel (Joe), named after our grandfather R. Yosele, was born in 1915, and I was born in 1918. In Zhetl we both went to school. I went to the Yiddish Folkshule for a year and then a Cheder for two to three years.

My parents did not get on and about 1926 my father sold or gave up his pharmacy and in 1928 went off to South Africa on his own. My mother, from aggravation, developed a tumor of the brain, sold her practice to an unqualified dental practitioner who paid her a retainer for a while and displayed her diploma on his desk in case an inspector came. Her sister took her to Vienna, but it was too late and she died at a resort between Warsaw and Othock in 1930. After she took ill, my mother had taken me back to Nowogrodek where I stayed with relatives and my brother went to live with an aunt in Warsaw. We both came to South Africa in January 1932. Life in South Africa was very hard. My father lost his job at the end of 1931 and in the first year we moved eight times, usually at night, as we could not pay the rent. Eventually I qualified and practiced as a chartered accountant, BCOMM.

I have two sons, Hilton in Vancouver and Julian in Pennsylvania. My brother Joe died in 1990 and his wife Sheila and four children live in South Africa and one in Israel. Both my brother and I lived for a few years in Israel at different times. Isel

Hinda (top, right) and graduates,
early 20th century

A book from Hinda Shluper
Krynski's library with her stamp

We began to correspond and in 1998 Isel came to visit. We had long talks about the family and he told me he had collections of all the books written by his grandfather and great-grandfather, some of which he had bought in Jerusalem during the '70s and which he had put on exhibition in the synagogue that he attended. He remembered that his mother had copies of R. Shluper's book מרכבת יוסף. He thus had a very strong identification with the family (great-grandson, one generation ahead of me) and was more aware of his background than other relatives I had met. He was the only one that I was aware of who actually carried R. Isel's name, though I once had a letter from an ex-Slonimer who was also named Aisel although he was not a relative. I know my father had a brother who was called Isaac, or Aisek, but Isel was called Isel. He was a man of many interest and hobbies, but his difficult and unhappy childhood had left its mark.

I was quite upset when he told me that he had been in Israel in the '70s, but apparently had not had the time or the means to look for any family. My parents were alive at that time and my father would have been overjoyed to meet any relatives, since his own large immediate family were victims of the Shoah.

In a subsequent biographical article-letter Isel told me more about his past:

> The first time I came to Vilna was in 1924/25 when I was six or seven years old when my family was living in Szetl (Zdienciol) and my mother brought me to see Dr. Kawarski, the child specialist... As for my uncle Modechai, known as Mottl, my mother's brother, I visited Slonim once as a child and seem to remember him joining us for a holiday in Nowojelna and the Pine Forests.
>
> I next visited Vilna some two-and-a-half years

ago when my son Julian was keen to see his 'roots.' Before coming to Vilna we went from Warsaw to Krakow and Oswiecim (Auschwitz) and saw the crematorium and other devices.

My visit in Navaredok (Nowogrodek), where I was born, was disappointing. I thought I would be able to show my son where I had lived with my cousin Leah Berlinerblau, in Ulica Mickiewicza 8, where I went to school ... nothing of the sort. Fifty years of Russian domination saw the complete elimination of homes, as I knew them, of all businesses around the marketplace, no hotels, no restaurants, no places of Jewish interest. The only places of interest were the home where Adam Mickiewicz [the Polish poet] had lived which is now a museum, and the historically famous ruins on a hill outside of town. On our way out we stopped at a small three-cornered monument erected by a Jack Kagan of London, inscribed in Hebrew, Russian and English, commemorating the extermination and burial of 5,500 Jews of Nowogrodek and two adjoining villages. At that spot I stood on the soil where my two cousins Leah and Miriam, both chemists, were buried.

It had always been my intention to visit Slonim, now in Belarus, where my mother was born, and to find the tombstones of Reb Isel Harif, my great-grandfather after whom I am named, and Reb Yosel Harif, my Grandfather, after whom my late brother was named, both famous Rabbis in their day. I found the entrance gate to the cemetery in a state of disrepair. What was once the cemetery is now a green field, but alongside a few tombstones dated 1941–1943, stands a concrete monument with an inscription in Hebrew commemorating the extermination of 35,000 of our brethren from Slonim and its environs. It was graced with a beautiful wreath of artificial flowers from the association of Ex-Slonim residents living in Israel. (However, the synagogue still stands on its original site, empty, one of the main buildings in the town. It is one of the few large synagogues in Belarus not converted to other purposes, but is in very bad condition. The Slonimer Society in Israel has funded the repair of the roof, but cannot undertake the large-scale repair necessary. They are hoping some 'angel' will come to its rescue — ER).

When I came to the Communty Center looking for more envelopes, possibly First Day Covers commemorating the anniversary of the death of the Vilna Gaon, I met Yosef Shapiro, who seemed to have infinite energy and unlimited interests and hobbies. In no time he produced a genealogical record of the Shapiro family and he gave me copies of the photos of Reb Yosel Szluper, my mother's father, and Moshe Shapiro, the son of Reb Isel Harif. He, R. Moshe, became the Chief Rabbi of Riga. Yosef also gave me copies of the seforim (Talmudic

Works) of Reb Isel Harif which were reprinted in Jerusalem and I in turn promised to let him have photocopies of the original seforim printed from 1840 onwards in Vilna and Warsaw which I managed to acquire in Jerusalem, Tel Aviv, and New York over a number of years. I have already written to Esther Rafaeli, Yosef's fourth cousin in Jerusalem for the book she published in English and Hebrew about Reb Aisel Harif Shapira, and to Esther's brother Alec Shapiro in London.

Isel subsequently sent me old photos of his family and it seemed to me that I could detect a resemblance between his mother Hinda and her cousin Pauline Shapiro Stavisky, who lived in New York.

After leaving Jerusalem, Isel met with my brother in London. Some time after his return to Canada he was taken ill and suffered a number of minor strokes. His health began to deteriorate and his sons found it necessary to place him in a nursing home. He died in 2001. In the meantime my brother has visited Julian in Philadelphia where he is involved in sport education and summer camps and we both keep in contact with him. I also met with Isel's niece in Tel Aviv, Ruth Cohen, and she contacts me whenever she is in Jerusalem.

My brother's attention was recently brought to some letters which appeared in the Slonim Yizkor Book, vol. 4, published in 1977. It seems there was a family by the name of Limon who lived next door to the Shlupers. The two daughters Miriam and Hinda were inseparable during their early and adolescent years, and enjoyed studying and discussing literature and poetry, as well as Torah studies. Apparently, Hinda was highly educated in secular as well as religious subjects, although I cannot imagine that R. Shluper was an active supporter of the Haskalah. Miriam's father on the other hand, admired the Haskalah but was not sure about advanced education for women. Still, he was persuaded by the example of Hinda, daughter of the leading rabbi of Slonim, to give his own daughter equal opportunity with his sons, and they all studied together with a private tutor, at home. Miriam was extremely talented, and with her literary knowledge and elegant style soon became known as a woman author. She wrote articles and stories in fluent literary Hebrew, which appeared in the newspapers *Ha-Tzfirah* and *Ha-Magid* in the late 1890's. Professionally she used the name Mirka Limon. She married Dr. Isaak Wernikovsky of Slonim in 1897, when he was twenty-one and she a little younger. The name Wernikovsky has already been mentioned in connection with the Slonim Yeshiva, so this young man may have been the son of the noted scholar. They immigrated in the early years of the 20th century to America, where her husband, now Dr. Werne, writer and educator, became the Chief Orthodox Rabbi of the congregation in Los Angeles. Amongst his papers, which were brought to light some 40 years later, there is a letter in Hebrew in which Miriam asks a mutual friend for information about the whereabouts of Hinda's sister Rasche, whom she knew to be in Minneapolis with her son Shmuel, and for information about the whereabouts of her girlhood friend Hinda Shluper (she refers to her as Hindka), who was her neighbor in Slonim. Miriam knew that Hinda had married a pharmacist, and thought she had emigrated to America, but the contact between the two friends had gradually weakened and finally ceased, and Miriam was now asking for information about her whereabouts. This letter appears to have been written in Los Angeles in 1914, and although Miriam passed away in 1920, her husband kept it amongst his papers, which were found in the 1970s. They have been researched by Naomi Jacobs, a direct descendant of Miriam (Mary) Limon Werne.

The Decendants Of Pauline Shapiro Stavisky

My book generated much interest among the extended family in the U.S. and in this way I was able to meet many of them when they visited Israel. I was also in touch with other relatives who were not in the habit of coming to visit. Ruth Picker, a granddaughter of Pauline Stavisky, and her husband Martin made yearly visits to Oxford because of his work as a musicologist, and they became friendly with my brother and sister-in-law in London. Geography plays a very important role in keeping up family connections.

I would like to recount a little of my meeting with Pauline Stavisky. I had always known about her existence because my father knew her still in Poland before her family went to America at the beginning of the twentieth century, and he occasionally spoke about her. I have already told how my father and Pauline met in Palestine in 1925 and I met her personally in the early fifties. In 1952, my brother went to the States for business purposes and on that occasion drove from Nashville, Tennessee down to St. Petersburg, Florida to meet with Pauline and Sam Stavisky. It was also during this visit that while pottering around the Lower

East Side, my brother found a copy of *Emek Yehoshua,* which Pauline's father had published in 1926. Pauline and Sam visited Israel many times, and I remember the occasion when she phoned me from Paris and told me that they were coming for dinner on Friday night … she would bring some kosher meat with her from Paris (this was the period of extreme austerity in Israel). And so she did. She brought the meat, I cooked it, and we had a delicious dinner.

Pauline's memory is kept alive and meaningful in her family partly because of a small purchase that she once made in Europe. Shortly after World War I ended, the Staviskys sailed to Europe, which was suffering from the devastation of the war and from a severe winter. They were approached in their hotel in Brussels by a man who wanted to sell a lace veil. He explained that the veil had been made by nuns living in a convent nearby who were desperately in need of money. Although Pauline's oldest daughter Fritzie (Feige Devorah) was barely in her teens, Pauline prevailed on her husband to purchase the veil, which was handmade in Rose Point lace, a popular style at the time, and which is now considered museum quality. Fritzie was the first to wear the veil in December 1926 when she married Herman Gottesman and Martha wore it in May 1928 when she married Gerson Bernstein. After Pauline passed away, the veil was found in her closet carefully wrapped in tissue paper, waiting for the next bride.

As of June 2000, four generations of Pauline and Samuel's daughters, granddaughters, great-granddaughters, and two great-great-granddaughters have worn the veil. And so the family maintains the original stipulation that the veil should remain in the family and be used at their weddings. The veil is presently in the keeping of Ann Schapiro and has undergone a preservation process. I suggested to her that this whole subject would make a beautiful family album, but the idea has not yet come to fruition.

I had close connections with Fritzie and with Martha. They came to Israel often and my husband and I saw them whenever we were in New York and Florida. Martha surprised her family by going to college and earning her B.A. degree when she was in her eighties. She and Fritzie celebrated that by making a special visit to Jerusalem.

Martha's family has distinguished itself in that the families of two of her daughters, Ann Schapiro and Ruth Levitz, have made aliya.

Gerson Schapiro

In 1988 Martha informed me that her grandson Gerson was coming to Israel to serve in the army, as he intended eventually to make aliya and wanted to have his army service behind him. During this period Ann and her husband Tobi (Tuvia), and Martha visited him several times. After eighteen months he returned to New York to gain more business experience, and to marry his wife Mindy Leibowitz. In October 1993 they made aliya with their daughter Zehava who was then ten months old. They have since added three more children to their family, Yehoshua, Eitan and Amihai. Mindy's parents also live here, and Gerson's parents visit at least twice a year.

Ann's sister Ruth, the youngest of Martha's five daughters, is married to Phil Levitz. Their older daughter, Cynthia, her Iranian-born husband Yitzhak Rahmani, and their five sons made aliya in June 1997. The younger daughter Shoshana married Steven Arnold and made aliya with their first son in October 1997. The parents, Ruth and Philip, after years of careful planning and execution, which I found most impressive, made aliya in July 2002 directly to their own fully-furnished home. Their son, Gerson made aliya with his wife Michelle and three children, in June 2003, also according to plan.

I understand that other members of the younger generation, whom I have not yet met, are also living in Israel. Shalva, daughter of Michael and Toby (Tova) Gottesman, granddaughter of Fritzie Gottesman, made aliya with her husband Yaacov ben David in 1988, and has four children. Mindie, daughter of Edith Schimmel and granddaughter of Mordecai Stavisky, made aliya in 1991. She is married to Benjamin Wurzburger and has a little girl. Her cousin Karen, daughter of Miriam Rich, granddaughter of Mordecai Stavisky, is married to Howie (Hanina) Schifmiller. They made aliya in 1992 and have six children. All the people mentioned in this chapter are descendants of Pauline (Shapiro) and Sam Stavisky. I find some poetic justice in the fact that Mordecai, the short-lived son of Reb Aisel who fathered only one child, now has the most flourishing branch of the family to his credit. What if his son Avraham had not emigrated to America? That branch of the family would not have come into existence, or would have disappeared with the other victims of the Shoah.

Fruma Schiffenbauer

In the summer of 1990, a wedding in the family of the relatives in Florida touched off an exciting development. A great-granddaughter of Martha's, the granddaughter of her oldest daughter, Adele Turoff, was getting married, and during the ceremony the rabbi spoke, amongst other matters, of the *yichus* of the family, their being descendants of the illustrious Reb Aisel Harif through his third son Mordecai. After the ceremony a very excited woman, a guest of the groom's from out of town, approached the mother of the bride and asked about this reference to Reb Aisel. After the matter was verified she exclaimed "but I am also a descendant of Reb Aisel! And my mother always supposed that we were the only surviving members of the family!"

After the excitement caused by this statement subsided, the woman told her story. Her name was Fruma and she was married to Milton Schiffenbauer of New York, but she had grown up in Seattle to which her parents emigrated from Europe after World War II. Her mother Fania was the youngest of the four daughters of R. Shabtai Aharon, of whom I have already written. His wife's name was Fruma Lifshitz. During Fania's childhood and youth the family had been very friendly with their cousins in Vilna, the Kolpanitsky family, and for the first years of the war, they were all in the Vilna ghetto, together with Ella Eisman, who I have already mentioned.

Ella and her two cousins named Fania were together at first but eventually Fania Kolpanitsky and Ella were sent to the Kaiserwald camp near Riga, and Fania Shapira was sent to other camps and eventually on a Death March of which she was one of the few survivors. After the war she went to Lodz, like many other survivors, to look for relatives, and she had one meeting with Fania Rolnitsky. I had quite forgotten that Fania mentioned this to me at our first meeting, but at that time she had no other information about her cousin and did not know if she was alive. However, Fania S. met a man by the name of Hersch Potok from Tartakow, Galicia, and after they married they moved to Badgastein, a DP Camp in Austria situated in the American Zone, where they lived for several years. She was presumed dead by her relatives and she similarly thought that no one else of her family had survived. In 1946 she gave birth to her daughter Fruma, and in 1949 Potok's family brought them over to the States where they settled in Seattle. In 1956 information was imparted to Paula Ben Gurion, wife of the then Prime Minister, about a solitary woman who had survived the camps in Estonia and was in a desperate situation. This woman turned out to be Esther, Fania's older sister. Fania was traced and contact was established between them and with the subsequent intervention of Senator 'Scoop' Jackson, she was brought over to Seattle. Esther died in 1972 of T.B., having spent her last years in a sanitorium.

In 1964 Fruma went to study in New York and eventually met and married her husband, Milton Schiffenbauer. Since the revelation of the family ties at the Florida wedding, Fruma has been in touch with her relatives in NY and has visited Israel twice, giving us the opportunity to get better acquainted, to exchange information about family history, and to clarify or verify what happened to the families during the war. Besides the above information, she also told me that she and her mother had paid several visits to Israel over the years, always trying to find out whether there might be some surviving relatives living here, but were never successful in locating those who were indeed in the country. What a rejoicing there would have been if the cousins who were so friendly in their youth would have succeeded in reuniting, fifty years on. As it was, Fruma did talk to Ella Eisman by phone on her visit in 1998, although they did not actually meet, and on her second visit, she met with Fania Rolnitsky (Kolpanitsky), now at 85 the only surviving member of that family.

Fruma's mother passed away in Seattle in 1979, and after her father's death four years ago, both parents were brought to burial in Israel, where there is also family from Mr. Potok's side, the Genauers. Fruma tries to come every year to visit their graves but sometimes other matters take precedence. She is also actively looking into her immediate family history and has visited the town of Badgastein where she was born, and has seen the house where the family lived. She even managed to get copies of her birth certificate from the local authorities. In the meantime, she has visited Slonim, Vilna, and Gorzhd. Even though she was aware that there was nothing Jewish to see in Gorzhd, she wanted to see the place where her grandfather had served as rabbi, and where her mother grew up in what she was always told were extremely comfortable and elegant surroundings.

The Schiffenbauers have three children. BenZion, the oldest, was born in June 1970. He is the rabbi of a large congregation in Flatbush, Brooklyn and teaches at Yeshiva Torah veDa'as, where he took his *smicha*, and in the Ma'alot Seminary for Girls. He is married to Chanie Schwartz, a teacher, and they have four children. Haya Rivka was born in 1971. A C.P.A. by profession, she is married to Lieby Gutman who has *smicha* from the Mir Yeshiva and is a director of a nursing home. They have six children including a pair of twins. Shabsie (Shabtai) Aron was born in 1974 and is a computer operator. He is married to Tzippie Ostrich, a speech therapist and they have three children.

In Conclusion

In spite of all the new material I was able to include in this chapter, the number of books I examined, and my brother's extensive genealogical research, I did not succeed in finding answers to all my questions. However, we have to take into consideration that many records, both Jewish and governmental, have been unavailable because the area about which I have written was a disputed region for centuries and therefore may have been destroyed in wars or been lost. As I was anxious to complete and publish this book, I decided to forego the possibility of new data from this direction.

One major question, however, has remained obstinately unanswered. For fifteen years my brother and I have tried to discover why there is no mention of the father of R. Mordecai, Aisel's grandfather. Mordecai is never referred to as 'ben ...' (son of ...) and so we have been unable to establish his direct paternal antecedents. There could be many possible explanations and suppositions to indulge in, such as fire damage or loss of records, family rivalry or feuds, incomplete records, and so on, but without real proof or evidence, such musings remain just musings. In the preface to their published works, Reb Aisel and his sons refer only to the lineage of Mordecai's wife, the Heilprin family, as the family tree. No mention is made of R. Aryeh Leib Shapira, 'Aryeh haKatan' (1701–1761), a great

Alec and I with our parents, Frema and Ze'ev Shapiro, 1973

scholar in religious and secular subjects whose daughter married R. Moshe Heilprin. Aryeh Leib himself was married to the daughter of Mordecai ben Azriel whose two sons were great grammarians and well known teachers in Germany and Europe. Perhaps our Mordecai was a lesser descendant of his. Or it could be possible that Mordecai's father is a descendant of Nathan Nata Shapira (Megaleh Amukot, 17th century) and had been a victim of rabbinical sectarianism; perhaps there had been a connection to the Shabtai Tzvi debacle in the previous century, which caused him to be dishonored. There are many cases of Jewish philosophers and rabbis who were ostracized because of their ideas, and their books were even burned, as we can see in the conflict between Mitnagdim and Hassidim.

Nathan Nata, who died in 1633, had three sons, and four daughters who are not recorded, so it is possible to follow the ramifications of the family. Aryeh haKatan did have a brother by the name of Nathan, but is this enough evidence for a connection between the two families? We also consulted with Paul Jacoby z'l, the genealogist, who supported the idea that there could have been a connection to the family of R. Nathan Nata Shapira, but he also did not find definite proof. Yet we know that Mordecai was a rabbi and Av Beit Din in Glussk, which was then a sizeable little town in the Ukraine, and was a respected citizen of Vilna who moved in the circle of the Vilna Gaon. Whatever the reason, in spite of the time and effort we devoted to this problem, we have not succeeded in finding a definite answer to the question: 'Who was R. Mordecai's father?'

One interesting piece of information I discovered in my searches was that R. Nathan Nata Shapira was one of the first exiles from Speyer to bear this name. This Jewish community began early in the twelfth century and developed gradually into an important economic and religious center under the patronage of the local Bishop Rudiger. Nevertheless, over the years there were pogroms and mass expulsions and the community declined. It seems that many of those who left took on the name of the town in some form or another — Spero, Spier, Shpira, Shapira, Shapiro — a common means of identification in Jewish social history. This could account for the widespread use of the name and for the fact that not all Shapiras or Shapiros are related.

July 2004

I have returned from my long-awaited 'pilgrimage' to Slonim, which I made in the company of a group of ex-Slonimer under the auspices of the Association of Slonimer living in Israel. Of course we visited other cities as well — Minsk and Grodno in Belarus, Vilna and Kovna in Lithuania, but for our group the main focus was on Slonim. Most of the twenty-five participants had been born there, were second or third generation, if not more, and had spent many years in Slonim before leaving in good time for Palestine, at the last minute by train to Russia and Siberia, or eventually caught up by the war. There was one family group of eight, first cousins and their spouses, and a second group of six, two brothers — one with his wife and two daughters, and the other with a daughter. Another of our travelers had been left by her mother at the church door in 1941, when she was 10 months old, after her father had already been murdered. Fortunately her identity was known and she was placed in the orphanage until she was discovered towards the end of the war by an uncle serving in the Red Army. He took her to an orphanage in Warsaw, since he was not in a position to care for her himself, and subsequently she spent some years at school in Israel and was then brought to America by another relative. Over the years she had maintained contact with the woman who had found and cared for her, and now she was coming to pay her a visit. The rest of the group were from nearby villages and from Vilna. For most of them it was the first visit since they had left and it was very moving to witness their reactions when they found their homes, and recalled their lives and relatives there. They had amazing stories to tell, and I, whose connection to Slonim was tenuous in comparison, felt I was stepping back in time and witnessing history in the making. These personal reminscences added an extra human dimension to our tour so that it was not merely a dry museum visit.

I already knew that there was little of Slonim's Jewish history remaining, yet it was enough, together with the personal stories we heard, to resurrect the town and its atmosphere. And of course, to feel the horror of the atrocities committed there.

We flew from Tel Aviv to Minsk and spent a couple of days there. It was fortunate that many of the group spoke Russian, otherwise we would have been lost. Our visit coincided with the 60th anniversary of the end of World War II and the twelfth anniversary of the independence of Belarus from the U.S.S.R.

We visited the Jewish Community Center, which occupies the grounds of the former synagogue, and various

Memorial at Czaplova
for the 10,000 Slonim
Jews murdered there

amenities have been established there — a museum, an old
age home, a summer day camp for young children, a public
meeting-hall and other offices. The JCC is very active in the
town. Minsk is now a well-laid out city, with wide roads and
beautiful parks, and it was a great surprise when we found
a quiet spot at a busy corner where a most moving memorial has been established, I think the most moving of all we
saw. In an area that was originally a quarry on the outskirts
of the town, the Jews of Minsk were murdered and buried
en masse in 1941. Today a long flight of steps leads down a
large paved area and a monument. A sculpture flanks the
flight of steps, depicting a file of men, women and children
going down to their death, and a violinist bringing up the

rear. It was created by the Israeli sculptress Elsa Pollak.

During the bus ride to Slonim, we stopped at the Czaplova killing site, where some 10,000 Jews from the Slonim Ghetto were murdered in November, 1941. There is a general monument here in memory of the Belarus soldiers killed in the war, now decorated with wreaths of plastic flowers in honor of the national holiday. In recent years the government permitted placing this memorial to the Jews of Slonim, with inscriptions in Hebrew and Yiddish sponsored by the Israel Association of ex-Slonimer.

Of the three cemetaries which had existed in Slonim for some hundreds of years, only the site of the most recent remains, that in which Reb Aisel and his son-in-law R. Yossel Shlupper had been buried. It is situated on a grassy slope of decent size, closed off with a metal fence and large iron gates. Inside at the entrance, several *matsevot* of marble and of granite have been placed, also by the Slonimer Organization, to commemorate the slaughters of the Jews, with inscriptions in Russian, Hebrew and Yiddish. There are no original tombstones. There are new large residential blocks nearby, and the locals living in the area use a footpath which runs alongside the graveyard. During the time of the Soviets only Russian inscriptions were permitted 'in memory of the victims of the Nazis,' but in recent years the Belarus government has permitted the addition of Hebrew and Yiddish texts, with details of the particular atrocity which was committed, and many more memorials have been erected.

We visited the two synagogue buildings which have survived, out of the twenty-odd *shteiblach* and prayer-halls which existed before the war. Then, each guild had its own

The author at the gate of the Slonim cemetery.
Photo by Rahel Rabinovitch

**External view of the
Great Synagogue**

place of worship, as did the political and religious factions. The so-called 'Zionist' synagogue, where R. Mordecai Shlupper prayed, is part of a row of buildings and is now used as a sports center. No vestiges of its previous character remain. The main synagogue however, 'Die Groisse Schul,' is a free-standing building of red brick faced with stucco surrounded with a wooden fence whose purpose seems to be to protect the building from intruders and the intruders from coming to any harm. It is in a very sad state indeed, yet there are still traces of its past grandeur.

The main prayer-hall is arranged as a square with an imposing canopy-style *bima* reaching to the ceiling. Its four columns are decorated with a 'tromp l'oeil' floral design, and along the eastern wall are panels of paintings

The majestic bimah of the Great Synagogue

which may be suggestive of the Holy Land, or are simply rural scenes. The Aron haKodesh still bears traces of the Ten Commandments and of a crown borne by two lions. There are also the skeletal remains of the women's gallery and at each side of the entrance doors we could see where the *zedaka* boxes had once been placed. There was a sudden moment of drama when one of the men found fragments of a prayerbook amongst the rubble of the bima. He carefully gathered them together as if he had discovered a buried treasure, storing them temporarily in a plastic bag. When we visited the synagogue in Grodno the following day we saw what a little restoration and a coat of whitewash can do. Similar in plan to the Slonim shul, it is impressive in its stark simplicity and its magnificent towering bima. Although only containing a few chairs, prayers are held there on Shabbat, under the auspices of Habad, who also run a *heder* in one of the side rooms.

The old *Schulhof*, the large area next to the synagogue, used to serve as a commercial district, market and artisans' center. Some of their synagogues were also situated there. Today the area serves as the local open-air market. The Beit Midrash 'HaHoma,' where Reb Aisel prayed on weekdays, had been across the road from the synagogue, and is replaced now by a large shop.

Unlike the Polish government, which is interested in restoring and preserving its Jewish past, the Belarus government seems to show no inclination in this direction, though it is allowing educational and cultural programs to be conducted by the Jewish community.

The old residential areas of Slonim are very picturesque and except for TV antennae and saucers, look as if they

The Zionist Synagogue

Interior of the Zionist Synagogue today

The approach to Slonim and coat of arms

haven't changed in centuries. Small, mostly well-kept wooden houses, painted in various colors, with vegetable or flower gardens, cover quite a large area. White lace curtains are seen through the double-glazed windows, which incorporate a small pane which opens for ventilation, probably the only window that can be opened in the winter. Here and there we could see muddy unpaved lanes and an occasional new elegant brick house. This was largely

Scenes of Slonim today

the Jewish area of Slonim, where many of our group found their family homes. In its best days the Jewish population amounted to 75% of the total, or about 11–12,000 people. When the ghetto was established in 1941, the number had risen to about 15,000 because of the numerous refugees who had flocked in from Poland in their attempt to reach Vilna and the northern ports. There were 80 survivors after the war. The beautiful river Szczara [Schara] has been depleted to a stream because of over-consumption.

Although we were officially received by the mayor of Slonim, with whom the chairman of the Slonimer Organisation has developed personal relations over the years, and received souvenirs of our visit, which included an album of old picture-postcards of Slonim, our stay at the Szczara Hotel was unfortunately not a pleasant one because of extensive construction work and a lack of an elevator. There was also an attempt to increase the agreed tariff. Since there is no other hotel in the town, we cut our visit short and proceeded to Grodno where we stayed over Shabbat. I have already mentioned the highlight of this visit.

It was an hour's drive to the border of Belarus and on the way we visited the village of Kremenytze where the family of the Righteous Gentile who had rescued the father/uncle of the group of cousins lived. We also stopped at the site of the Petrelovitch massacre of 1942, where long flights of steps lead up to the monument at the top of the hill.

At the border there was a wait of almost three hours to leave Belarus to cross into Lithuania. We had no permission to leave the bus, and one couldn't help thinking of other journeys which Jews had made in the area, under

Memorial to the Vilna Jews massacred at Ponar

One of the pits used in Ponar

Main memorial to the Vilna Jews massacred at Ponar

less comfortable conditions. Finally we arrived in Vilna. It was wonderful to come to a country with European standards and where English was widely spoken and the language was written in Latin letters. We revelled in the comfort of the hotel.

We toured the two Jewish ghettos, saw the building which served as the Judenraat, the Jewish Theater, and the house where the Vilna Gaon lived and also visited his grave in the large Jewish cemetary which had been moved after the war. We saw an unusual custom in this cemetery. Small heaps of stones and large pebbles were placed here and there, smooth, washed, and of fairly uniform size, prepared for visitors to place on the graves, in the ancient Jewish tradition. They looked very aesthetic and revealed a thoughtful attitude towards the public. We heard about the plans to rebuild the ghetto area, and visited the H.K.P work camp where one lady of our group from Vilna told us of her life there with her family, the hardships they endured, her escape from the scene of the massacre and her walk back to Vilna. She was thirteen years old at the time and survived by sheer willpower.

We went of course to see the 'killing fields' of Ponar where thousands of Vilna Jews were murdered and buried. Here the work of the Nazis was made easy. The pits had already been dug by the Lithuanians for storing fuel, and a railway ran alongside the forest area. For a long time the Jews of Vilna did not know what was happening there to those who disappeared until one day two women managed to escape from the shooting, and begged for help at a nearby house. These people brought them to the Jewish hospital in Vilna and the story came out.

I skipped the tour of Kovno in order to visit my relative Yosef and his wife Margarita and to exchange family news with them. The last years have not been kind to them, although he is still keeping active with his collections and his museum. His grandson Eugene, who spent some years in Jerusalem on an educational program, has returned to Vilna with a Ukranian-born wife, whom he met and married in Jerusalem, and is now working with his father in a family-owned printing shop.

A visit to Trokei the next day, the original picturesque capital of Lithuania, brought our trip to its close and we returned to Vilna to eat lunch and pick up our luggage, and proceeded directly to the Minsk airport to catch our midnight flight home. It had been a strenuous week, physically and emotionally, but I was glad I had participated. For just a few days we had stepped back into the legendary Jewish world of our parents and grandparents, that is no more. We had given a nod of recognition and a salute to those who had lived out their lives in Slonim. We also touched the reality of those whose lives ended so cruelly and tragically in those beautiful birch forests of Lithuania and Belarus.

THE PUBLISHED WORKS OF
R. YEHOSHUA AISEK SHAPIRA

R. Aisel's works fall into four groups. The first, being mainly his responsa, consists of his first two works, Emek Yehoshua (The Valley of Yehoshua) and Nahlat Yehoshua (The Inheritance of Yehoshua). These books are not merely lists of questions and answers but evince a delving down to the basic principals of the Shas and the Poskim, thereby making that basic law clearly understood through straight logic rather than by tortuous pilpul. The revelation of this basic truth was more important to R. Aisel than any particular question and its answer. Thus, the aim of his study was always to "understand the argument and the reasoning behind it (וכל העיקר היגיעה היא להבין הסברות והטעמים). In so doing, R. Aisel always brings support for his ideas from the Babylonian and Jerusalem Talmuds.

The second category, that of *pilpul* and commentary, contains the four volumes of *Noam Yerushalmi*, his commentary and glosses on the Jerusalem Talmud. Here, it was important first to establish the correct text, and only then could R. Aisel follow his usual critical method of establishing the basic principles and then examining each point accordingly. It was Aisel's profound knowledge of both Talmuds and his brilliant critical comparison of the texts that rendered his work so important.

A third category of R. Aisel's work consists of *drash* or homilies that he gave on the Shabbat and Festivals. All in all, he published eighty-eight sermons, sixteen in the second part of *Emek Yehoshua*, and thirteen in the second part of *Nahlat Yehoshua*. In the latter volume there is also a hesped that Aisel delivered on the death of his father. The *Sefat HaNahal* (The Language of the Valley, but possibly also the Language of the Stream) contains twenty-eight sermons, and *Ibbei HaNahal* (The Blossoms of the Valley, a quotation from the Song of Songs) contains thirty-one.

The three small books published by my father in one volume make up the fourth category, in which R. Aisel examines the Aggadic literature of the *Shas*. These are: *Aizat Yehoshua* (The Counsel of Yehoshua), on questions asked by the Sages of Athens of the *tana* R. Yehoshua ben Hanania concerning his knowledge of Nature, and his replies to them. Athens was often mentioned in the Talmud as a center of wisdom and wit; *Marbeh Aiza* (Increasing Counsel), a commentary on the legends of Rabba bar Bar Hanna who told fantastic stories about his travels; and *Marbeh Tevunah* (Increasing Wisdom), devoted to *Mussar*, or moral behaviour, based on the principles of the *Shas* and both Talmuds.

As R. Aisel was steeped in all branches of Torah and Talmudic studies, he was able to bring all this knowledge into play when clarifying a question of *halakhah*, a difficult passage in the Talmud or other forms of commentary. He said, "The words of the Torah and the Talmud are like showers which rain down... and each oak, fig and vine takes from it according to its needs."

The following is a list of the published works of R. Yehoshua Aisek Shapira, otherwise known as R. Aisel Harif:

1. *Emek Yehoshua* (The Valley of Yehoshua), Warsaw, 1842.

Responsa on the *Shulhan Arukh,* and in Part 2, *drash.*

2. *Nahlat Yehoshua* (The Inheritance of Yehoshua), Warsaw, 1851. Responsa on various *halakhot,* and selected subjects in the Babylonian and the Jerusalem Talmuds. In Part 2, *drash* for Shabbat and Festivals, and a eulogy for his father.

3. *Noam Yerushalmi* (The Beauty of the Jerusalem Talmud).
   Zera'im, 1863;
   Mo'ed, 1866;
   Nashim, 1868;
   Nezikin, 1869. All published in Vilna.

4. *Ibbei HaNahal* (The Blossoms of the Valley), Koenigsberg, 1855.

5. *Sefat HaNahal* (The Language of the Valley), Koenigsberg, 1859.

6. *Aizat Yehoshua* (The Counsel of Yehoshua), Vilna, 1868.

7. *Marbeh Aiza* (Increasing Counsel), Vilna, 1870.

8. *Marbeh Tevuna* (Increasing Understanding), Vilna, 1872.

GLOSSARY

admor	Acronym of the Hebrew title used by *hassidim* when talking of pious rabbis — "*adonenu morenu vera-benu*," our master, our teacher and rabbi
baalei batim	Landlords, men of property. Often used in a negative sense meaning bourgeois or men of selfish interests.
Beit Din	Religious court of law; literally, the house of judgement.
din torah	A law suit in the religious court.
darshan	One who preaches on Torah subjects, or clarifies difficult passages by referring to other sources. This method is called "drash."
eruv	The cord used to demarcate the boundaries of an area within which it is permitted to carry objects on Shabbat.
gabbai	Warden of the synagogue, dealing with finances and other practical matters.

gematria	The system of interpreting verses of the Torah through the sum of the numerical value of the letters, and interchanging them with verses or phrases of equal value.
Guberna	Russian province.
haredim	The God-fearing; a term applied to the ultra-orthodox.
Halakhah	The body of Jewish religious law accumulated throughout the ages, covering all aspects of human behavior. Also, each single law within the comprehensive *Halakhah*.
Haskalah	Hebrew name for the Enlightenment, a Jewish movement seeking modernisation of religious observance and secular education. It began in Germany in the late eighteenth century and gathered strength in the nineteenth century.
heder	The first stage of traditional Jewish education for young children, originally held in a room (*heder*) in the teacher's house.
heter	Rabbinical permission to perform an act, or eat food normally forbidden.

heter v'issur	Term covering questions concerning what is allowed and what is forbidden, particularly in dietary matters.
lashon hara	Slander or malicious gossip; literally, "evil tongue."
maggid	From the Hebrew verb "to say." A preacher who devotes his sermons to moral issues in human behavior.
melamed	A teacher, particularly of young children in *heder.*
Mishnah	From the verb "to study and repeat." The work of the *Tannaim,* the great scholars of the second and third centuries, who discussed and interpreted the laws of the Torah, passing on their knowledge and arguments, orally, to the next generation of scholars. Put into final form and written down by R. Yehuda HaNassi, in the years 200–220 C.E., for fear that the numerous laws would be forgotten. Comprises six sections, therefore called by its Hebrew acronym the *Shas, Shisha Sidrei Mishnah.*

misnagdim	Yiddish form of the Hebrew word for opponents, *mitnagdim*, or specifically, those who opposed the *hassidim*.
nigun	Hebrew and Yiddish. A wordless melody sung by *hassidim* to express sad or happy emotions. The various hassidic courts had their own repertoires.
pilpul	A method of talmudic study which elaborates on infinitesimal variations of meaning. Commonly called "hair-splitting."
poskim	The great rabbis who make decisions on problematic questions and set them down as laws of the *Halakhah* for practical usage. Also abbreviation of generic term "Books of the Poskim," which are referred to by the rabbis when seeking solutions to problems brought before them.
rebbe	Title of hassidic rabbi, Yiddish.
reb	Common Yiddish form of address; the equivalent of "mister," in English.
seforim	Yiddish for *sefarim*, or books, especially those on rabbinical literature.

shamash	Caretaker, servant, rabbi's factotum.
shtiebel	In Yiddish, a small room. Used in reference to prayer-rooms for small groups of people, a style initiated by the *hassidim*.
Talmud	From the Hebrew verb "to learn." A general term covering the Oral Law, which consists of the Mishnah, Tosefta, Gemara, Midrash or Homilies on the *Halakhah* and Aggadah (legend). A vast literature, often called "the sea of Talmud," which is in essence a repository of religious laws, rabbinic commentary, philosophic discussion, stories and legends, and the wisdom derived from the full spectrum of human experience. Until modern times, the main source of education for the Jews, which shaped their lives and lifestyles.
Talmud Yerushalmi	The Talmud that developed in Eretz Yisrael, and was shaped mainly by R. Yohanan ben Nafkha who lived c. 200–280 C.E., although it was only completed at the beginning of the fifth century. It developed in the study centers of

Tiberias, Sepphoris, and Caesarea, not in Jerusalem, well before the Babylonian Talmud, but it fell into disuse because of the political and economic deterioration of the country after the destruction of Jerusalem, and with the ascendancy of the Babylonian centres of learning. Parts of it were lost, and the remainder became fragmented and corrupted by faulty transmission. It consists of four sections.

Talmud Bavli   The Talmud that developed in the great learning centres of Babylon and gradually took precedence over the *Talmud Yerushalmi,* It was finalized in the sixth century by the great teachers R. Ashi and R. Ravina. It consists of six sections.

Tehillim   Psalms.

tekiat kaf   A formal handshake on an agreement or promise, considered as binding as an oath.

tish   In Yiddish, a table, but referring to the communal meal held by the hassidic rebbe for his followers on Shabbat and festivals.

yiches, yichus   In Yiddish and Hebrew, lineage or pedigree.

BIBLIOGRAPHY

Alperowitz, Y. ed. *Gorzhd Yizkor Book*, Lahav, T. A. 1980.

Chones, S.M. *Toldot HaPoskim*. Warsaw, 1910.

Drouyanov, A. *Sefer HaBdiha v'HaHidud*. Eretz Yisrael, 1922.

Eisenstadt, B. *Dor Rabbanav Usfarav*, Vols. 2, 4, 1900.

Encyclopedia Judaica, Vol 8, p. 268; Vol. 14, Jerusalem, 1971, p. 1299.

Encyclopedia Judaica, Vol. 14. pp. 1299, 1302; Vol. 15, p. 778.

Engelshar, A. *Der Yiddisher Oitzar*. B'nei Brak: Yahadut Press, 1966. 2nd ed.

Fishman, Y.L. *Sarei HaMeah*. Jerusalem: Mossad HaRav Kook, 1956.

Freidman, N.Z. ed. *Otsar Rabbanim*.

The Jews in Latvia. Association of Latvian and Estonian Jews in Israel, 1971.

Katz, D. *T'nuat HaMussar*. Vols. 1–2. Eretz Yisrael, 1945.

Levin, Dov, ed. *Pinkas HaKehillot. Latvia and Estonia*. Jerusalem: Yad Vashem, 1988.

Levin, Dov, ed. *Pinkas HaKehillot. Lita*. Jerusalem: Yad VaShem.

Levin, Y.L. *Rabbi Aisel Harif*. Jerusalem: Nahliel Press, 1971. 2nd ed.

— *Megillat Polin. Sidrath Kehilloth Yisrael*, Vol. 1, 1966.

Levin, Y.L. (Yehallel) *Zichronot VeHegionot*. Jerusalem: Mossad Bialik, 1968. 2nd ed.

Lichtenstein, K. *Toldot HaYishuv HaYehudi b'Slonim*. Tel Aviv, 1960.

Lunsky, H. *Gaonim un Gedolim fun Nenten Avar*. Vilna, 1931.

Minsk, Ir v'Em, Memorial Volume. Kiryat Sefer, 1985, p. 626.

Reitzeson, M. *Fun R. Aisel's Moil.* Slonim, 1931.

Shapira, M. *Prefaces to Pnei Moshe,* Vilna 1872; *D'rashot Meharam,* Pietrkow, 1900; *Birkat Moshe,* Pietrkow, 1909.

Shapira, Y.A. *Prefaces to Emek Yehoshua,* Warsaw, 1842, and Jerusalem, 1925. 3rd ed.

Torat Avot. Jerusalem: Yeshivat Beth Avraham, 1973.

Yahadut Latvia, Sefer Zikaron. Israel, 1953.

Yahadut Lita, vol. 3, Irgun Yotzei Lita b'Yisrael, 1951.

GENEALOGY

Moshe ben Noah LIPSHUETZ
& Unknown LURIA

Eliezer Lipman HEILPRIN
bp. Szklow
& Unknown

R. Katriel HEILPRIN b. Szklow & Unk.
LURIA descendant of Maharshal

R. Solomon (Shlomo)
HEILPRIN
bp. Szklow
& Unknown LURIA

R.Yitzhak
SHAPIRA

R.Arieh Leib
(HaKatan)
SHAPIRA
1701-1761
&Daughter
of Azriel
ben MOSHE

R. Yehiel HEILPRIN
b.1660 d.1746 Minsk
'Seder Hadorot'
& Rachel bat Yosef Moshe

Isaac Aisek
HEILPRIN
& unknown FALK

Shlomo
HEILPRIN ?

Unknown 1
HEILPRIN
&Yitzhak
Hacohen
RAPPAPORT

Unknown 2
HEILPRIN
& R. Moshe
Unknown
bp. Russia

ben Menahem
of Russia.ABD
of DOBRAIYA

R. Moshe HEILPRIN
& unknown SHAPIRA

R. Arieh Yehuda
HEILPRIN

R. Yehiel Michael
HEILPRIN

unknown HEILPRIN
& R. Mordehai SHAPIRA
b.abt 1750,Glovenka

R. Yehiel SHAPIRA
b. 1772, d. 1847
& Rasha Unknown

Shlomo
Unknown

Yitzhak
Unknown

R. Mordecai
of USHATZ
& Unknown

Mendel &
Unknown

R. Yehoshua Aisek SHAPIRA
b.1801 Glovenka
d.1873 Slonim
& Haya FINE
m. Minsk

R. Issahar Dov SHAPIRA
b. 1828 d. 1902

R. Moshe SHAPIRA
b.1835 d.1911 Riga

R. Mordehai SHAPIRA
b.1838 d.1863 Slonim

Nehama SHAPIRA
b.1840 d. Slonim

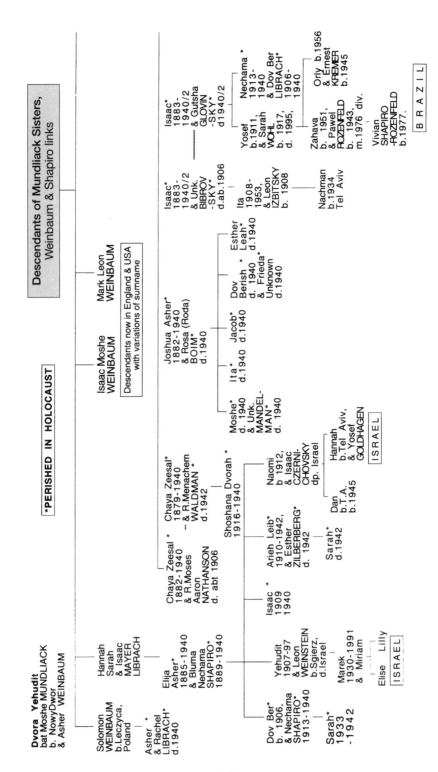

Descendants of Mundliack Sisters,
Weinbaum & Shapiro links

*PERISHED IN HOLOCAUST

354

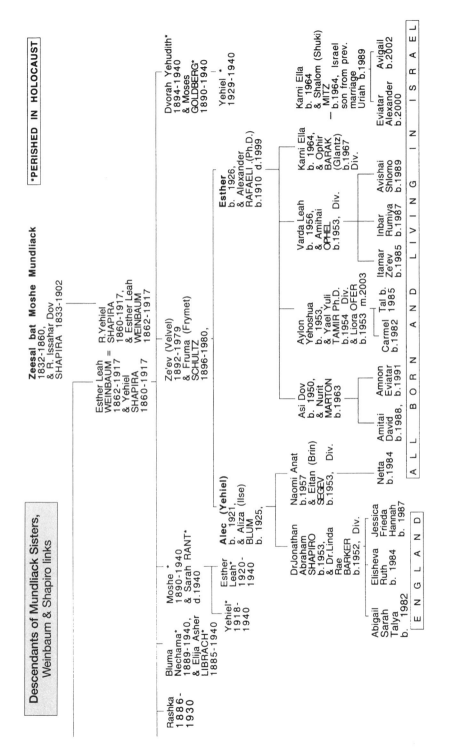

Descendants of Mundliack Sisters, Weinbaum & Shapiro links

Zeesal bat Moshe Mundliack 1832-1860, & R. Issahar Dov SHAPIRA 1833-1902

*PERISHED IN HOLOCAUST

Rashka 1886-1930

Bluma Nechama* 1889-1940, & Elija Asher LIBRACH* 1885-1940

Moshe * 1890-1940 & Sarah RANT* d.1940

Yehiel* 1918-1940

Esther Leah* 1920-1940

Esther Leah WEINBAUM 1862-1917 & Yehiel SHAPIRA 1860-1917

R.Yehiel SHAPIRA 1860-1917, & Esther Leah WEINBAUM 1862-1917

Ze'ev (Velvel) 1892-1979 & Fruma (Frymet) SCHULTZ 1896-1980,

Alec (Yehiel) b. 1921, & Aliza (Ilse) BLUM b. 1925,

Dr.Jonathan Abraham SHAPIRO b.1953, & Dr.Linda Rae BARKER b.1952, Div.

Abigail Sarah Talya b. 1982

Elisheva Ruth b. 1984

Jessica Frieda Hannah b. 1987

Naomi Anat b.1957 & Eitan (Brin) SEGEV b.1953, Div.

Netta b.1984

Asi Dov b. 1950, & Nurit MARTON b.1963

Amitai David b.1988,

Amnon Eviatar b.1991

Aylon Yehoshua b. 1953, & Yael Yuli TAMIR Ph.D. b.1954 Div. & Liora OFER m.2003

Carmel b.1982

Tal b. 1985

Dvorah Yehudith* 1894-1940 & Moses GOLDBERG* 1890-1940

Yehiel * 1929-1940

Esther b. 1926, & Alexander RAFAELI .(Ph.D.) b.1910 d.1999

Varda Leah b. 1956, & Amihai OPHEL b.1953, Div.

Itamar Ze'ev b.1985

Inbar Rumiya b.1987

Karni Ella b. 1964, & Ophir BARAK (Glantz) b.1967 Div.

Avishai Shlomo b.1989

Karni Ella b. 1964, & Shalom (Shuki) MITZ — b.1964, Israel son from prev. marriage Uriah b.1989

Eviatar Alexander b.2000

Avigail b.2002

ALL BORN AND LIVING IN ISRAEL

ENGLAND

355

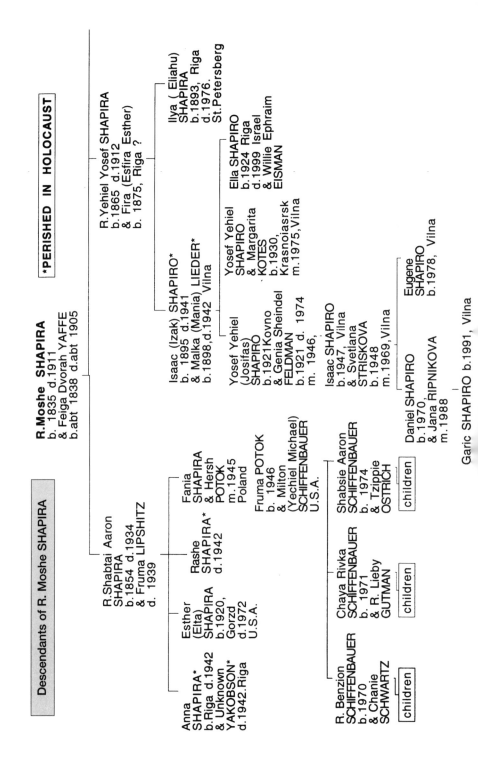

Descendants of R. Moshe SHAPIRA

R.Moshe SHAPIRA
b. 1835 d.1911
& Feiga Dvorah YAFFE
b.abt 1838 d.abt 1905

PERISHED IN HOLOCAUST

R.Shabtai Aaron
SHAPIRA
b.1854 d.1934
& Fruma LIPSHITZ
d. 1939

R.Yehiel Yosef SHAPIRA
b.1865 d.1912
& Fira (Esfira Esther)
b. 1875, Riga ?

Rashe
SHAPIRA*
d.1942

Fania
SHAPIRA
& Hersh
POTOK
m.1945
Poland

Isaac (Izak) SHAPIRO*
b. 1895 d.1941
& Malka (Mania) LIEDER*
b.1898,d.1942 Vilna

Ilya (Eliahu)
SHAPIRA
b.1893, Riga
d.1976.
St.Petersberg

Esther
(Elta)
SHAPIRA
b.1920,
Gorzd
d.1972
U.S.A.

Fruma POTOK
b. 1946
& Milton
(Yechiel Michael)
SCHIFFENBAUER
U.S.A.

Yosef Yehiel
(Josifas)
SHAPIRO
b.1921Kovno
& Genia Sheindel
FELDMAN
b.1921 d. 1974
m. 1946,

Yosef Yehiel
SHAPIRO
& Margarita
KOTES
b.1930,
Krasnoiasrsk
m.1975,Vilna

Ella SHAPIRO
b.1924 Riga
d.1999 Israel
& Willie Ephraim
EISMAN

Anna
SHAPIRA*
b.Riga d.1942
& Unknown
YAKOBSON*
d.1942.Riga

Chaya Rivka
SCHIFFENBAUER
b. 1971
& R. Lieby
GUTMAN

Shabsie Aaron
SCHIFFENBAUER
b. 1974
& Tzippie
OSTRICH

Isaac SHAPIRO
b.1947, Vilna
& Svetlana
STRISKOVA
b.1948
m.1969,Vilna

Eugene
SHAPIRO
b.1978, Vilna

R. Benzion
SCHIFFENBAUER
b.1970
& Chanie
SCHWARTZ

children

children

children

Daniel SHAPIRO
b.1970,
& Jana RIPNIKOVA
m.1988

Garic SHAPIRO b.1991, Vilna

356

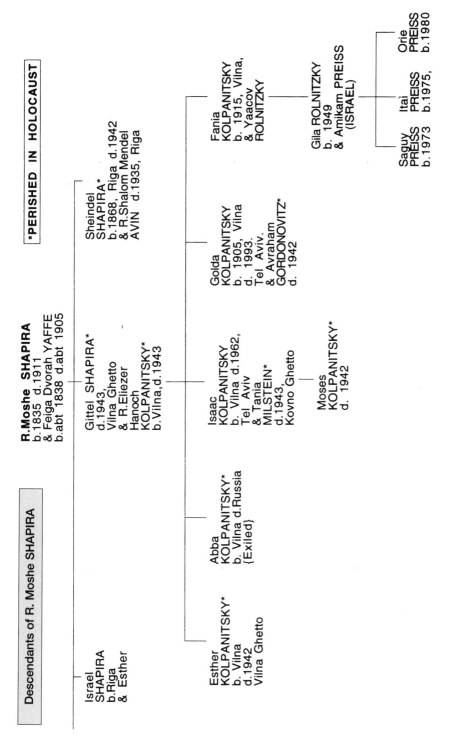

Descendants of R. Moshe SHAPIRA

*PERISHED IN HOLOCAUST

R.Moshe SHAPIRA
b.1835 d.1911
& Feiga Dvorah YAFFE
b.abt 1838 d.abt 1905

Israel
SHAPIRA
b.Riga
& Esther

Gittel SHAPIRA*
d.1943,
Vilna Ghetto
& R.Eliezer
Hanoch
KOLPANITSKY*
b.Vilna,d.1943

Sheindel
SHAPIRA*
b.1868, Riga d.1942
& R.Shalom Mendel
AVIN d.1935, Riga

Esther
KOLPANITSKY*
b. Vilna
d.1942
Vilna Ghetto

Abba
KOLPANITSKY*
b. Vilna d.Russia
(Exiled)

Isaac
KOLPANITSKY
b. Vilna d.1962,
Tel Aviv
& Tania
MILSTEIN*
d.1943,
Kovno Ghetto

Moses
KOLPANITSKY*
d. 1942

Golda
KOLPANITSKY
b. 1905, Vilna
d. 1993.
Tel Aviv.
& Avraham
GORDONOVITZ*
d. 1942

Fania
KOLPANITSKY
b. 1915, Vilna,
& Yaacov
ROLNITZKY

Gila ROLNITZKY
b. 1949
& Amikam PREISS
(ISRAEL)

Saguy
PREISS
b.1973

Itai
PREISS
b.1975,

Orie
PREISS
b.1980

357

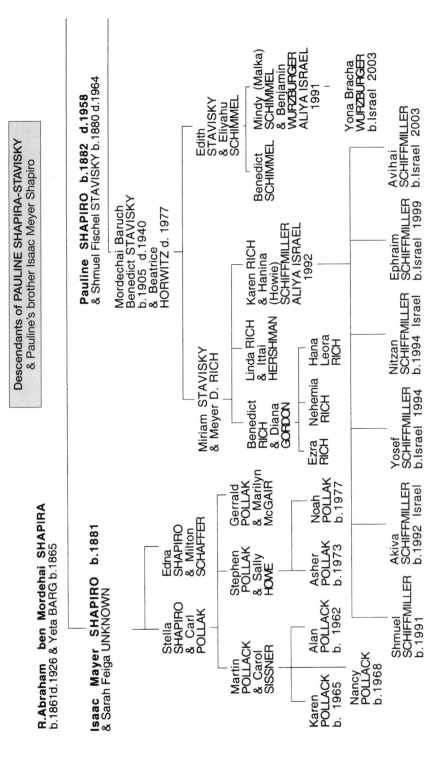

Descendants of PAULINE SHAPIRA-STAVISKY
& Pauline's brother Isaac Meyer Shapiro

R.Abraham ben Mordehai SHAPIRA
b.1861d.1926 & Yeta BARG b.1865

Isaac Mayer SHAPIRO b.1881
& Sarah Feiga UNKNOWN

Pauline SHAPIRO b.1882 d.1958
& Shmuel Fischel STAVISKY b.1880 d.1964

Mordechai Baruch
Benedict STAVISKY
b.1905 d.1940
& Beatrice
HORWITZ d. 1977

Edith
STAVISKY
& Eliyahu
SCHIMMEL

Mindy (Malka)
SCHIMMEL
& Benjamin
WURZBURGER
ALIYA ISRAEL
1991

Benedict
SCHIMMEL

Yona Bracha
WURZBURGER
b.Israel 2003

Miriam STAVISKY
& Meyer D. RICH

Karen RICH
& Hanina
(Howie)
SCHIFFMILLER
ALIYA ISRAEL
1992

Linda RICH
& Ittai
HERSHMAN

Avihai
SCHIFFMILLER
b.Israel 2003

Ephraim
SCHIFFMILLER
b.Israel 1999

Benedict
RICH
& Diana
GORDON

Nehemia
RICH

Hana
Leora
RICH

Nitzan
SCHIFFMILLER
b.1994 Israel

Ezra
RICH

Yosef
SCHIFFMILLER
b.Israel 1994

Edna
SHAPIRO
& Milton
SCHAFFER

Gerrald
POLLAK
& Marilyn
McGAIR

Akiva
SCHIFFMILLER
b.1992 Israel

Stella
SHAPIRO
& Carl
POLLAK

Stephen
POLLAK
& Sally
HOWE

Noah
POLLAK
b.1977

Asher
POLLAK
b.1973

Martin
POLLACK
& Carol
SISSNER

Alan
POLLACK
b. 1962

Shmuel
SCHIFFMILLER
b.1991

Karen
POLLACK
b. 1965

Nancy
POLLACK
b.1968

358

R.Abraham ben Mordehai SHAPIRA
b.1861 d.1926 & Yeta BARG b.1865

Pauline SHAPIRO b.1882 d.1958
& Shmuel Fischel STAVISKY b.1880 d.1964

Feiga (Fritzi)
STAVISKY
b.1907 d.1985
& Herman
GOTTESMAN
b.1899 d.1975

Masha Martha
STAVISKY
b.1908, d.2000
& Gerson
BERNSTEIN
b.1904 d.1965
See Separate Chart

Michael Judah
GOTTESMAN
& Toby PASCHER

Baruch
Yisrael
Kalman
GOTTESMAN
& Mindy
SHIDLOVSKY

Sharon (Shalva)
GOTTESMAN
& Jeff Yaakov
BEN DAVID
(DAVIS)
ALIYA ISRAEL
1988

Mendel
GOTTESMAN
& Haya
SPIEGELMAN

Haim
GOTTESMAN
& Dana
BLUMENSTEIN

Laurie
GOTTESMAN
& Yehuda
MINCHENBERG

Benjamin
Samuel
GOTTESMAN

Rachel
Leah
GOTTESMAN

Orit
Tchiya
GOTTESMAN

TUVIA
MINCHENBERG

Asher Anshel
MINCHENBERG

Samuel
MINCHENBERG

Reena
Zippora
GOTTES
-MAN

Yosef
Yehiel
GOTTES
-MAN

Ariella
Ahuva
GOTTESMAN

Dovid
Mordechai
GOTTESMAN

Shalom
Asher
GOTTESMAN

Zvi Shemaya
BEN DAVID
Israel

Sari
BEN DAVID
Israel

Bat Zion
BEN DAVID
Israel

Elisheva
BEN DAVID
Israel

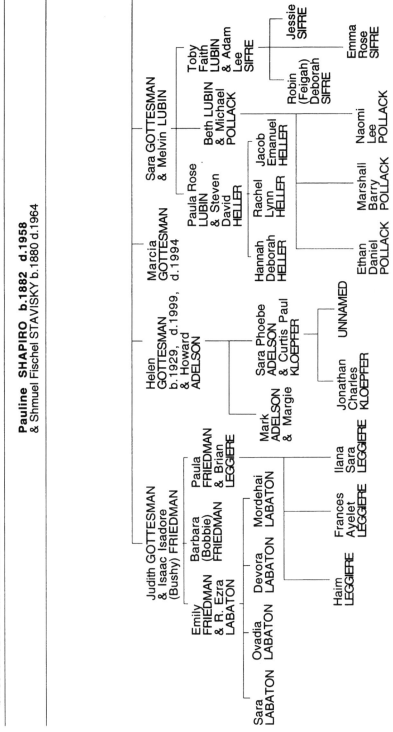

Descendants of
PAULINE SHAPIRA-STAVISKY

R.Abraham ben Mordehai SHAPIRA
b.1861d.1926 & Yeta BARG b.1865

Pauline SHAPIRO b.1882 d.1958
& Shmuel Fischel STAVISKY b.1880 d.1964

Judith GOTTESMAN
& Isaac Isadore
(Bushy) FRIEDMAN

Emily
FRIEDMAN
& R. Ezra
LABATON

Barbara
(Bobbie)
FRIEDMAN

Paula
FRIEDMAN
& Brian
LEGGIERE

Sara
LABATON

Ovadia
LABATON

Devora
LABATON

Mordehai
LABATON

Haim
LEGGIERE

Frances
Ayelet
LEGGIERE

Ilana
Sara
LEGGIERE

Helen
GOTTESMAN
b.1929, d.1999,
& Howard
ADELSON

Mark
ADELSON
& Margie

Sara Phoebe
ADELSON
& Curtis Paul
KLOEPFER

Jonathan
Charles
KLOEPFER

UNNAMED

Marcia
GOTTESMAN
d.1994

Paula Rose
LUBIN
& Steven
David
HELLER

Hannah
Deborah
HELLER

Rachel
Lynn
HELLER

Jacob
Emanuel
HELLER

Sara GOTTESMAN
& Melvin LUBIN

Beth LUBIN
& Michael
POLLACK

Ethan
Daniel
POLLACK

Marshall
Barry
POLLACK

Naomi
Lee
POLLACK

Toby
Faith
LUBIN
& Adam
Lee
SIFRE

Robin
(Feigah)
Deborah
SIFRE

Jessie
SIFRE

Emma
Rose
SIFRE

360

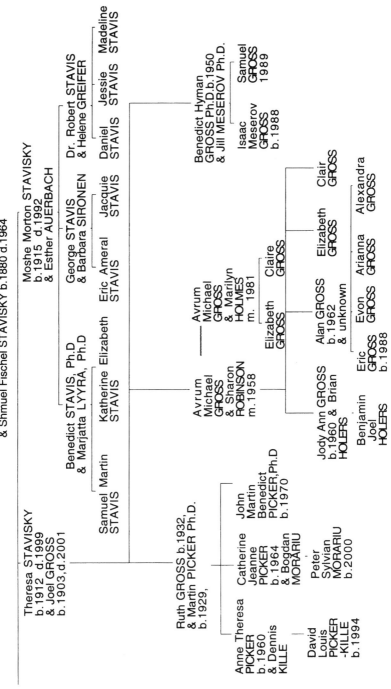

R.Abraham ben Mordehai SHAPIRA
b.1861d.1926 & Yeta BARG b.1865

Descendants of
PAULINE SHAPIRA-STAVISKY

Pauline SHAPIRO b.1882   d.1958
& Shmuel Fischel STAVISKY b.1880 d.1964

Moshe Morton STAVISKY
b.1915 d.1992
& Esther AUERBACH

Theresa STAVISKY
b.1912 d.1999
& Joel GROSS
b.1903,d.2001

Benedict STAVIS, Ph.D
& Marjatta LYYRA, Ph.D

George STAVIS
& Barbara SIRONEN

Dr. Robert STAVIS
& Helene GREIFER

Samuel Martin
STAVIS

Katherine Elizabeth
STAVIS

Eric Ameral
STAVIS

Jacquie
STAVIS

Daniel
STAVIS

Jessie
STAVIS

Madeline
STAVIS

Benedict Hyman
GROSS Ph.D.b.1950
& Jill MESEROV Ph.D.

Isaac
Meserov
GROSS
b.1988

Samuel
GROSS
1989

Avrum
Michael
GROSS
& Sharon
ROBINSON
m.1958

Avrum
Michael
GROSS
& Marilyn
HOLMES
m. 1981

Elizabeth
GROSS

Claire
GROSS

Jody Ann GROSS
b.1960 & Brian
HOLERS

Alan GROSS
b.1962
& unknown

Elizabeth
GROSS

Clair
GROSS

Benjamin
Joel
HOLERS

Eric
GROSS
b.1988

Evon
GROSS

Arianna
GROSS

Alexandra
GROSS

Ruth GROSS b.1932,
& Martin PICKER Ph.D.
b.1929,

Catherine
Jeanne
PICKER
b.1964
& Bogdan
MORĂRIU

John
Martin
Benedict
PICKER,Ph.D
b.1970

Anne Theresa
PICKER
b.1960
& Dennis
KILLE

Peter
Sylvian
MORĂRIU
b.2000

David
Louis
PICKER
-KILLE
b.1994

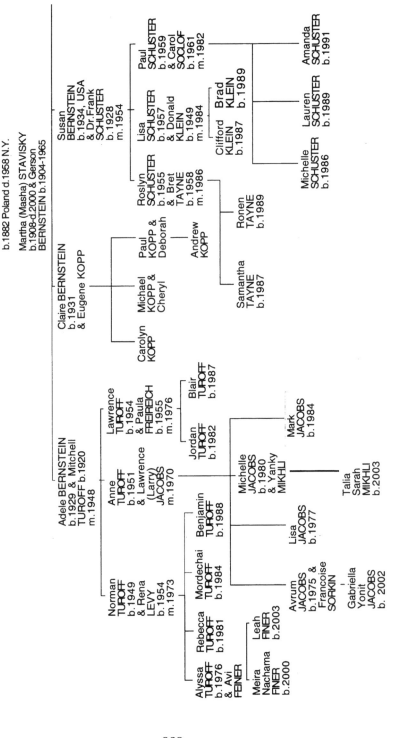

Family of MARTHA and GERSON BERNSTEIN

Samuel Fischel STAVISKY
b.1882-1964, N.Y.
& Peshe Reisel (Pauline)
bat R.Abraham SHAPIRO
b.1882 Poland d.1958 N.Y.

Martha (Masha) STAVISKY
b.1908-d.2000 & Gerson
BERNSTEIN b.1904-1965

Adele BERNSTEIN
b.1929 & Mitchell
TUROFF b.1920
m.1948

Claire BERNSTEIN
b.1931
& Eugene KOPP

Susan
BERNSTEIN
b.1934, USA
& Dr.Frank
SCHUSTER
b.1928
m.1954

Norman
TUROFF
b.1949
& Rena
LEVY
b.1954
m.1973

Anne
TUROFF
b.1951
& Lawrence
(Larry)
JACOBS
m.1970

Lawrence
TUROFF
b.1954
& Paula
FREIREICH
b.1955
m.1976

Carolyn
KOPP

Michael
KOPP &
Cheryl

Paul
KOPP &
Deborah

Andrew
KOPP

Roslyn
SCHUSTER
b.1955
& Bret
TAYNE
b.1958
m.1986

Lisa
SCHUSTER
b.1957
& Donald
KLEIN
b.1949
m.1984

Paul
SCHUSTER
b.1959
& Carol
SOCLOF
b.1961
m.1982

Rebecca
TUROFF
b.1981

Mordechai
TUROFF
b.1984

Benjamin
TUROFF
b.1988

Jordan
TUROFF
b.1982

Blair
TUROFF
b.1987

Michelle
JACOBS
b.1980
& Yanky
MIKHLI

Mark
JACOBS
b.1984

Samantha
TAYNE
b.1987

Ronen
TAYNE
b.1989

Clifford
KLEIN
b.1987

Brad
KLEIN
b.1989

Michelle
SCHUSTER
b.1986

Lauren
SCHUSTER
b.1989

Amanda
SCHUSTER
b.1991

Alyssa
TUROFF
b.1976
& Avi
FEINER

Leah
FINER
b.2003

Lisa
JACOBS
b.1977

Avrum
JACOBS
b.1975 &
Francoise
SORKIN

Talia
Sarah
MIKHLI
b.2003

Meira
Nachama
FINER
b.2000

Gabriella
Yonit
JACOBS
b. 2002

Family of MARTHA and GERSON BERNSTEIN

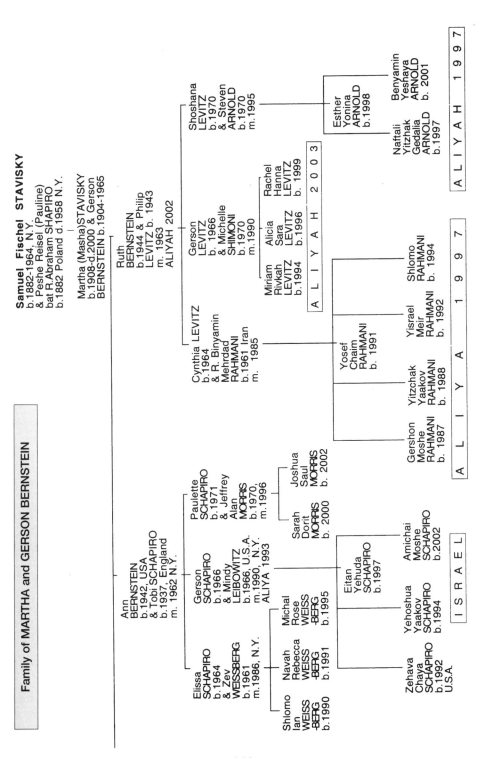

Samuel Fischel STAVISKY
b.1882-1964, N.Y.
& Peshe Reisel (Pauline)
bat R.Abraham SHAPIRO
b.1882 Poland d.1958 N.Y.

Martha (Masha)STAVISKY
b.1908-d.2000 & Gerson
BERNSTEIN b.1904-1965

Ann
BERNSTEIN
b.1942, USA
& Tobi SCHAPIRO
b.1937, England
m. 1962 N.Y.

Ruth
BERNSTEIN
b.1944 & Philip
LEVITZ b. 1943
m. 1963
ALIYAH 2002

Elissa
SCHAPIRO
b.1964
& Zev
WEISSBERG
b.1961
m.1986, N.Y.

Gerson
SCHAPIRO
b.1966
& Mindy
LEIBOWITZ
b.1966, U.S.A.
m.1990, N.Y.
ALIYA 1993

Paulette
SCHAPIRO
b.1971
& Jeffrey
Alan
MORRIS
b.1970,
m.1996

Cynthia LEVITZ
b.1964
& R. Binyamin
Mehrdad
RAHMANI
b.1961 Iran
m. 1985

Gerson
LEVITZ
b. 1966
& Michelle
SHIMONI
b.1970
m.1990

Shoshana
LEVITZ
b.1970
& Steven
ARNOLD
b.1970
m.1995

Shlomo
Ian
WEISS-
BERG
b.1990

Navah
Rebecca
WEISS-
BERG
b.1991

Michal
Rose
WEISS-
BERG
b.1995

Sarah
Dorit
MORRIS
b. 2000

Joshua
Saul
MORRIS
b. 2002

Gershon
Moshe
RAHMANI
b. 1987

Yitzchak
Yaakov
RAHMANI
b. 1988

Yosef
Chaim
RAHMANI
b. 1991

Yisrael
Meir
RAHMANI
b. 1992

Shlomo
RAHMANI
b. 1994

Miriam
Rivkah
LEVITZ
b.1994

Alicia
Sara
LEVITZ
b.1996

Rachel
Hanna
LEVITZ
b. 1999

Esther
Yonina
ARNOLD
b.1998

Naftali
Yitzhak
Gedalia
ARNOLD
b.1997

Benyamin
Yeshaya
ARNOLD
b. 2001

Zehava
Chaya
SCHAPIRO
b.1992
U.S.A.

Yehoshua
Yaakov
SCHAPIRO
b.1994

Eitan
Yehuda
SCHAPIRO
b.1997

Amichai
Moshe
SCHAPIRO
b.2002

I S R A E L

A L I Y A

A L I Y A H 1 9 9 7

A L I Y A H 2 0 0 3

A L I Y A H 1 9 9 7

363

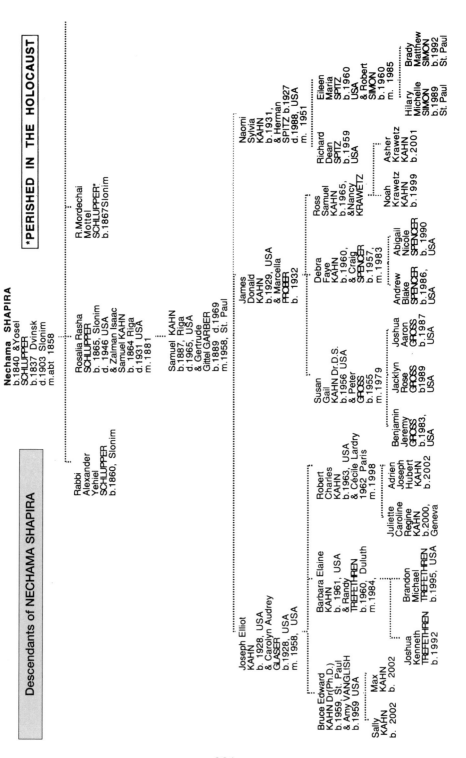

Descendants of NECHAMA SHAPIRA

*PERISHED IN THE HOLOCAUST

Nechama SHAPIRA
b.1840 &Yosel
SCHLUPPER
b.1837 Dvinsk
d.1903 Slonim
m.abt 1858

Rabbi
Alexander
Yeniel
SCHLUPPER
b.1860, Slonim

Rosalia Rasha
SCHLUPPER
b. 1865, Slonim
d. 1946 USA
& Zalman Isaac
Samuel KAHN
b.1864 Riga
d.1931 USA
m.1881

R.Mordechai
Mottel
SCHLUPPER*
b.1867Slonim

Samuel KAHN
b.1887, Riga
d.1965, USA
& Gertrude
Gittel GARBER
b.1889 d.1969
m.1958, St. Paul

James
Donald
KAHN
b.1929, USA
& Marcella
PROBER
b. 1932

Naomi
Sylvia
KAHN
b.1931,
& Herman
SPITZ b.1927
d.1988, USA
m. 1951

Susan
Gail
KAHN Dr.D.S.
b.1956 USA
& Peter
GROSS
b.1955
m.1979

Robert
Charles
KAHN
b.1963, USA
& Cécile Lardry
1962 Paris
m.1998

Debra
Faye
KAHN
b.1960,
& Craig
SPENCER
b.1957,
m.1983

Ross
Samuel
KAHN
b.1965,
&Nancy
KRAWETZ

Richard
Dean
SPITZ
b.1959
USA

Eileen
Maria
SPITZ
b.1960
USA
& Robert
SIMON
b.1960
m. 1985

Jacklyn
Rose
GROSS
b.1989
USA

Joshua
Aaron
GROSS
b.1987
USA

Benjamin
Jeremy
GROSS
b.1983,
USA

Adrien
Joseph
Hubert
KAHN
b.2002

Juliette
Caroline
Regine
KAHN
b.2000,
Geneva

Andrew
Blake
SPENCER
b.1986,
USA

Abigail
Nicole
SPENCER
b. 1990
USA

Noah
Krawetz
KAHN
b.1999

Asher
Krawetz
KAHN
b.2001

Hilary
Michelle
SIMON
b.1989
St. Paul

Brady
Matthew
SIMON
b.1992
St. Paul

Joseph Elliot
KAHN
b. 1928, USA
& Carolyn Audrey
GLASER
b.1928, USA
m. 1958, USA

Barbara Elaine
KAHN
b. 1961, USA
& Randy
TREFETHREN
b.1960, Duluth
m.1984,

Bruce Edward
KAHN Dr(Ph.D.)
b.1959, St. Paul
& Amy VANGLISH
b.1959 USA

Max
KAHN
b. 2002

Sally
KAHN
b. 2002

Joshua
Kenneth
TREFETHREN
b.1992

Brandon
Michael
TREFETHREN
b.1995, USA

364

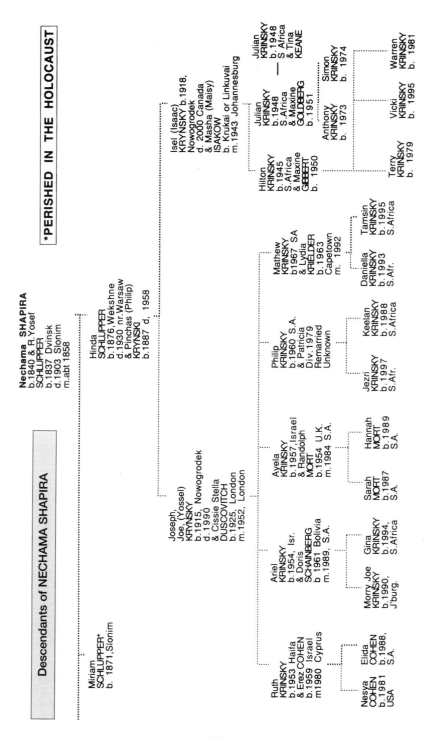

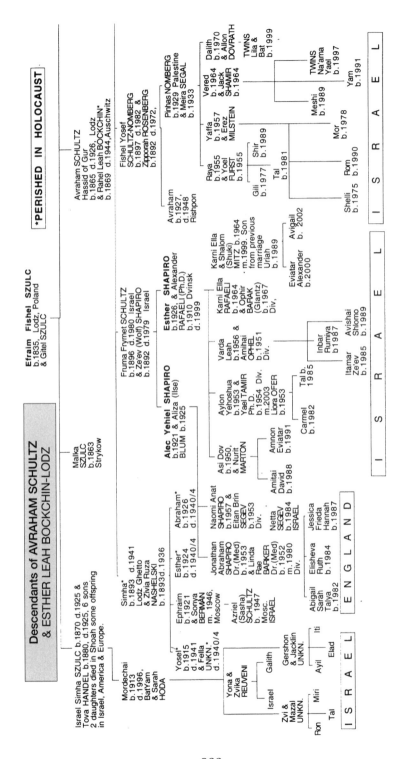

Descendants of AVRAHAM SCHULTZ & ESTHER LEAH BOCKCHIN-LODZ

Efraim Fishel SZULC
b.1835, Lodz, Poland
& Gitel SZULC

*PERISHED IN HOLOCAUST

366

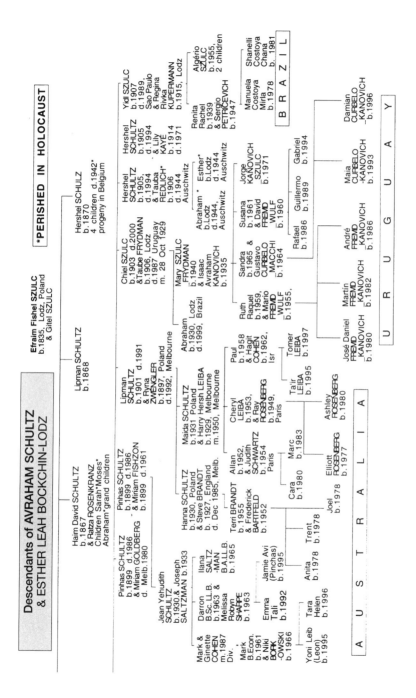

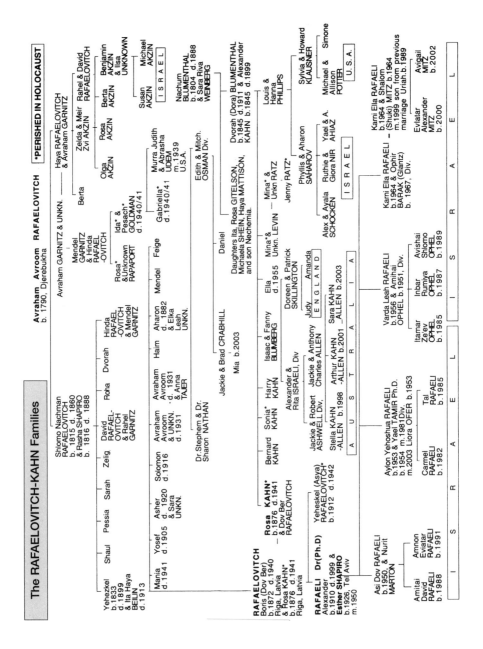

The RAFAELOVITCH-KAHN Families

*PERISHED IN HOLOCAUST

368